ON

月詠

つくよみ

PHASE

1

Keitaro Arima

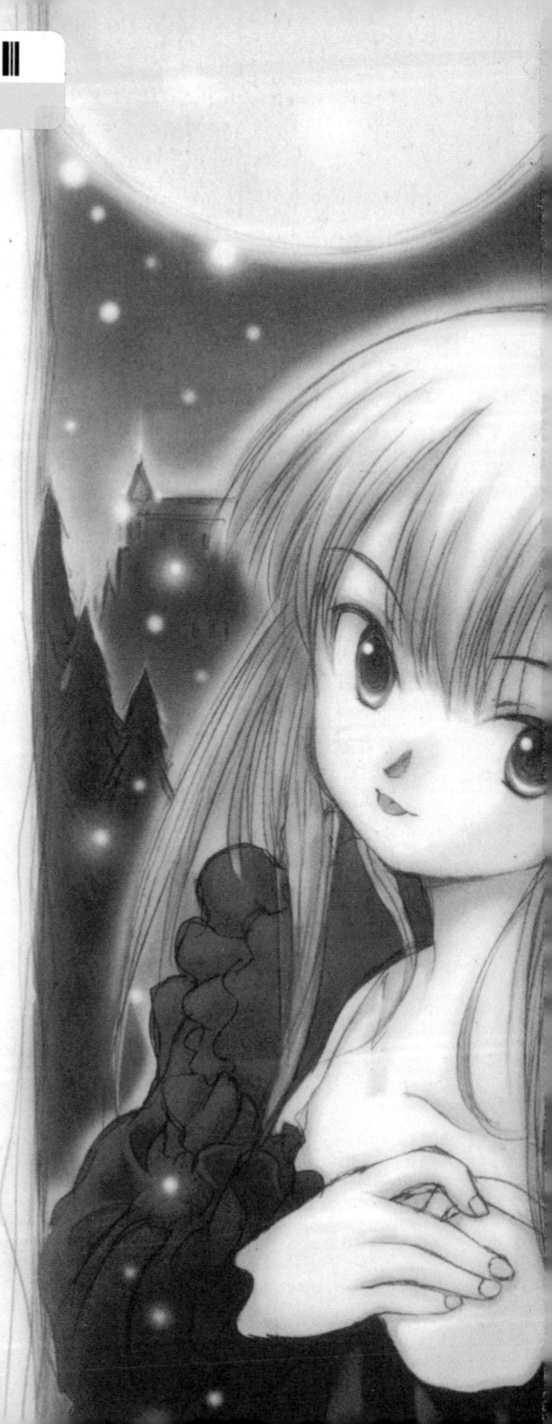

TSUKUYOMI

Moon Phase 月詠

CREATED BY: KEITARO ARIMA

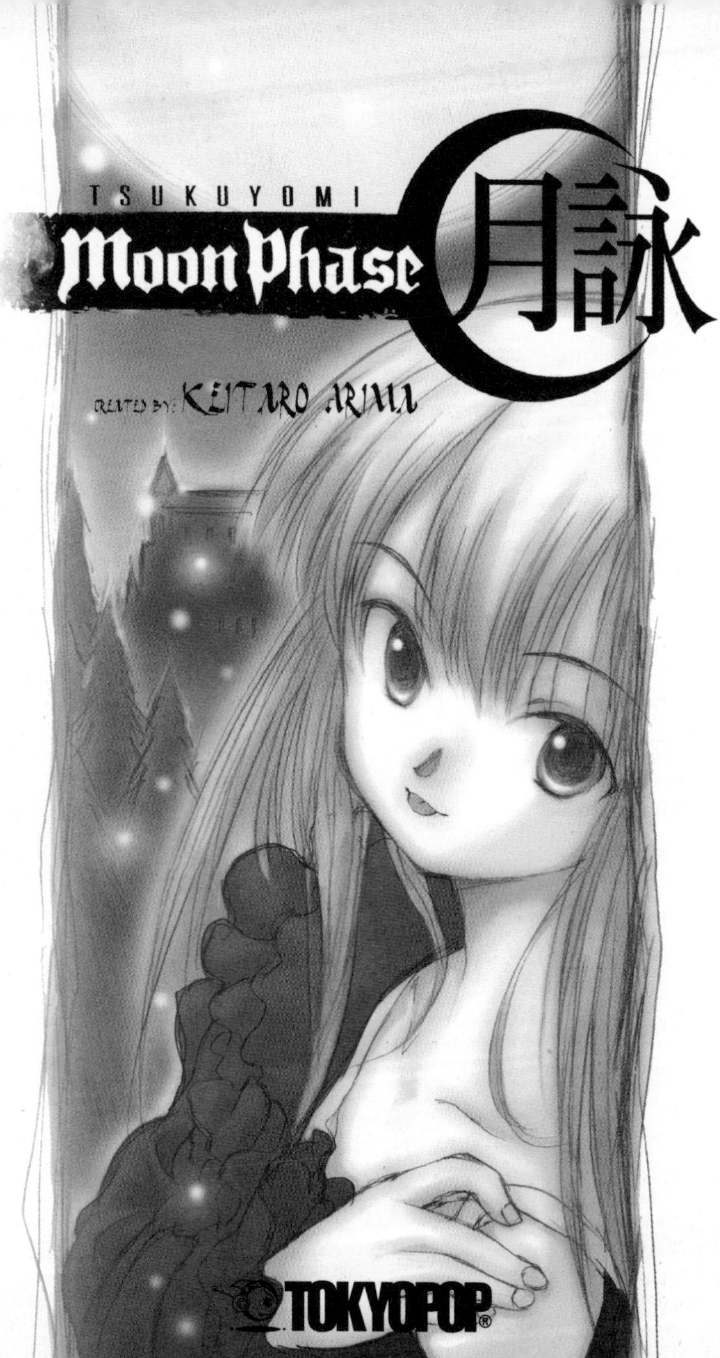

TOKYOPOP®

HAMBURG // LONDON // LOS ANGELES // TOKYO

Tsukuyomi - Moon Phase Vol. 1
created by Keitaro Arima

Translation - Yoohae Yang
English Adaptation - Jeffrey Reeves
Copy Editors - Hope Donovan and Eric Althoff
Retouch and Lettering - Chris Anderson
Production Artist - Rafael Najarian
Cover Design - Seth Cable

Editor - Julie Taylor
Digital Imaging Manager - Chris Buford
Production Managers - Jennifer Miller and Mutsumi Miyazaki
Managing Editor - Lindsey Johnston
VP of Production - Ron Klamert
Publisher and E.I.C. - Mike Kiley
President and C.O.O. - John Parker
C.E.O. - Stuart Levy

A  Manga

TOKYOPOP Inc.
5900 Wilshire Blvd. Suite 2000
Los Angeles, CA 90036

E-mail: info@TOKYOPOP.com
Come visit us online at www.TOKYOPOP.com

ISBN: 1-59532-948-X

First TOKYOPOP printing: December 2005
10 9 8 7 6 5 4 3 2
Printed in the USA

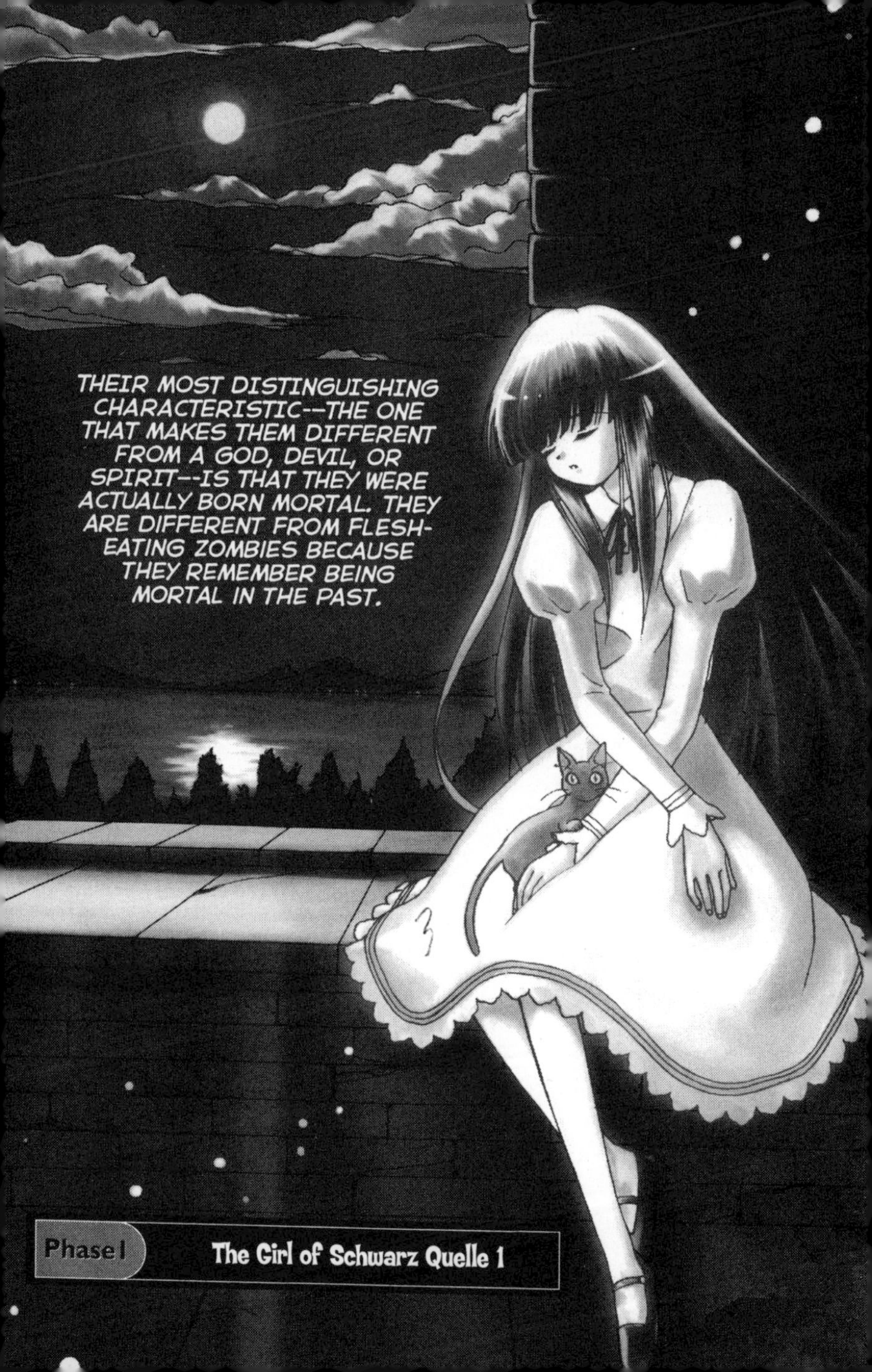
THEIR MOST DISTINGUISHING CHARACTERISTIC--THE ONE THAT MAKES THEM DIFFERENT FROM A GOD, DEVIL, OR SPIRIT--IS THAT THEY WERE ACTUALLY BORN MORTAL. THEY ARE DIFFERENT FROM FLESH-EATING ZOMBIES BECAUSE THEY REMEMBER BEING MORTAL IN THE PAST.
Phase I
The Girl of Schwarz Quelle 1

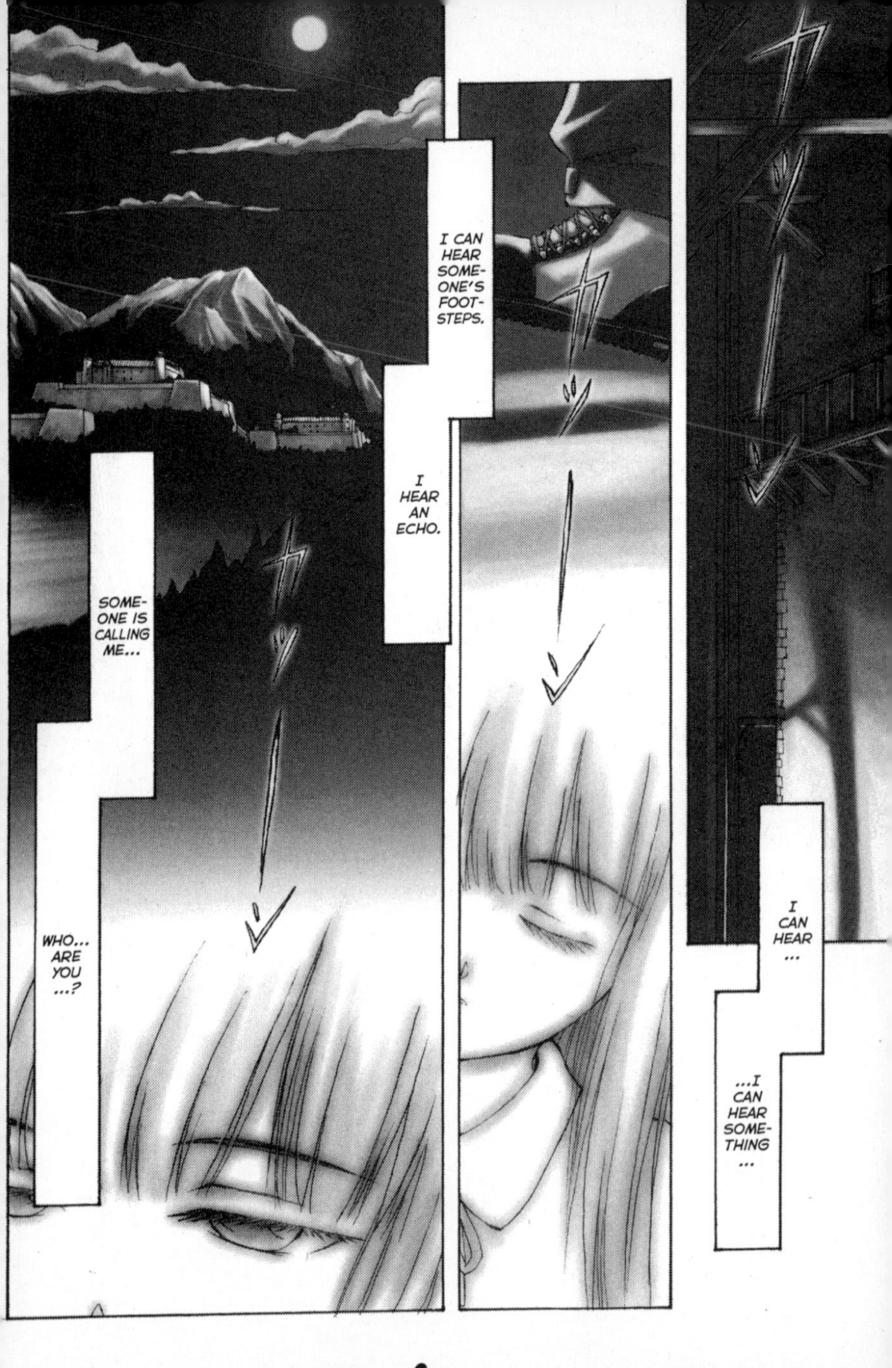
I CAN HEAR...
...I CAN HEAR SOMETHING...
I CAN HEAR SOMEONE'S FOOTSTEPS.
I HEAR AN ECHO.
SOMEONE IS CALLING ME...
WHO... ARE YOU ...?

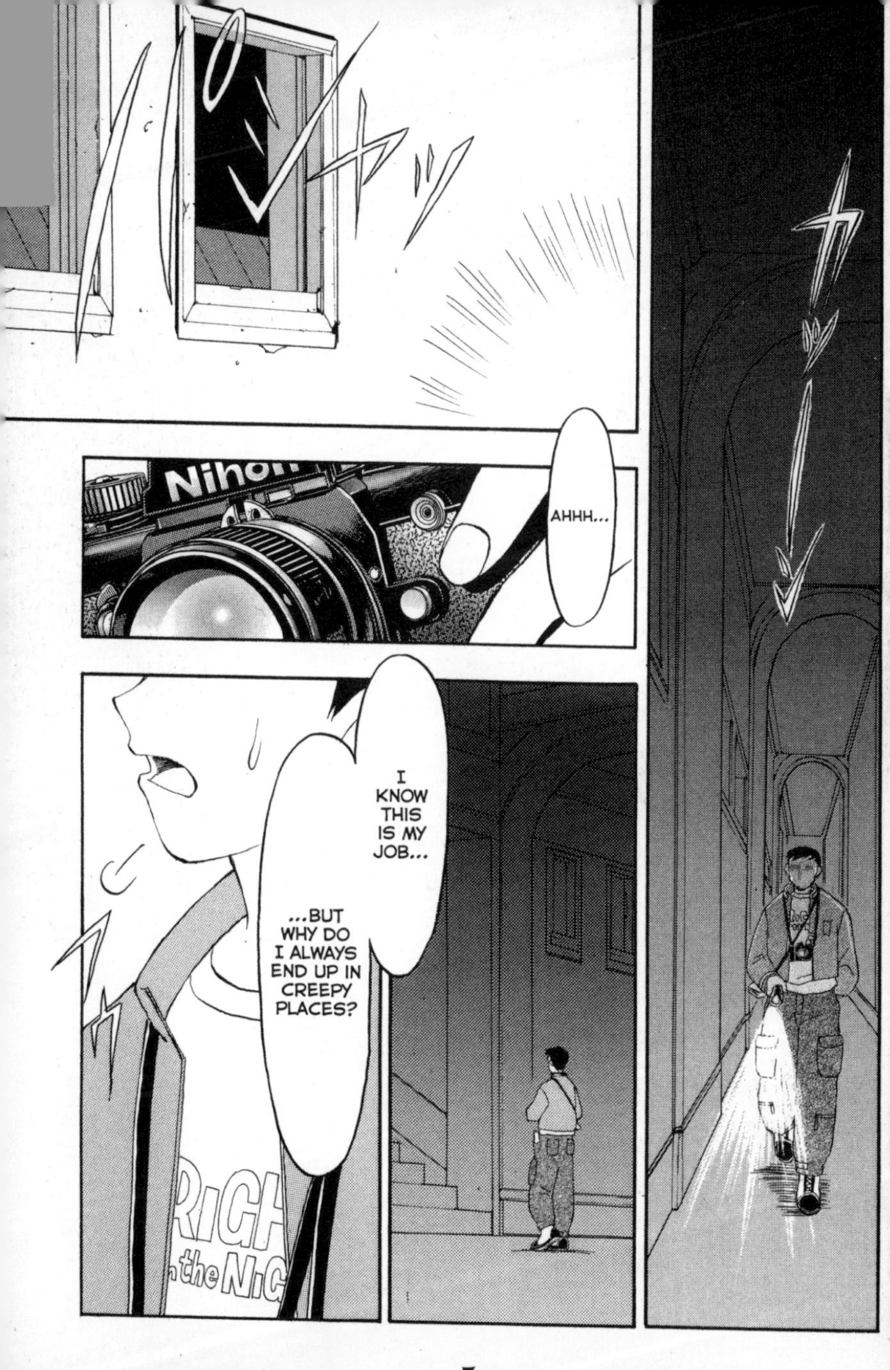
AHHH...
I KNOW THIS IS MY JOB...
...BUT WHY DO I ALWAYS END UP IN CREEPY PLACES?

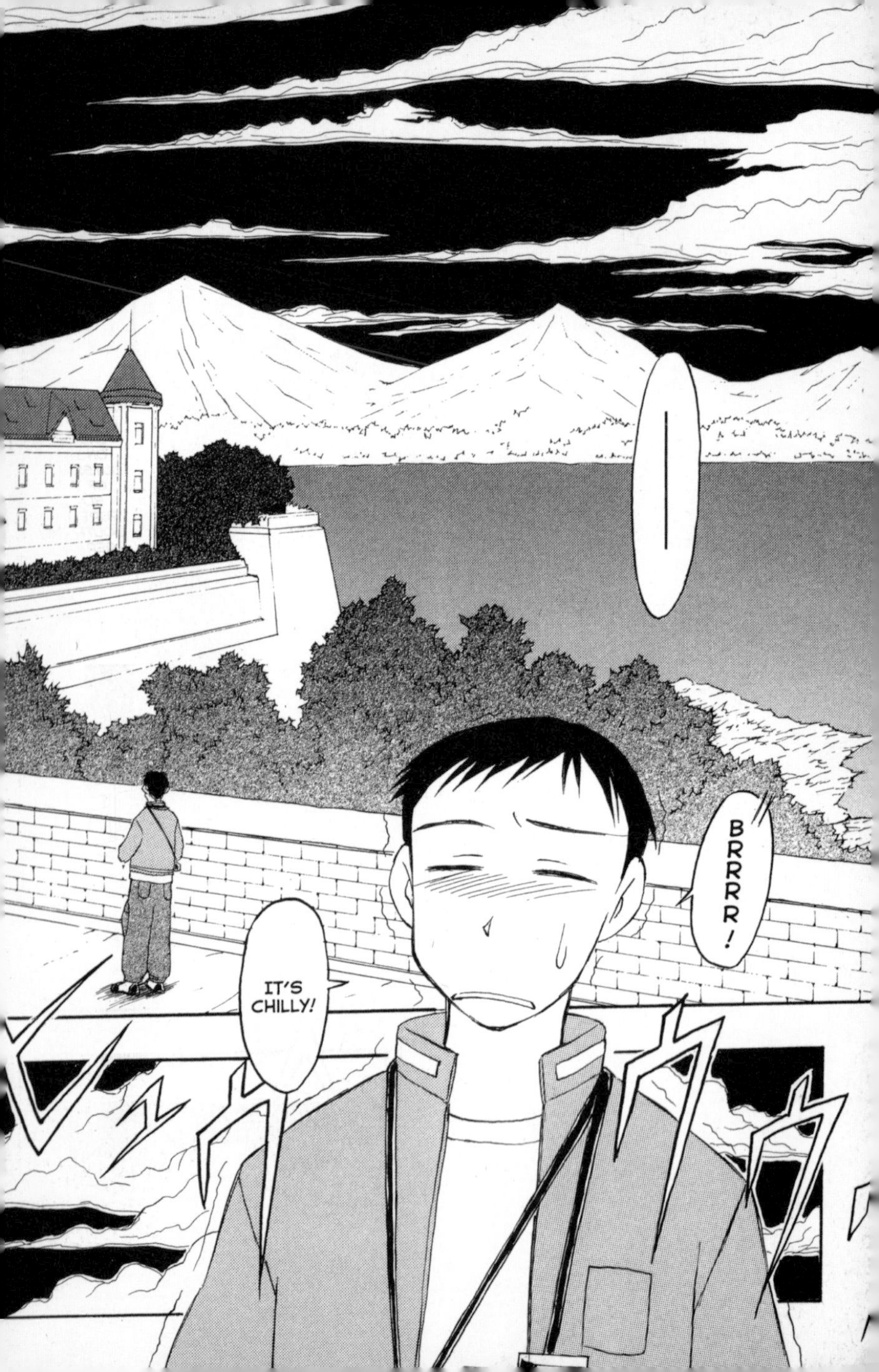
BRRRR!
IT'S CHILLY!

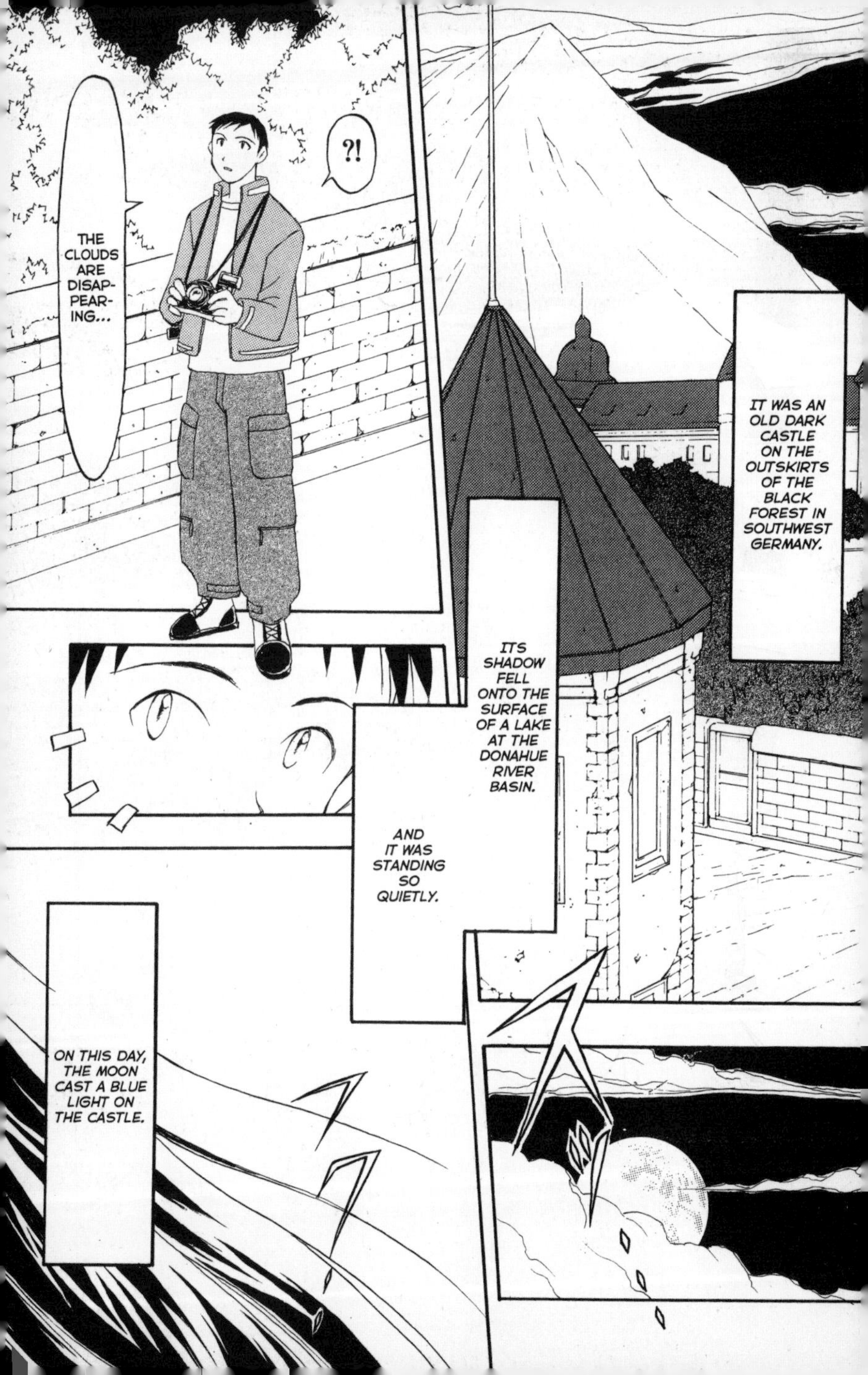
IT WAS AN OLD DARK CASTLE ON THE OUTSKIRTS OF THE BLACK FOREST IN SOUTHWEST GERMANY.
ITS SHADOW FELL ONTO THE SURFACE OF A LAKE AT THE DONAHUE RIVER BASIN.
AND IT WAS STANDING SO QUIETLY.
?!
THE CLOUDS ARE DISAPPEARING...
ON THIS DAY, THE MOON CAST A BLUE LIGHT ON THE CASTLE.

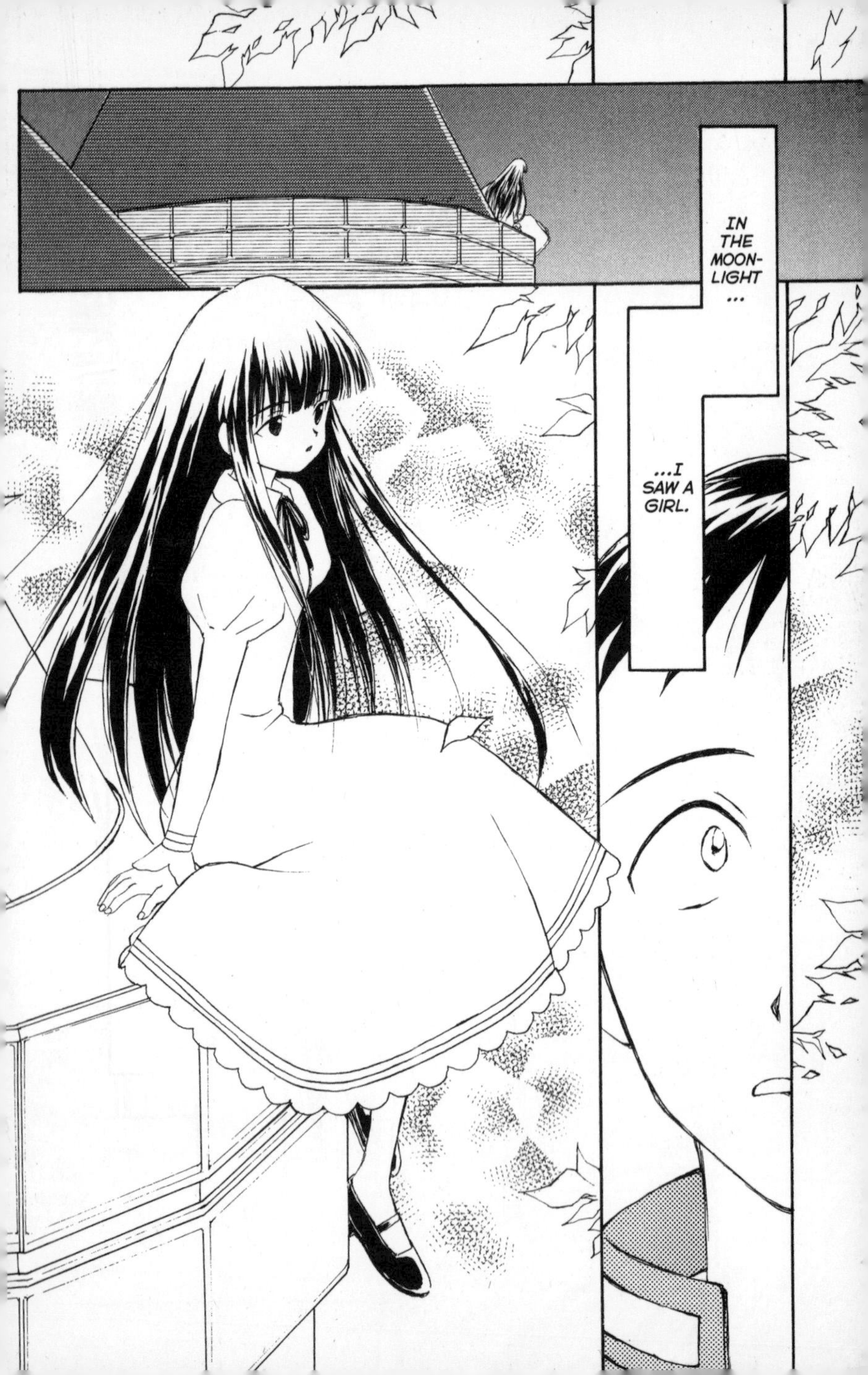

IN THE MOON-LIGHT ...
...I SAW A GIRL.

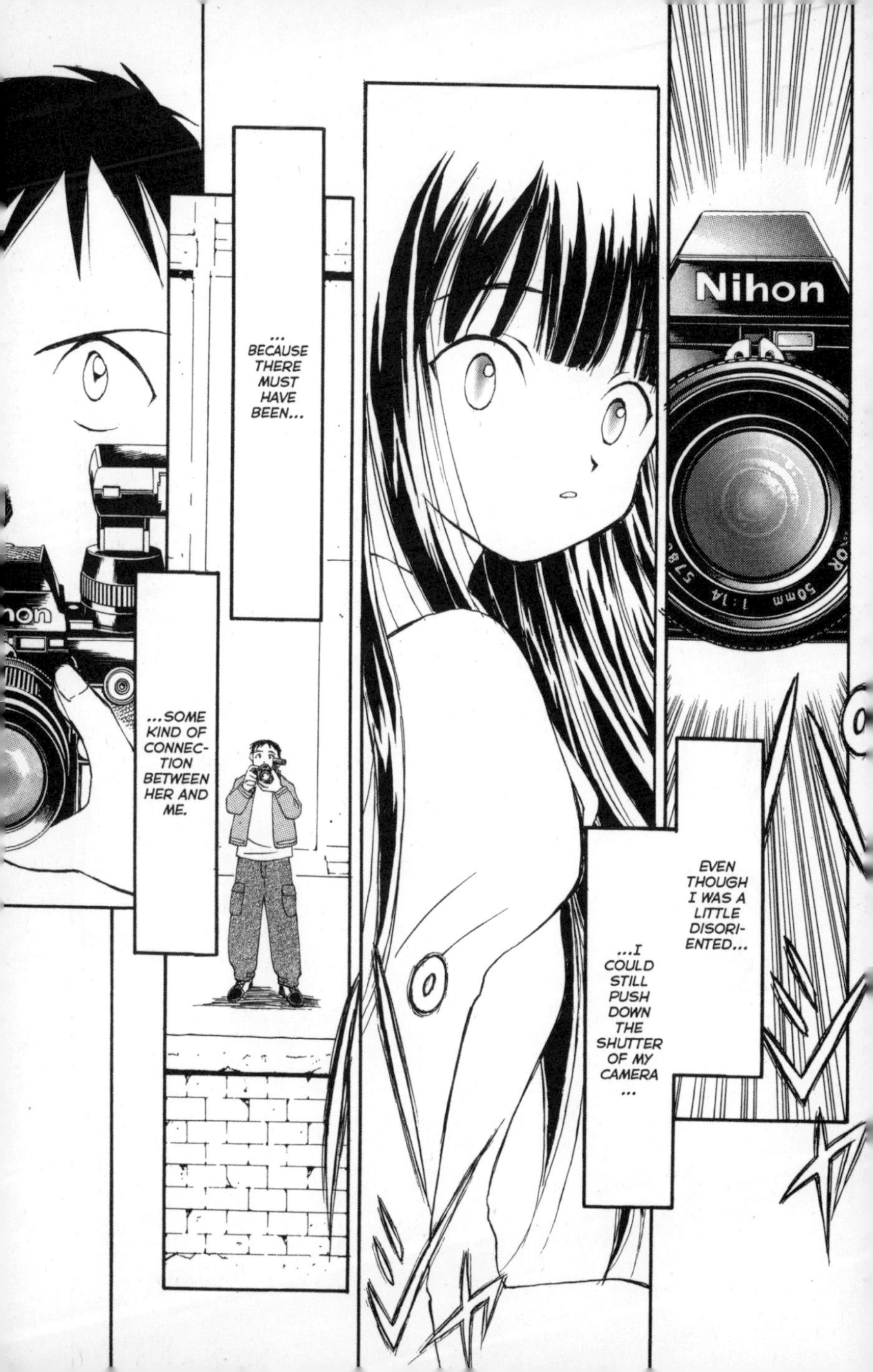
Nihon
EVEN THOUGH I WAS A LITTLE DISORIENTED...
...I COULD STILL PUSH DOWN THE SHUTTER OF MY CAMERA ...
... BECAUSE THERE MUST HAVE BEEN...
...SOME KIND OF CONNECTION BETWEEN HER AND ME.

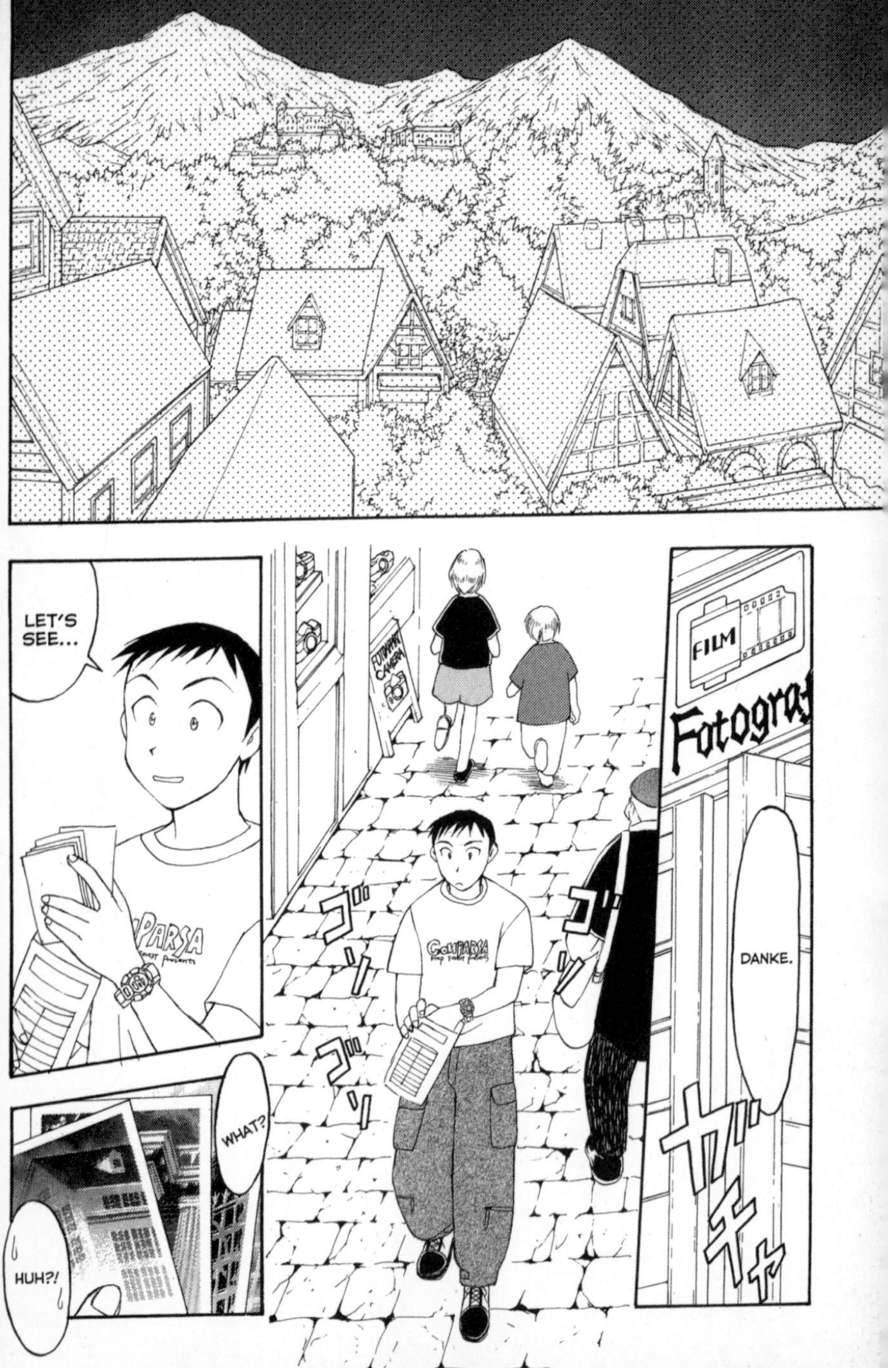
FILM
Fotograf
DANKE.
CAMERA
LET'S SEE...
WHAT?
HUH?!

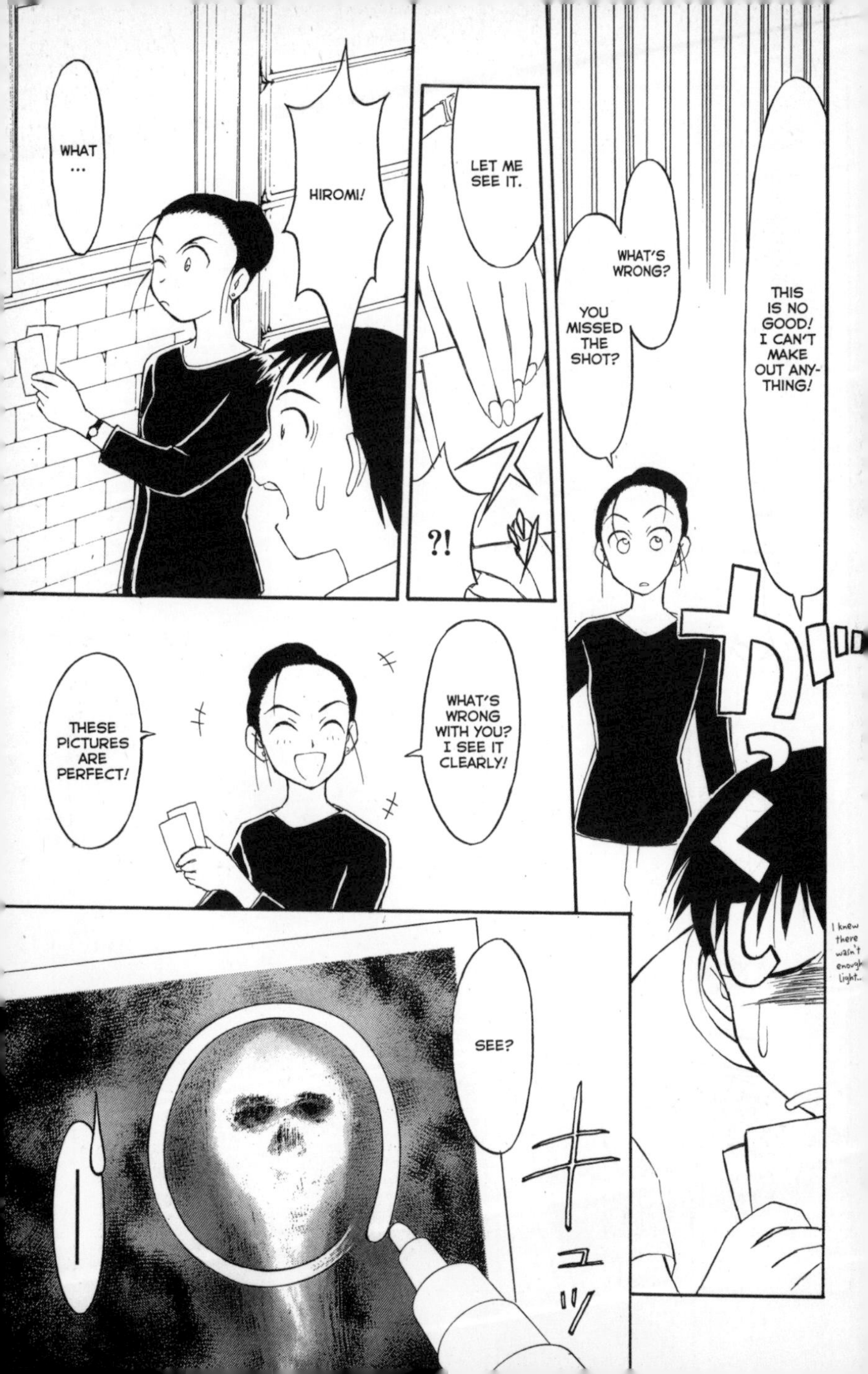

THIS IS NO GOOD! I CAN'T MAKE OUT ANYTHING!
WHAT'S WRONG?
YOU MISSED THE SHOT?
ガッ
I knew there wasn't enough light..
LET ME SEE IT.
?!
HIROMI!
WHAT ...
WHAT'S WRONG WITH YOU? I SEE IT CLEARLY!
THESE PICTURES ARE PERFECT!
SEE?
キュッ

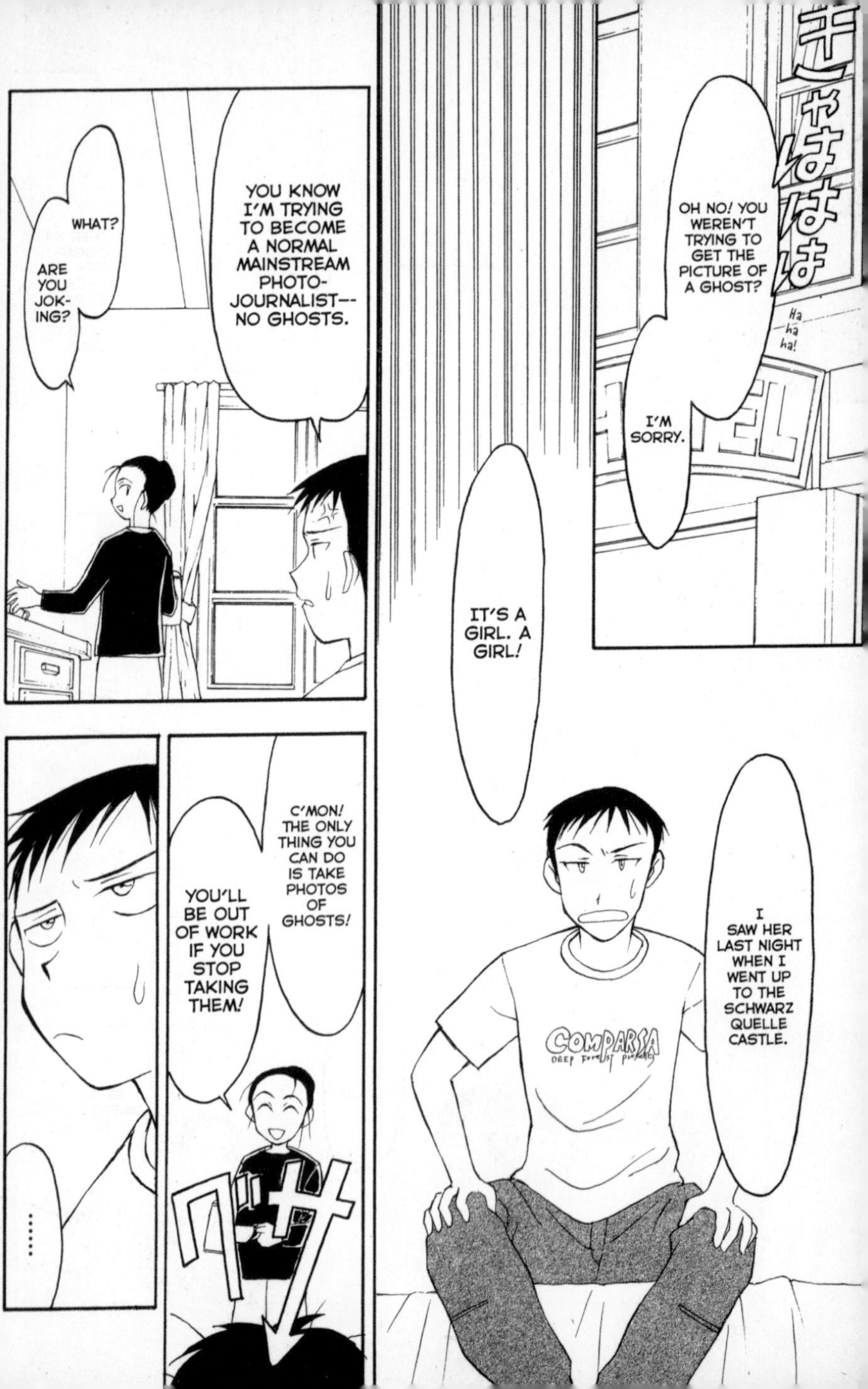
きゃははは
Ha ha ha!
OH NO! YOU WEREN'T TRYING TO GET THE PICTURE OF A GHOST?
I'M SORRY.
IT'S A GIRL. A GIRL!
I SAW HER LAST NIGHT WHEN I WENT UP TO THE SCHWARZ QUELLE CASTLE.
COMPARSA
YOU KNOW I'M TRYING TO BECOME A NORMAL MAINSTREAM PHOTO-JOURNALIST--NO GHOSTS.
WHAT?
ARE YOU JOK-ING?
C'MON! THE ONLY THING YOU CAN DO IS TAKE PHOTOS OF GHOSTS!
YOU'LL BE OUT OF WORK IF YOU STOP TAKING THEM!
......

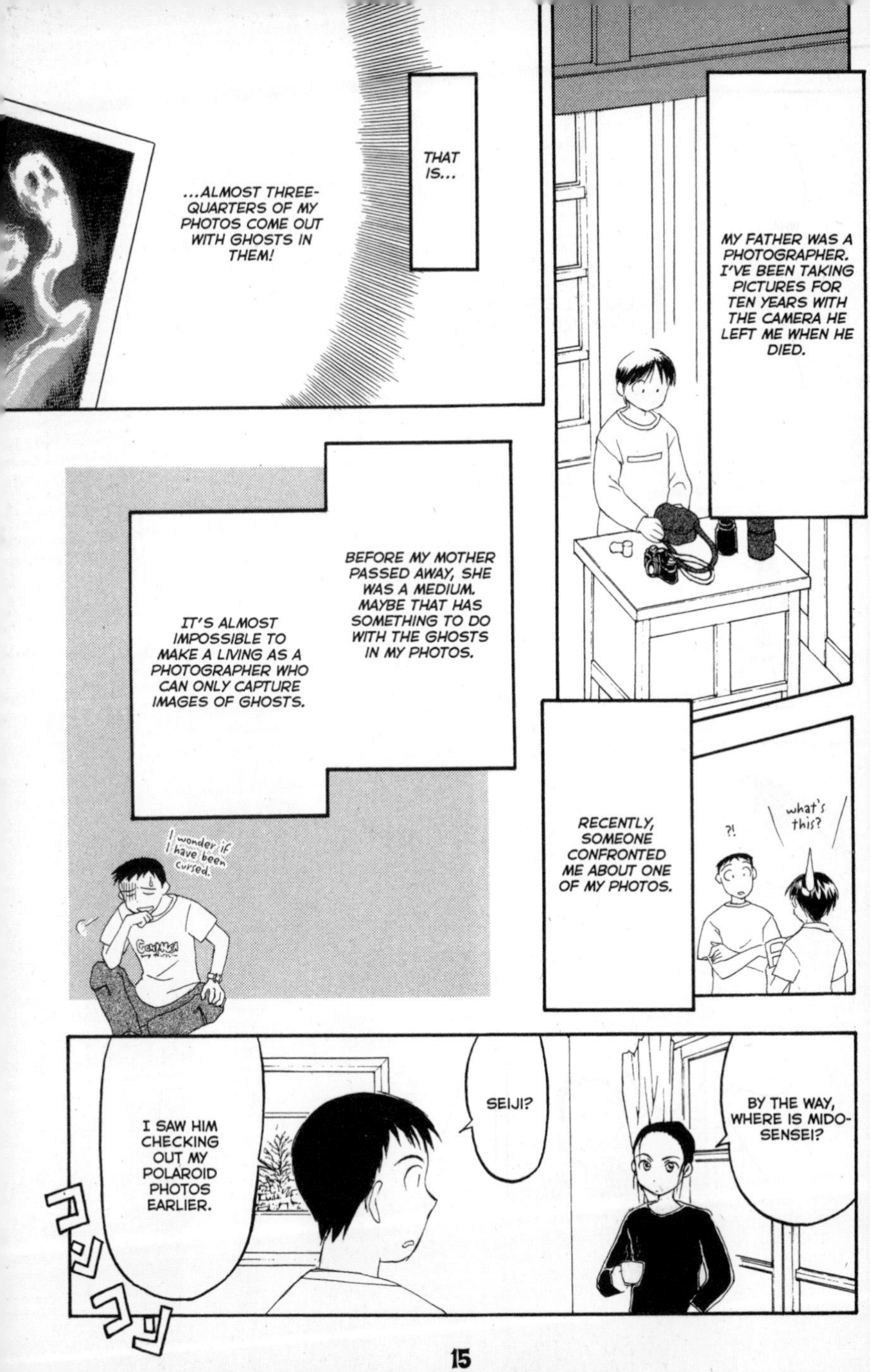
MY FATHER WAS A PHOTOGRAPHER. I'VE BEEN TAKING PICTURES FOR TEN YEARS WITH THE CAMERA HE LEFT ME WHEN HE DIED.
THAT IS...
...ALMOST THREE-QUARTERS OF MY PHOTOS COME OUT WITH GHOSTS IN THEM!
BEFORE MY MOTHER PASSED AWAY, SHE WAS A MEDIUM. MAYBE THAT HAS SOMETHING TO DO WITH THE GHOSTS IN MY PHOTOS.
IT'S ALMOST IMPOSSIBLE TO MAKE A LIVING AS A PHOTOGRAPHER WHO CAN ONLY CAPTURE IMAGES OF GHOSTS.
I wonder if I have been cursed.
RECENTLY, SOMEONE CONFRONTED ME ABOUT ONE OF MY PHOTOS.
what's this?
?!
BY THE WAY, WHERE IS MIDO-SENSEI?
SEIJI?
I SAW HIM CHECKING OUT MY POLAROID PHOTOS EARLIER.

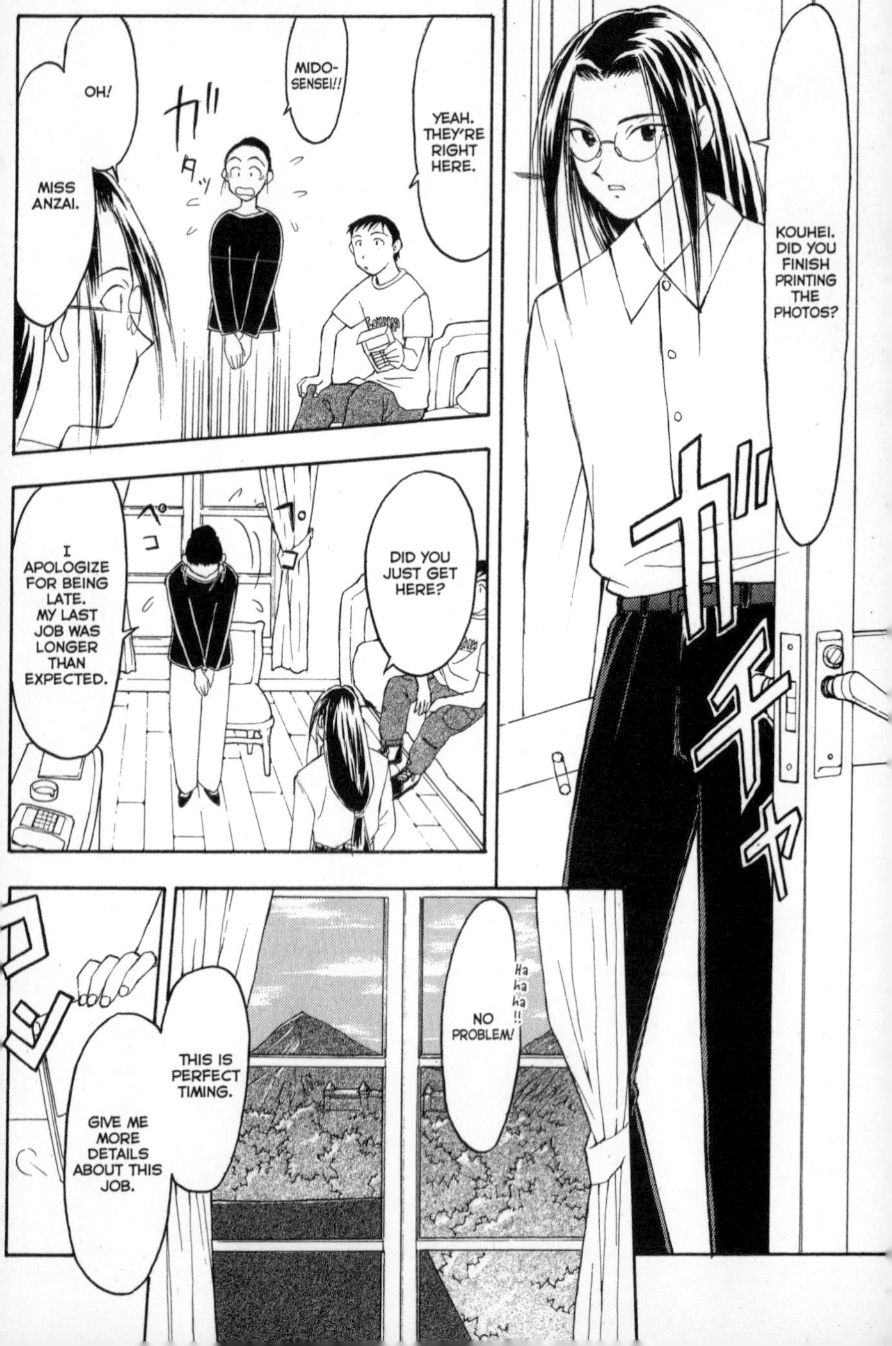
KOUHEI. DID YOU FINISH PRINTING THE PHOTOS?
ガチャ
YEAH. THEY'RE RIGHT HERE.
MIDO-SENSEI!!
ガタッ
OH!
MISS ANZAI.
DID YOU JUST GET HERE?
ペコ
I APOLOGIZE FOR BEING LATE. MY LAST JOB WAS LONGER THAN EXPECTED.
Ha ha ha!!
NO PROBLEM!
THIS IS PERFECT TIMING.
GIVE ME MORE DETAILS ABOUT THIS JOB.

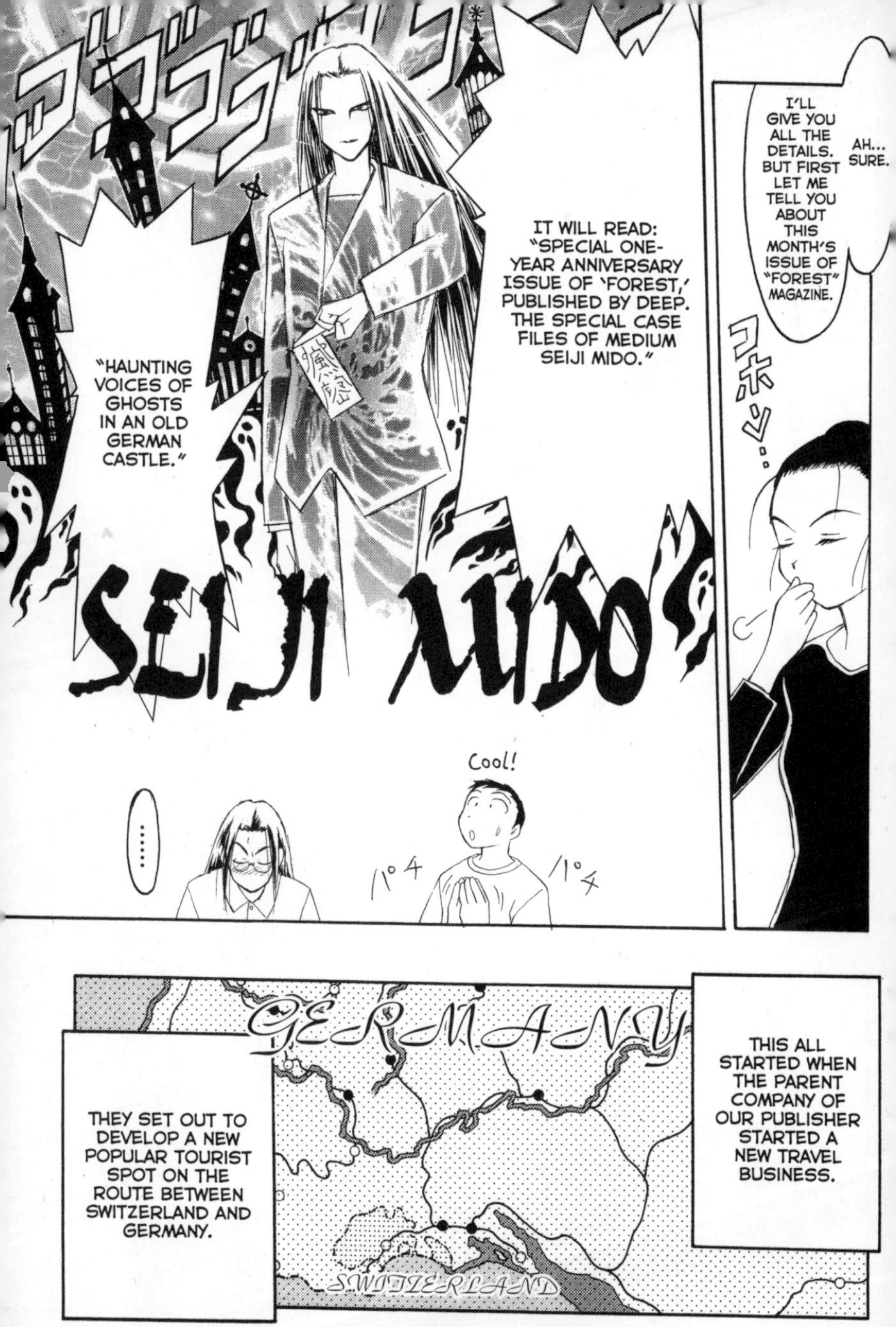
AH... SURE.
I'LL GIVE YOU ALL THE DETAILS. BUT FIRST LET ME TELL YOU ABOUT THIS MONTH'S ISSUE OF "FOREST" MAGAZINE.
コホン..
IT WILL READ: "SPECIAL ONE-YEAR ANNIVERSARY ISSUE OF 'FOREST,' PUBLISHED BY DEEP. THE SPECIAL CASE FILES OF MEDIUM SEIJI MIDO."
"HAUNTING VOICES OF GHOSTS IN AN OLD GERMAN CASTLE."
SEIJI MIDO
Cool!
......
THIS ALL STARTED WHEN THE PARENT COMPANY OF OUR PUBLISHER STARTED A NEW TRAVEL BUSINESS.
GERMANY
THEY SET OUT TO DEVELOP A NEW POPULAR TOURIST SPOT ON THE ROUTE BETWEEN SWITZERLAND AND GERMANY.
SWITZERLAND

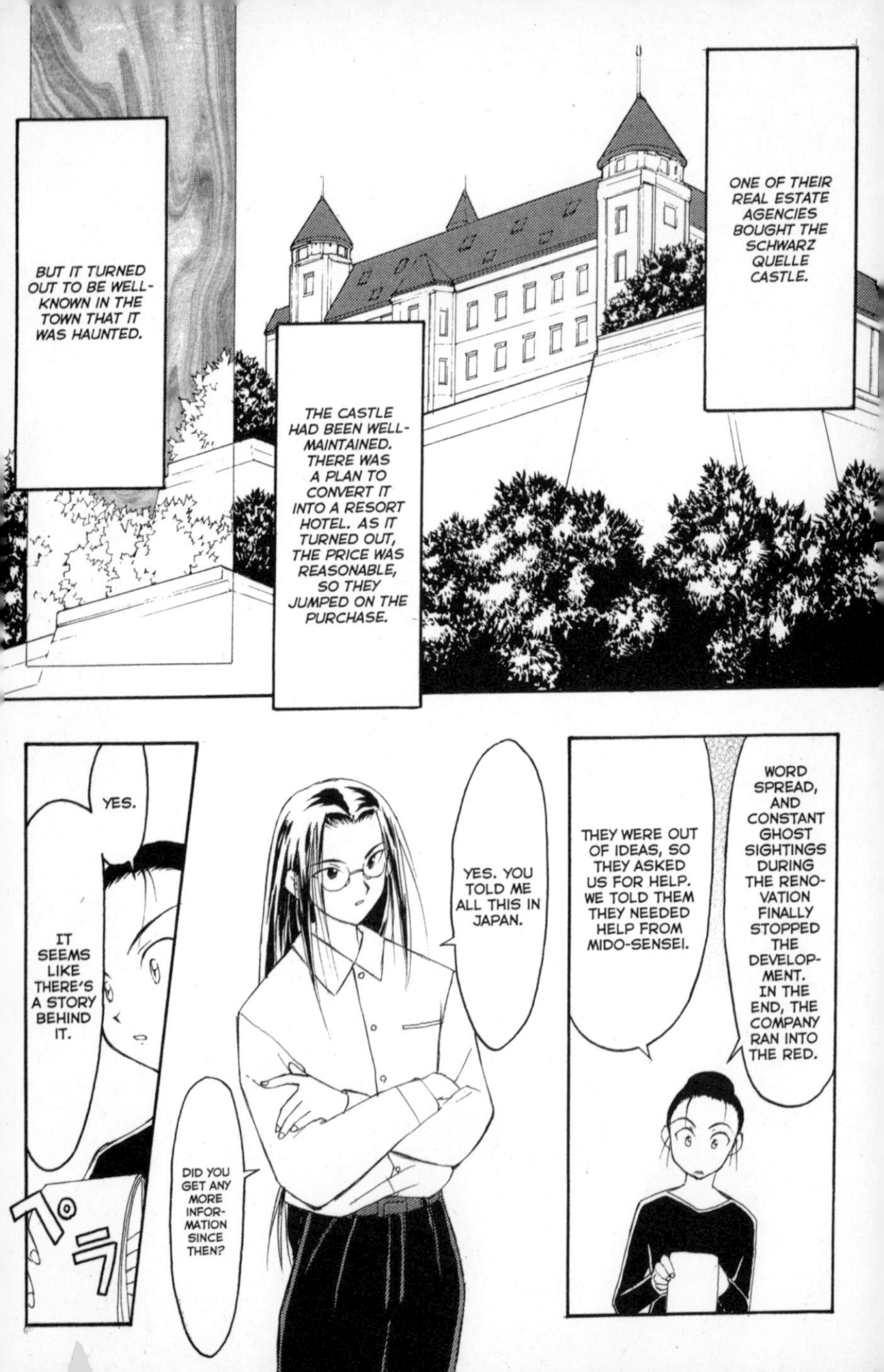
ONE OF THEIR REAL ESTATE AGENCIES BOUGHT THE SCHWARZ QUELLE CASTLE.
THE CASTLE HAD BEEN WELL-MAINTAINED. THERE WAS A PLAN TO CONVERT IT INTO A RESORT HOTEL. AS IT TURNED OUT, THE PRICE WAS REASONABLE, SO THEY JUMPED ON THE PURCHASE.
BUT IT TURNED OUT TO BE WELL-KNOWN IN THE TOWN THAT IT WAS HAUNTED.
WORD SPREAD, AND CONSTANT GHOST SIGHTINGS DURING THE RENOVATION FINALLY STOPPED THE DEVELOPMENT. IN THE END, THE COMPANY RAN INTO THE RED.
THEY WERE OUT OF IDEAS, SO THEY ASKED US FOR HELP. WE TOLD THEM THEY NEEDED HELP FROM MIDO-SENSEI.
YES. YOU TOLD ME ALL THIS IN JAPAN.
DID YOU GET ANY MORE INFORMATION SINCE THEN?
YES.
IT SEEMS LIKE THERE'S A STORY BEHIND IT.
ペラ

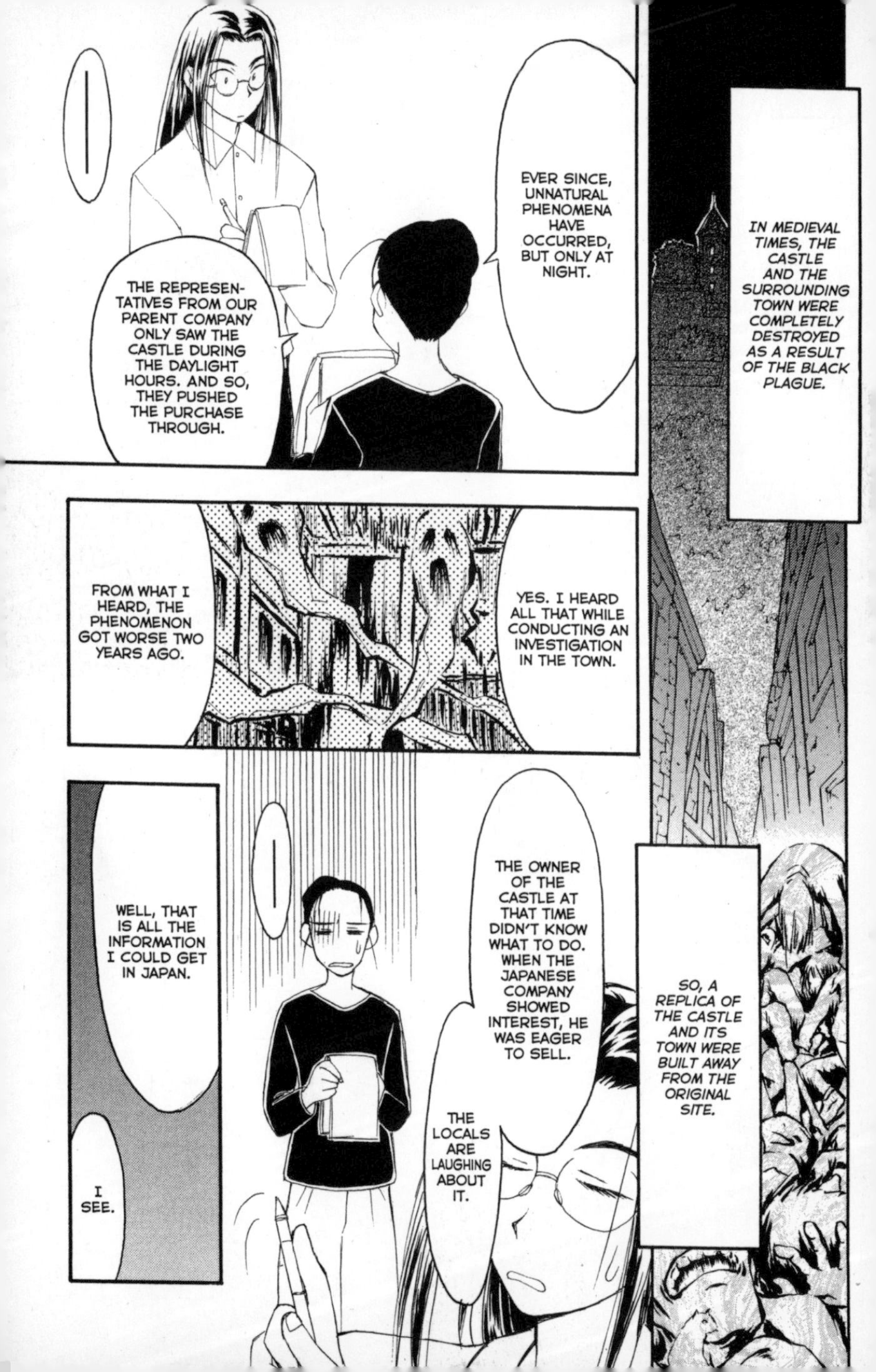
IN MEDIEVAL TIMES, THE CASTLE AND THE SURROUNDING TOWN WERE COMPLETELY DESTROYED AS A RESULT OF THE BLACK PLAGUE.
SO, A REPLICA OF THE CASTLE AND ITS TOWN WERE BUILT AWAY FROM THE ORIGINAL SITE.
EVER SINCE, UNNATURAL PHENOMENA HAVE OCCURRED, BUT ONLY AT NIGHT.
THE REPRESEN-TATIVES FROM OUR PARENT COMPANY ONLY SAW THE CASTLE DURING THE DAYLIGHT HOURS. AND SO, THEY PUSHED THE PURCHASE THROUGH.
YES. I HEARD ALL THAT WHILE CONDUCTING AN INVESTIGATION IN THE TOWN.
FROM WHAT I HEARD, THE PHENOMENON GOT WORSE TWO YEARS AGO.
THE OWNER OF THE CASTLE AT THAT TIME DIDN'T KNOW WHAT TO DO. WHEN THE JAPANESE COMPANY SHOWED INTEREST, HE WAS EAGER TO SELL.
THE LOCALS ARE LAUGHING ABOUT IT.
WELL, THAT IS ALL THE INFORMATION I COULD GET IN JAPAN.
I SEE.

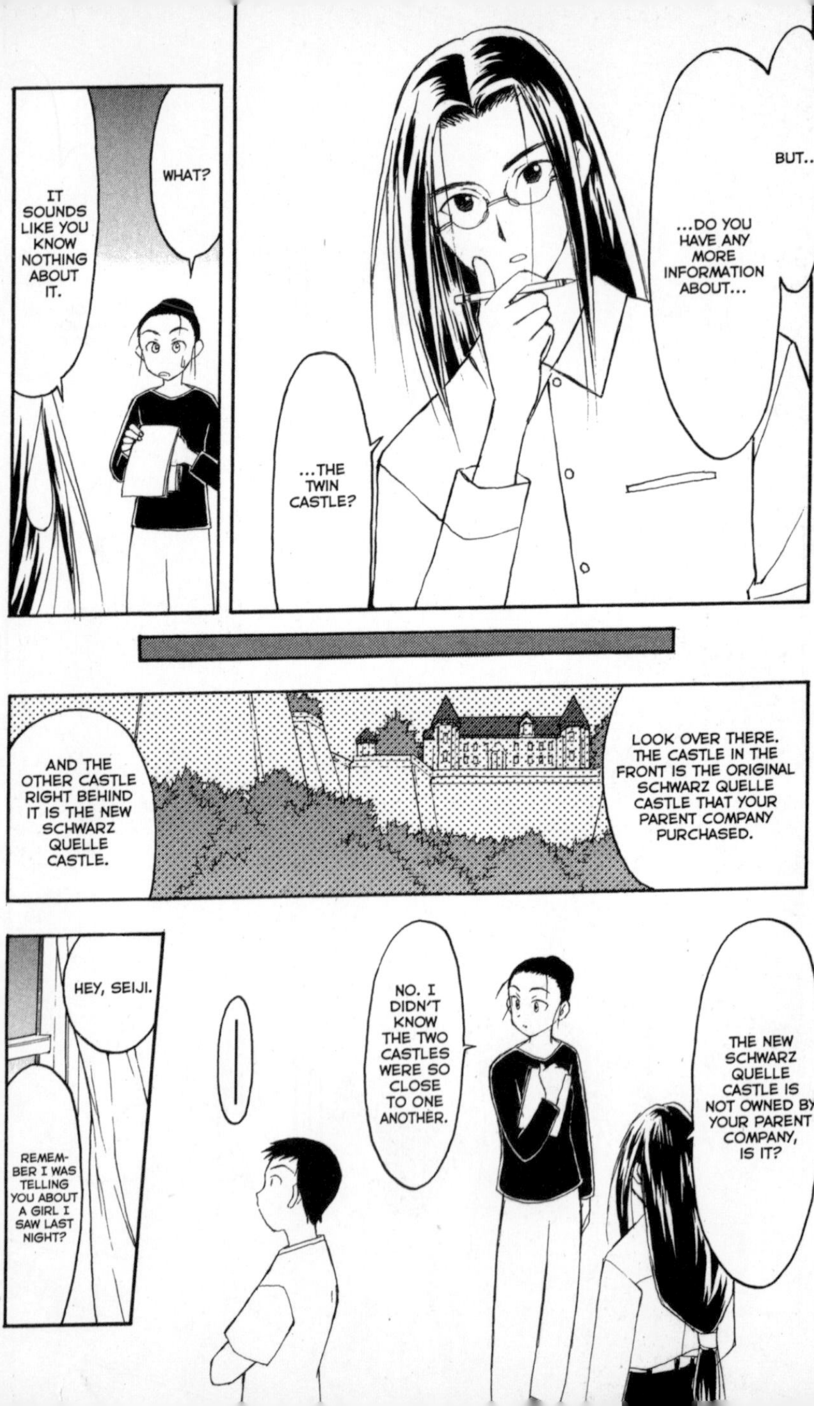
BUT...
...DO YOU HAVE ANY MORE INFORMATION ABOUT...
...THE TWIN CASTLE?
WHAT?
IT SOUNDS LIKE YOU KNOW NOTHING ABOUT IT.
LOOK OVER THERE. THE CASTLE IN THE FRONT IS THE ORIGINAL SCHWARZ QUELLE CASTLE THAT YOUR PARENT COMPANY PURCHASED.
AND THE OTHER CASTLE RIGHT BEHIND IT IS THE NEW SCHWARZ QUELLE CASTLE.
THE NEW SCHWARZ QUELLE CASTLE IS NOT OWNED BY YOUR PARENT COMPANY, IS IT?
NO. I DIDN'T KNOW THE TWO CASTLES WERE SO CLOSE TO ONE ANOTHER.
HEY, SEIJI.
REMEMBER I WAS TELLING YOU ABOUT A GIRL I SAW LAST NIGHT?

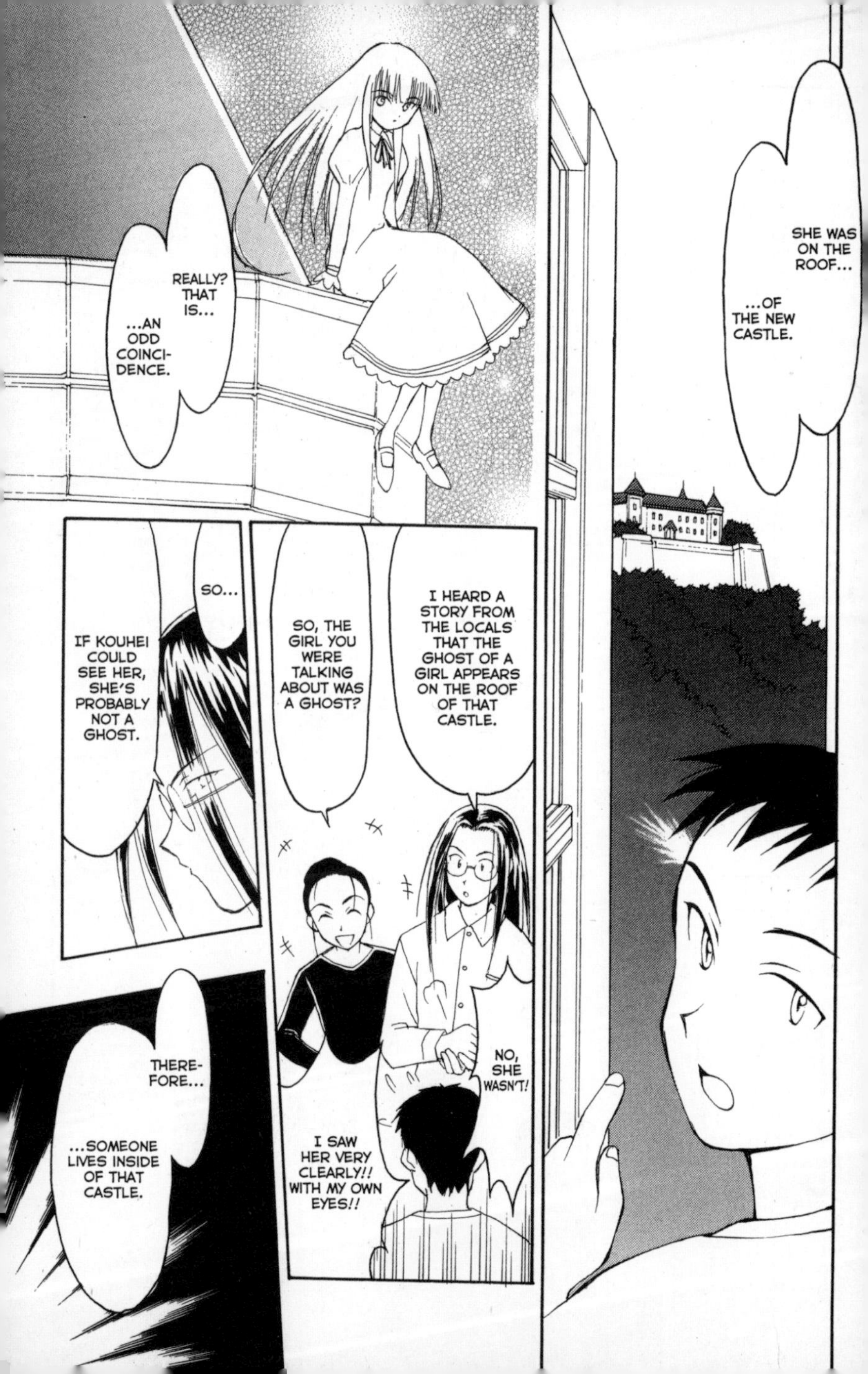
SHE WAS ON THE ROOF...
...OF THE NEW CASTLE.
REALLY? THAT IS...
...AN ODD COINCI-DENCE.
I HEARD A STORY FROM THE LOCALS THAT THE GHOST OF A GIRL APPEARS ON THE ROOF OF THAT CASTLE.
SO, THE GIRL YOU WERE TALKING ABOUT WAS A GHOST?
NO, SHE WASN'T!
I SAW HER VERY CLEARLY!! WITH MY OWN EYES!!
SO...
IF KOUHEI COULD SEE HER, SHE'S PROBABLY NOT A GHOST.
THERE-FORE...
...SOMEONE LIVES INSIDE OF THAT CASTLE.

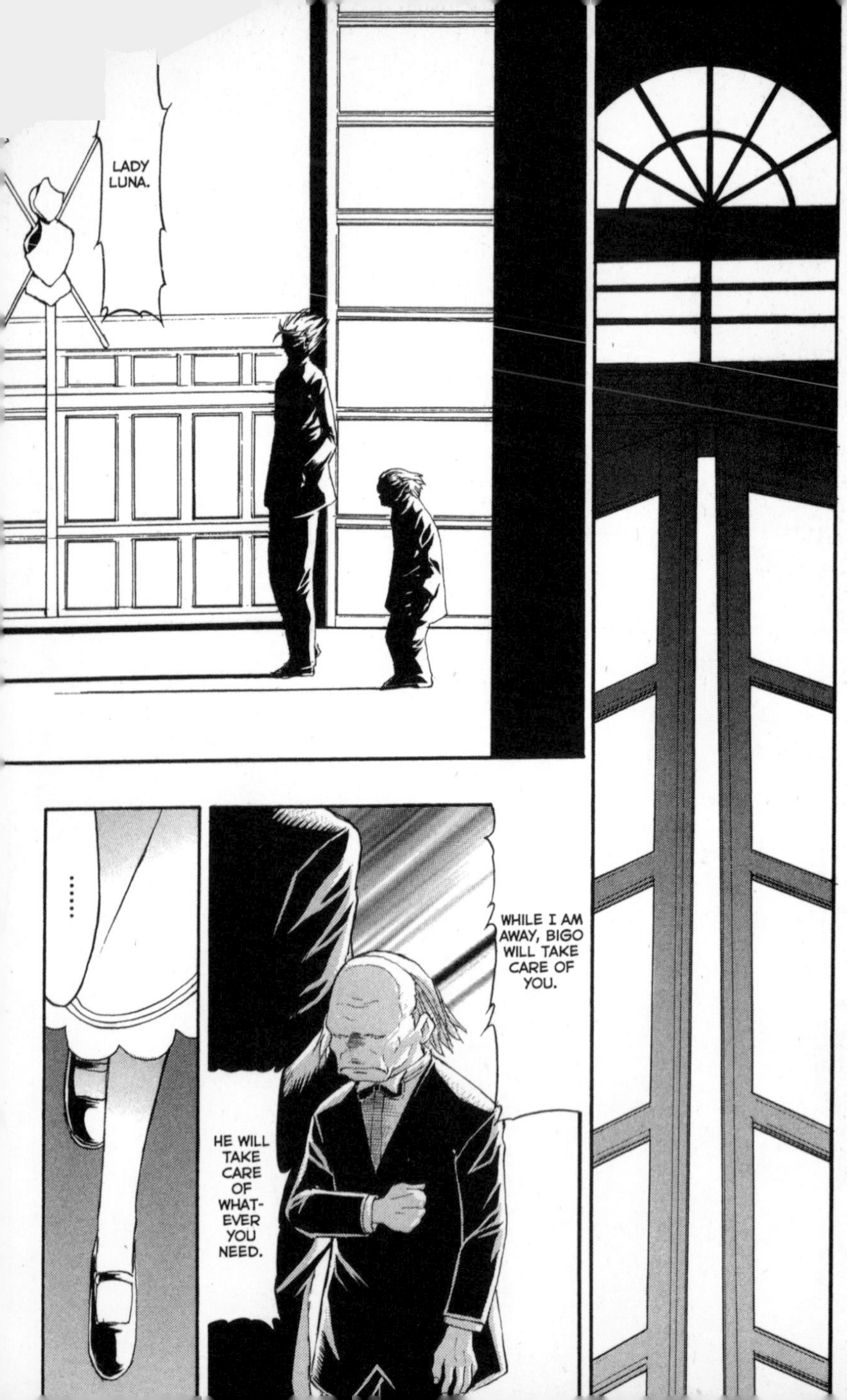
LADY LUNA.
WHILE I AM AWAY, BIGO WILL TAKE CARE OF YOU.
HE WILL TAKE CARE OF WHAT-EVER YOU NEED.
......

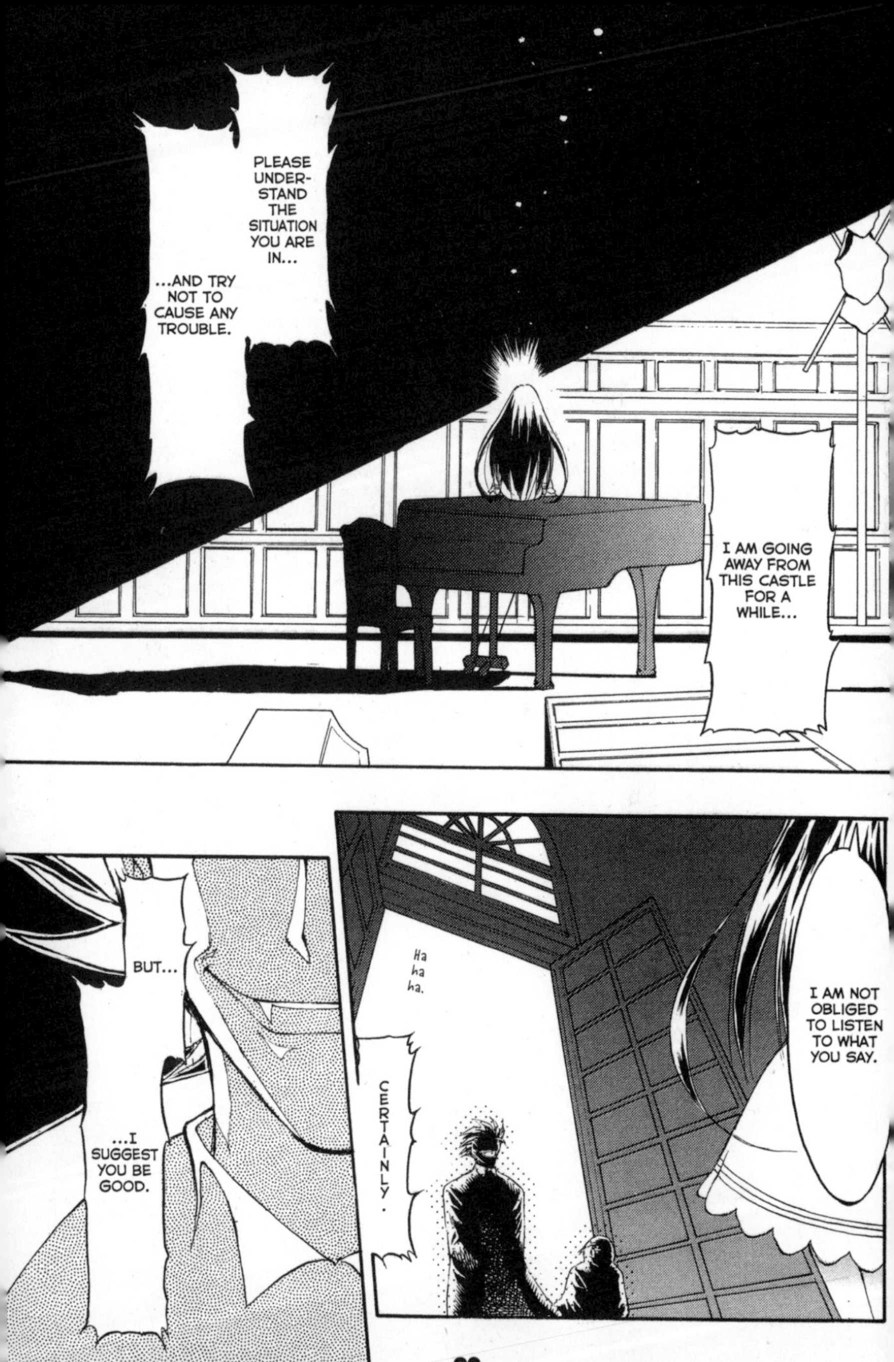
I AM GOING AWAY FROM THIS CASTLE FOR A WHILE...
PLEASE UNDER-STAND THE SITUATION YOU ARE IN...
...AND TRY NOT TO CAUSE ANY TROUBLE.
I AM NOT OBLIGED TO LISTEN TO WHAT YOU SAY.
Ha ha ha.
CERTAINLY.
BUT...
...I SUGGEST YOU BE GOOD.

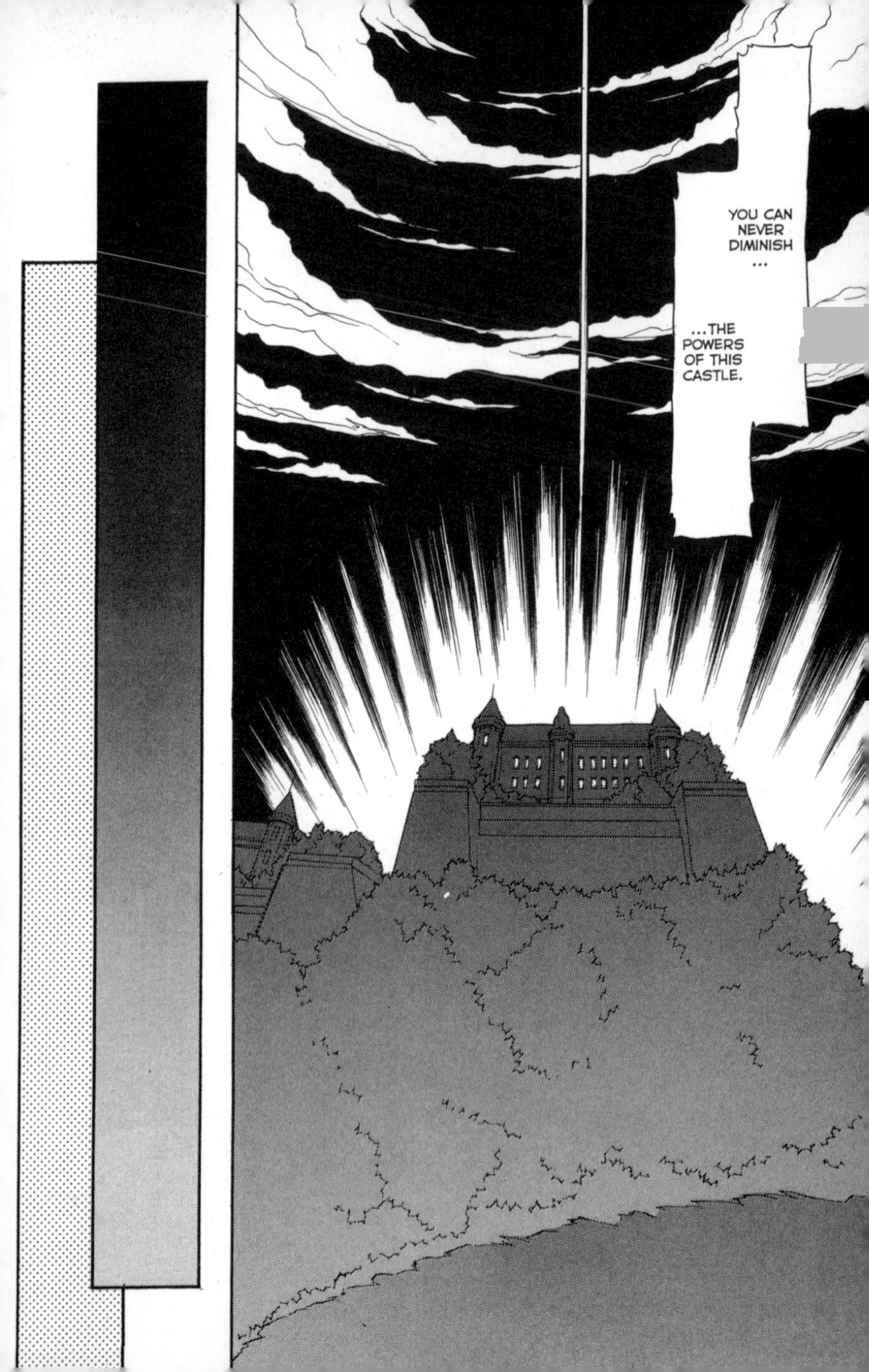
YOU CAN NEVER DIMINISH ...
...THE POWERS OF THIS CASTLE.

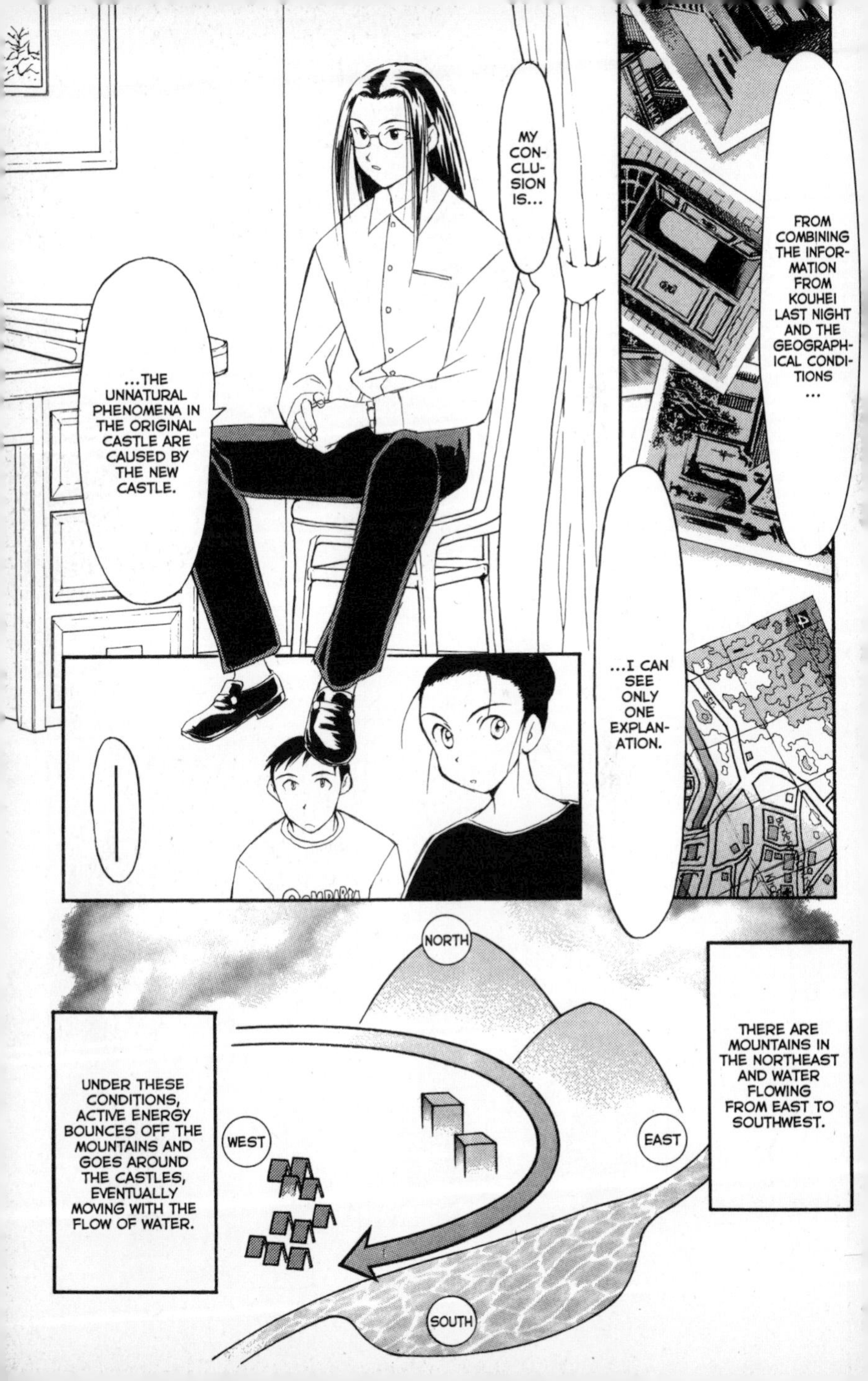

FROM COMBINING THE INFORMATION FROM KOUHEI LAST NIGHT AND THE GEOGRAPHICAL CONDITIONS...
...I CAN SEE ONLY ONE EXPLANATION.
MY CONCLUSION IS...
...THE UNNATURAL PHENOMENA IN THE ORIGINAL CASTLE ARE CAUSED BY THE NEW CASTLE.
THERE ARE MOUNTAINS IN THE NORTHEAST AND WATER FLOWING FROM EAST TO SOUTHWEST.
NORTH
EAST
WEST
SOUTH
UNDER THESE CONDITIONS, ACTIVE ENERGY BOUNCES OFF THE MOUNTAINS AND GOES AROUND THE CASTLES, EVENTUALLY MOVING WITH THE FLOW OF WATER.

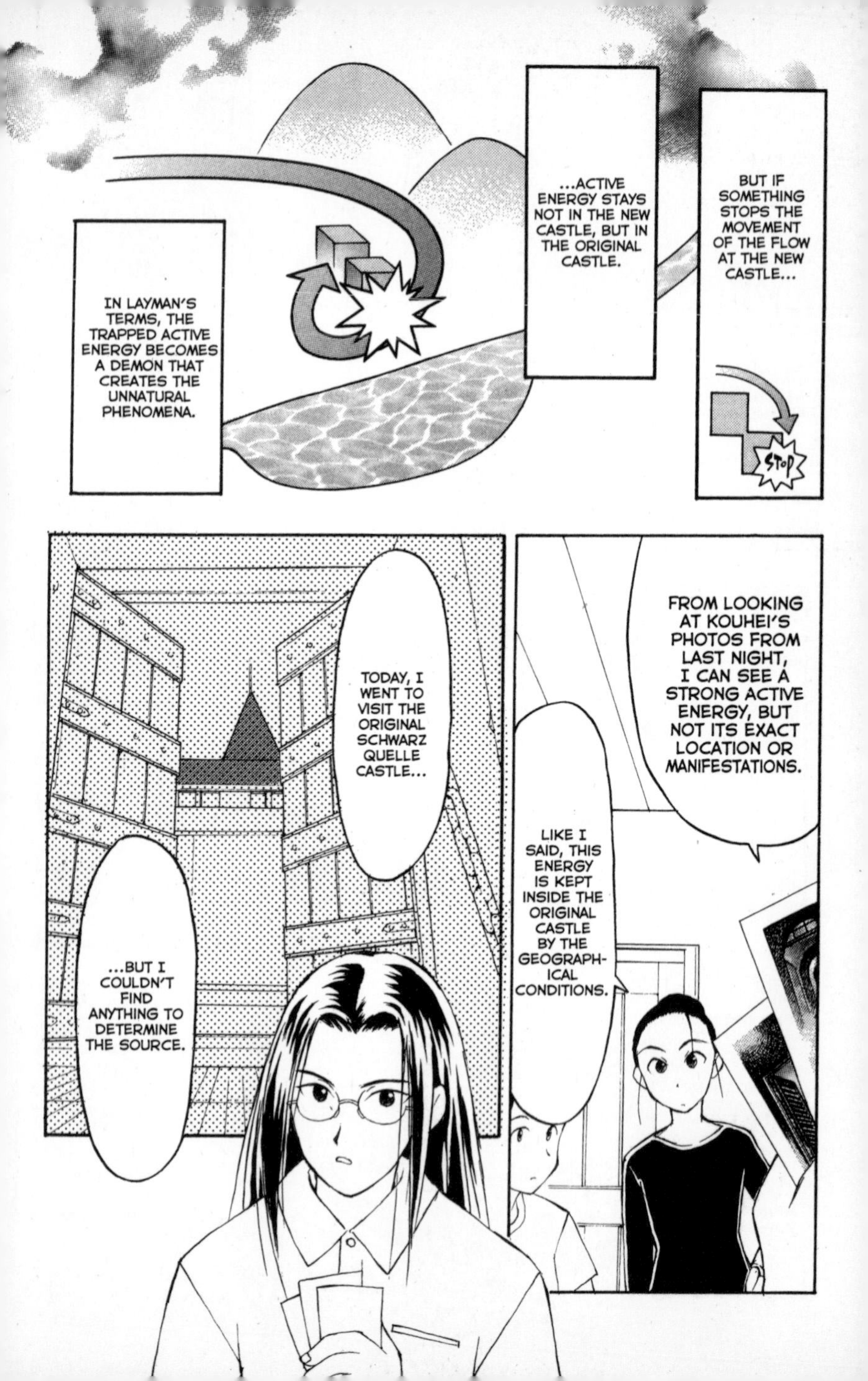
BUT IF SOMETHING STOPS THE MOVEMENT OF THE FLOW AT THE NEW CASTLE...
STOP
...ACTIVE ENERGY STAYS NOT IN THE NEW CASTLE, BUT IN THE ORIGINAL CASTLE.
IN LAYMAN'S TERMS, THE TRAPPED ACTIVE ENERGY BECOMES A DEMON THAT CREATES THE UNNATURAL PHENOMENA.
FROM LOOKING AT KOUHEI'S PHOTOS FROM LAST NIGHT, I CAN SEE A STRONG ACTIVE ENERGY, BUT NOT ITS EXACT LOCATION OR MANIFESTATIONS.
LIKE I SAID, THIS ENERGY IS KEPT INSIDE THE ORIGINAL CASTLE BY THE GEOGRAPH-ICAL CONDITIONS.
TODAY, I WENT TO VISIT THE ORIGINAL SCHWARZ QUELLE CASTLE...
...BUT I COULDN'T FIND ANYTHING TO DETERMINE THE SOURCE.

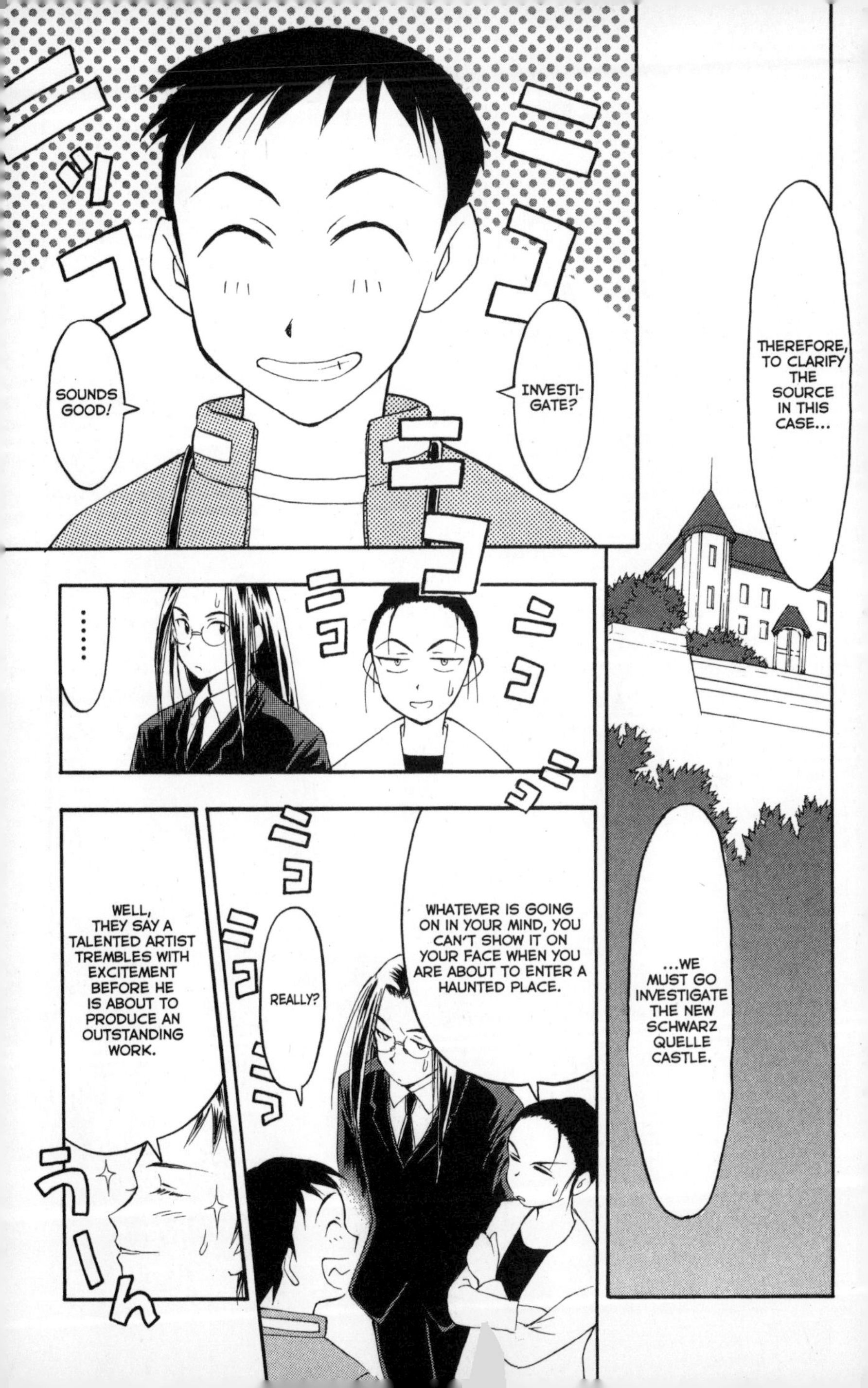
THEREFORE, TO CLARIFY THE SOURCE IN THIS CASE...
...WE MUST GO INVESTIGATE THE NEW SCHWARZ QUELLE CASTLE.
INVESTI-GATE?
SOUNDS GOOD!
......
WHATEVER IS GOING ON IN YOUR MIND, YOU CAN'T SHOW IT ON YOUR FACE WHEN YOU ARE ABOUT TO ENTER A HAUNTED PLACE.
REALLY?
WELL, THEY SAY A TALENTED ARTIST TREMBLES WITH EXCITEMENT BEFORE HE IS ABOUT TO PRODUCE AN OUTSTANDING WORK.

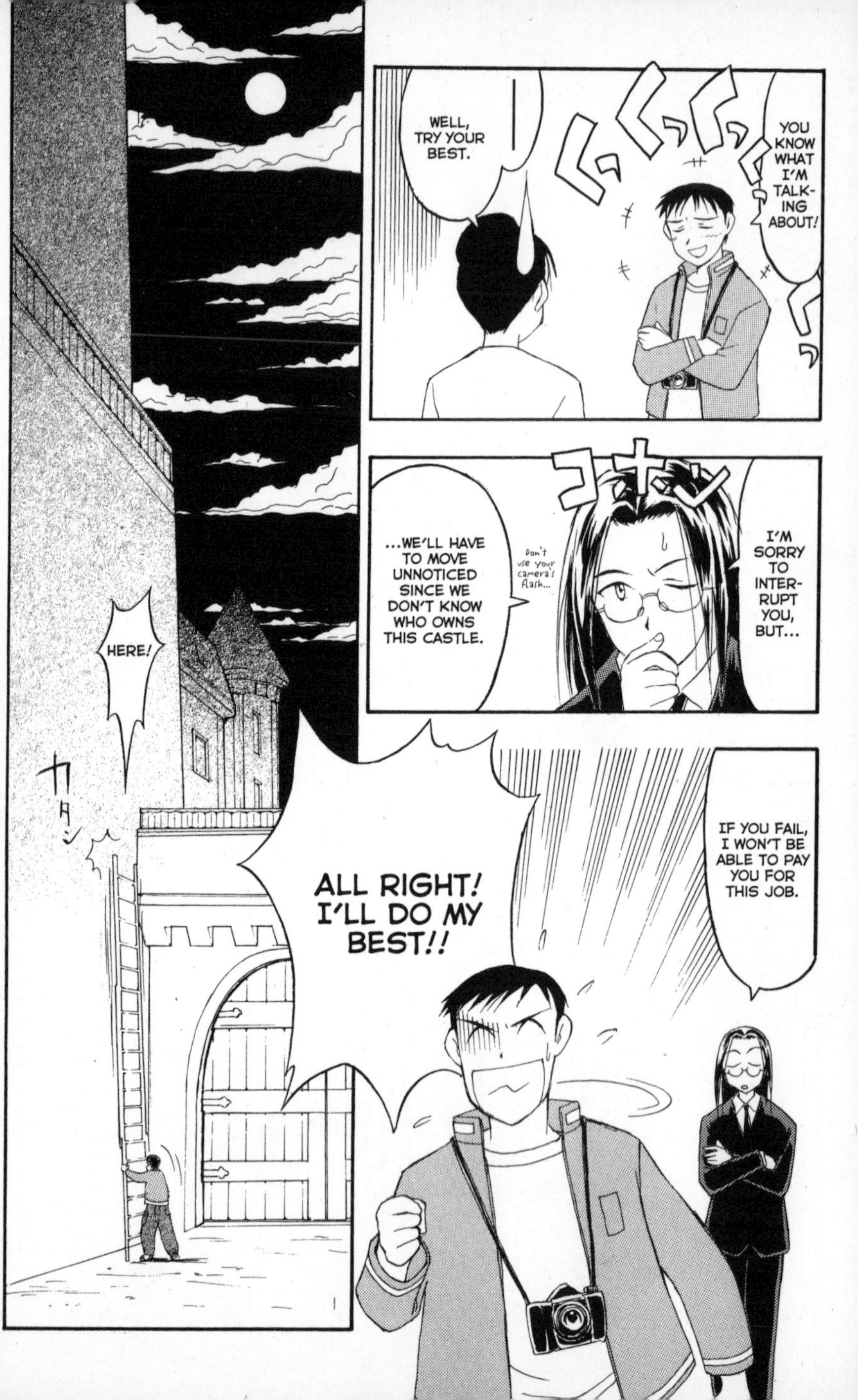
YOU KNOW WHAT I'M TALKING ABOUT!
WELL, TRY YOUR BEST.
コホン
I'M SORRY TO INTERRUPT YOU, BUT...
Don't use your camera's flash...
...WE'LL HAVE TO MOVE UNNOTICED SINCE WE DON'T KNOW WHO OWNS THIS CASTLE.
IF YOU FAIL, I WON'T BE ABLE TO PAY YOU FOR THIS JOB.
ALL RIGHT! I'LL DO MY BEST!!
HERE!
カタン

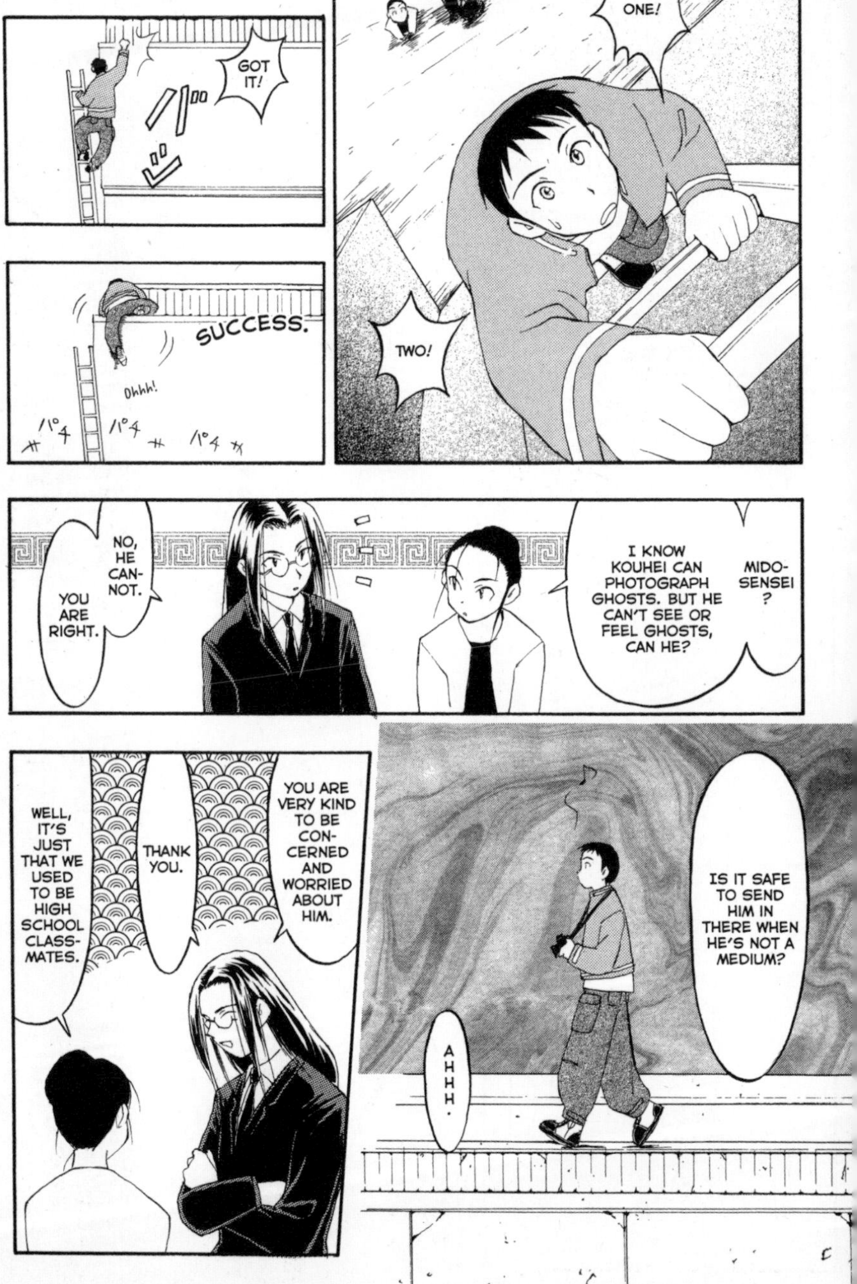
ONE!
TWO!
GOT IT!
SUCCESS.
Ohhh!
MIDO-SENSEI?
I KNOW KOUHEI CAN PHOTOGRAPH GHOSTS. BUT HE CAN'T SEE OR FEEL GHOSTS, CAN HE?
NO, HE CANNOT.
YOU ARE RIGHT.
IS IT SAFE TO SEND HIM IN THERE WHEN HE'S NOT A MEDIUM?
AHHH.
YOU ARE VERY KIND TO BE CONCERNED AND WORRIED ABOUT HIM.
THANK YOU.
WELL, IT'S JUST THAT WE USED TO BE HIGH SCHOOL CLASSMATES.

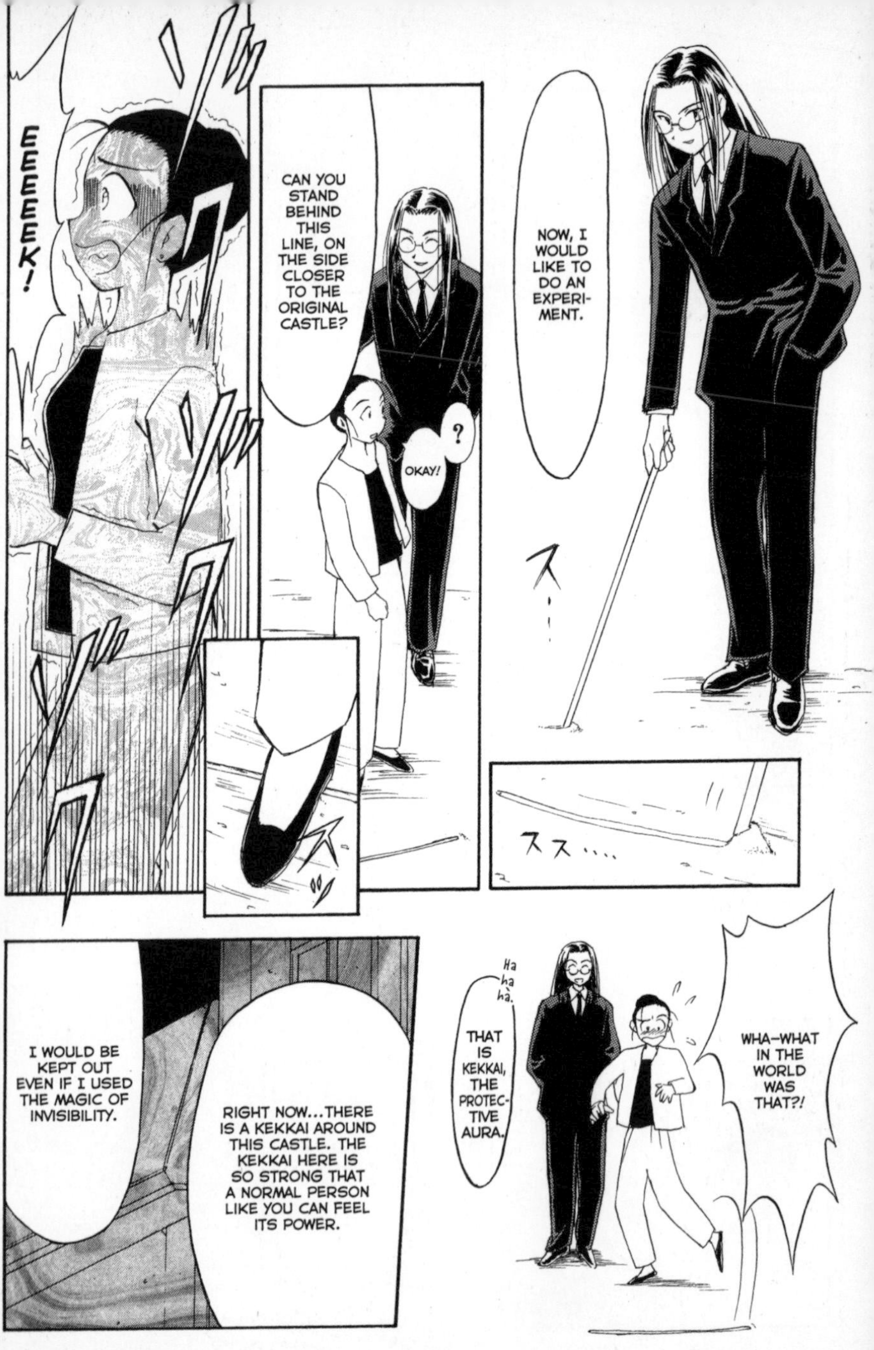

NOW, I WOULD LIKE TO DO AN EXPERIMENT.
ス…
スス…
CAN YOU STAND BEHIND THIS LINE, ON THE SIDE CLOSER TO THE ORIGINAL CASTLE?
?
OKAY!
EEEEEEK!
WHA–WHAT IN THE WORLD WAS THAT?!
Ha ha ha.
THAT IS KEKKAI, THE PROTECTIVE AURA.
RIGHT NOW...THERE IS A KEKKAI AROUND THIS CASTLE. THE KEKKAI HERE IS SO STRONG THAT A NORMAL PERSON LIKE YOU CAN FEEL ITS POWER.
I WOULD BE KEPT OUT EVEN IF I USED THE MAGIC OF INVISIBILITY.

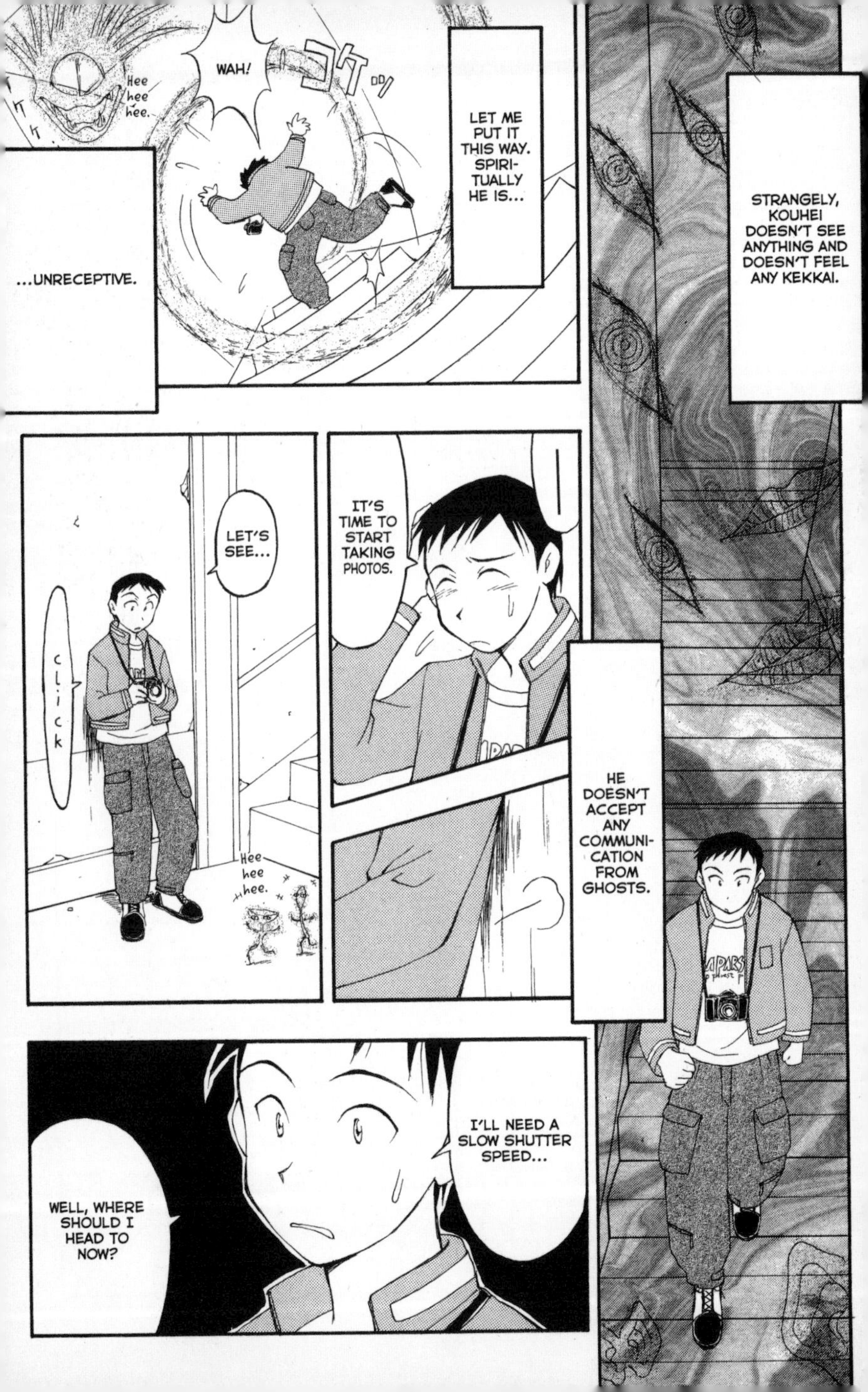
STRANGELY, KOUHEI DOESN'T SEE ANYTHING AND DOESN'T FEEL ANY KEKKAI.
HE DOESN'T ACCEPT ANY COMMUNICATION FROM GHOSTS.
LET ME PUT IT THIS WAY. SPIRITUALLY HE IS...
コケッ
WAH!
Hee hee hee.
...UNRECEPTIVE.
IT'S TIME TO START TAKING PHOTOS.
LET'S SEE...
click
Hee hee hee.
I'LL NEED A SLOW SHUTTER SPEED...
WELL, WHERE SHOULD I HEAD TO NOW?

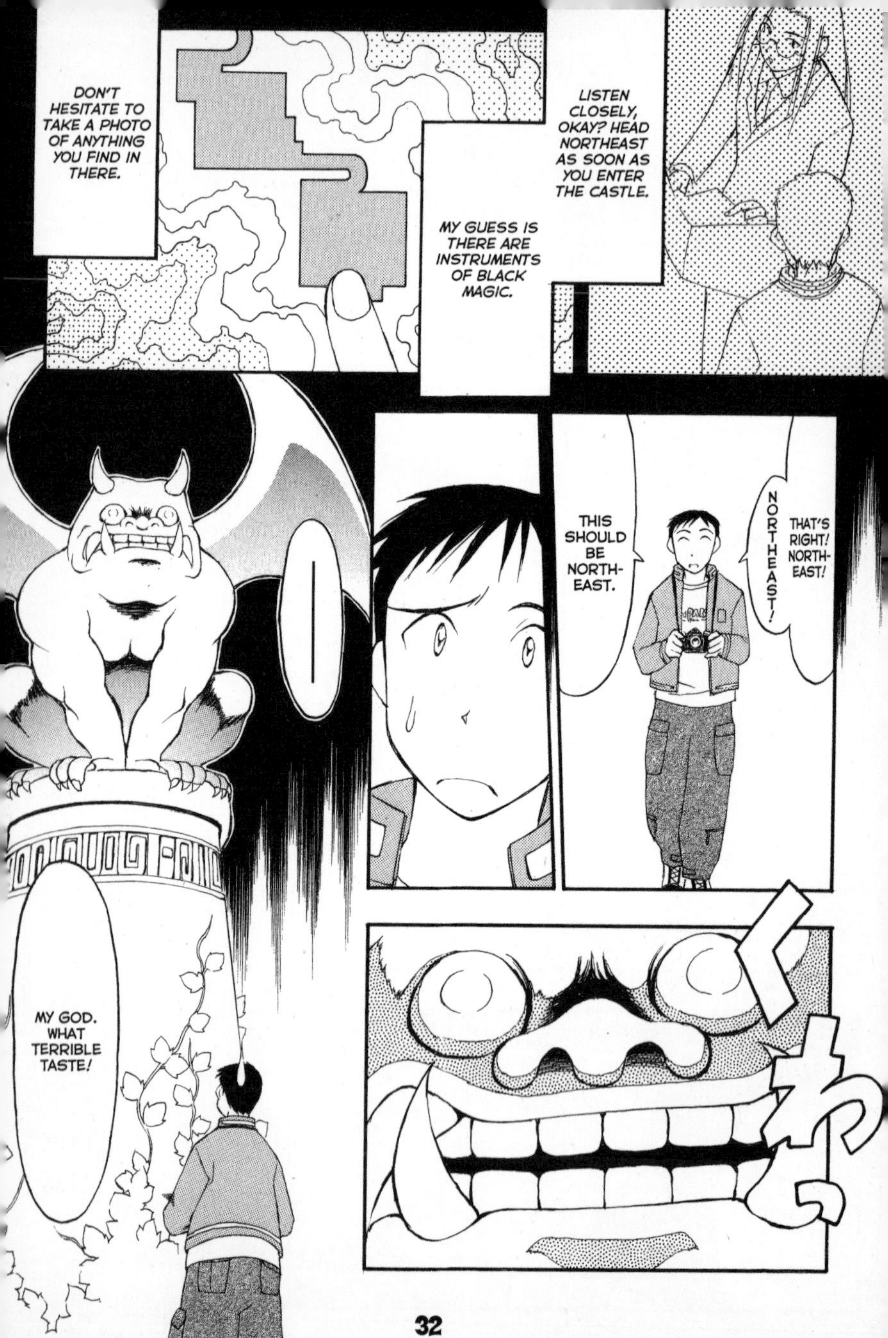
LISTEN CLOSELY, OKAY? HEAD NORTHEAST AS SOON AS YOU ENTER THE CASTLE.
MY GUESS IS THERE ARE INSTRUMENTS OF BLACK MAGIC.
DON'T HESITATE TO TAKE A PHOTO OF ANYTHING YOU FIND IN THERE.
THAT'S RIGHT! NORTH-EAST!
NORTHEAST!
THIS SHOULD BE NORTH-EAST.
くわっ
—
MY GOD. WHAT TERRIBLE TASTE!

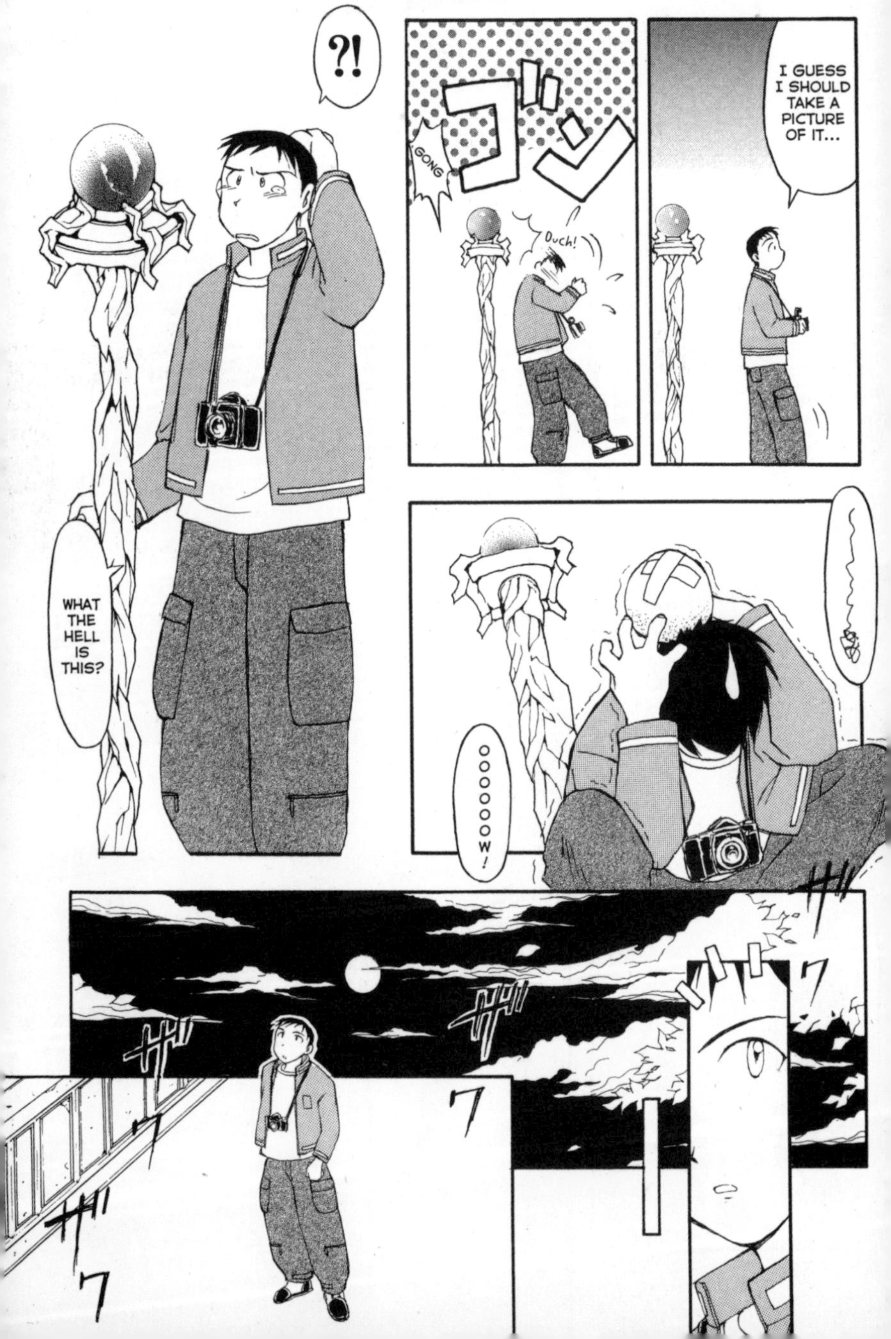
I GUESS I SHOULD TAKE A PICTURE OF IT...
ゴン
GONG
Ouch!
OOOOOOOW!
?!
WHAT THE HELL IS THIS?

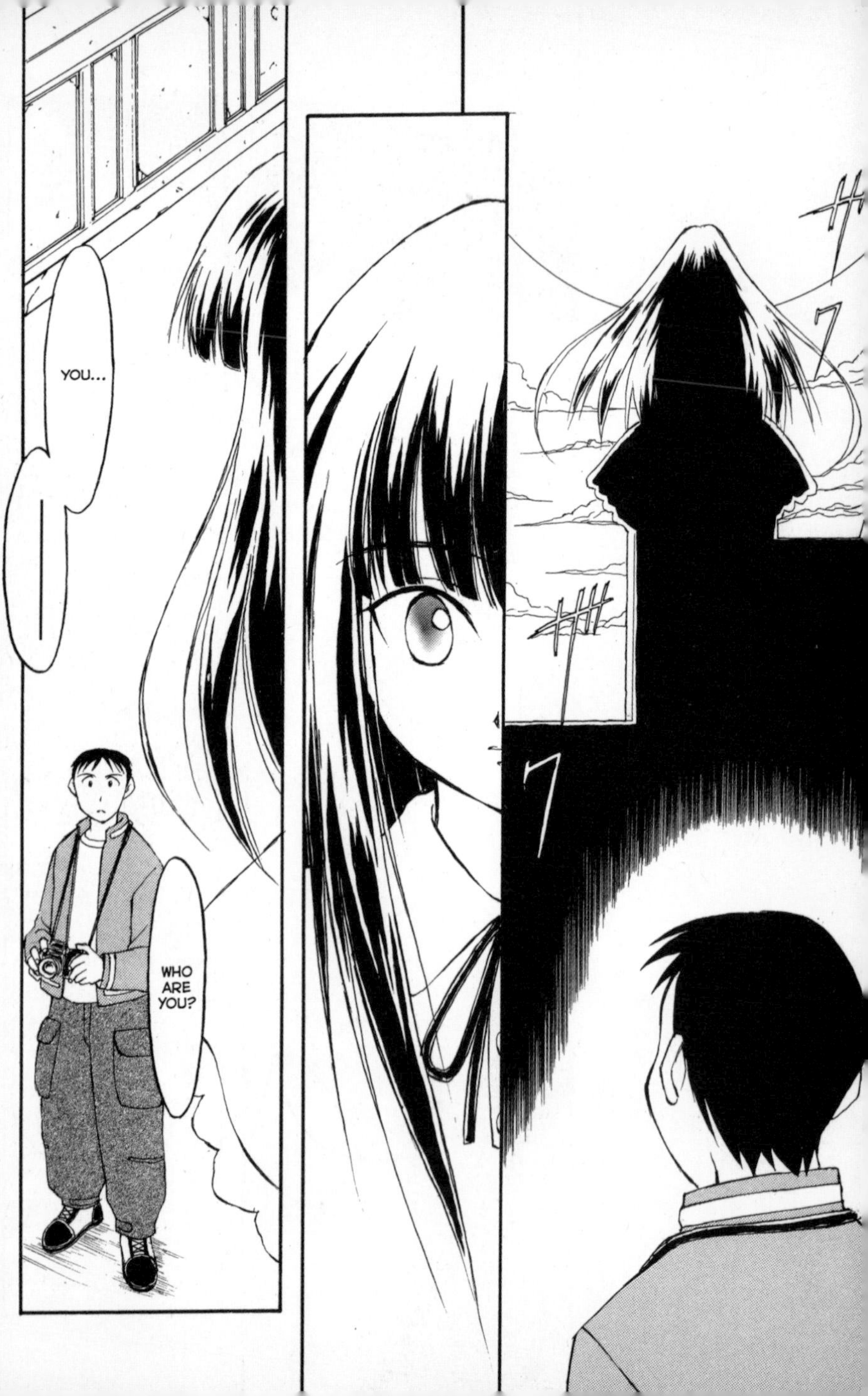
YOU...
WHO ARE YOU?

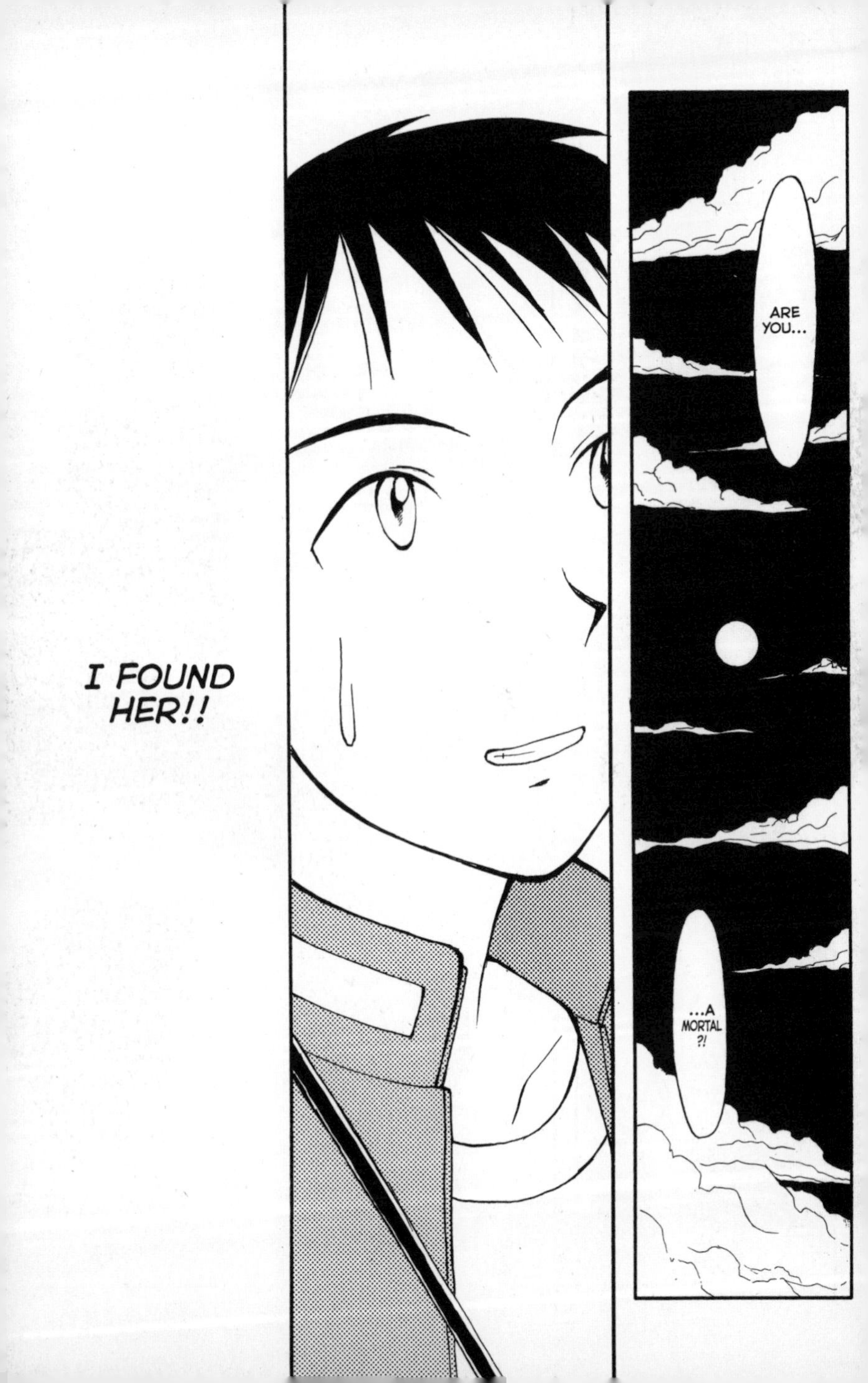
ARE YOU...
...A MORTAL ?!
I FOUND HER!!

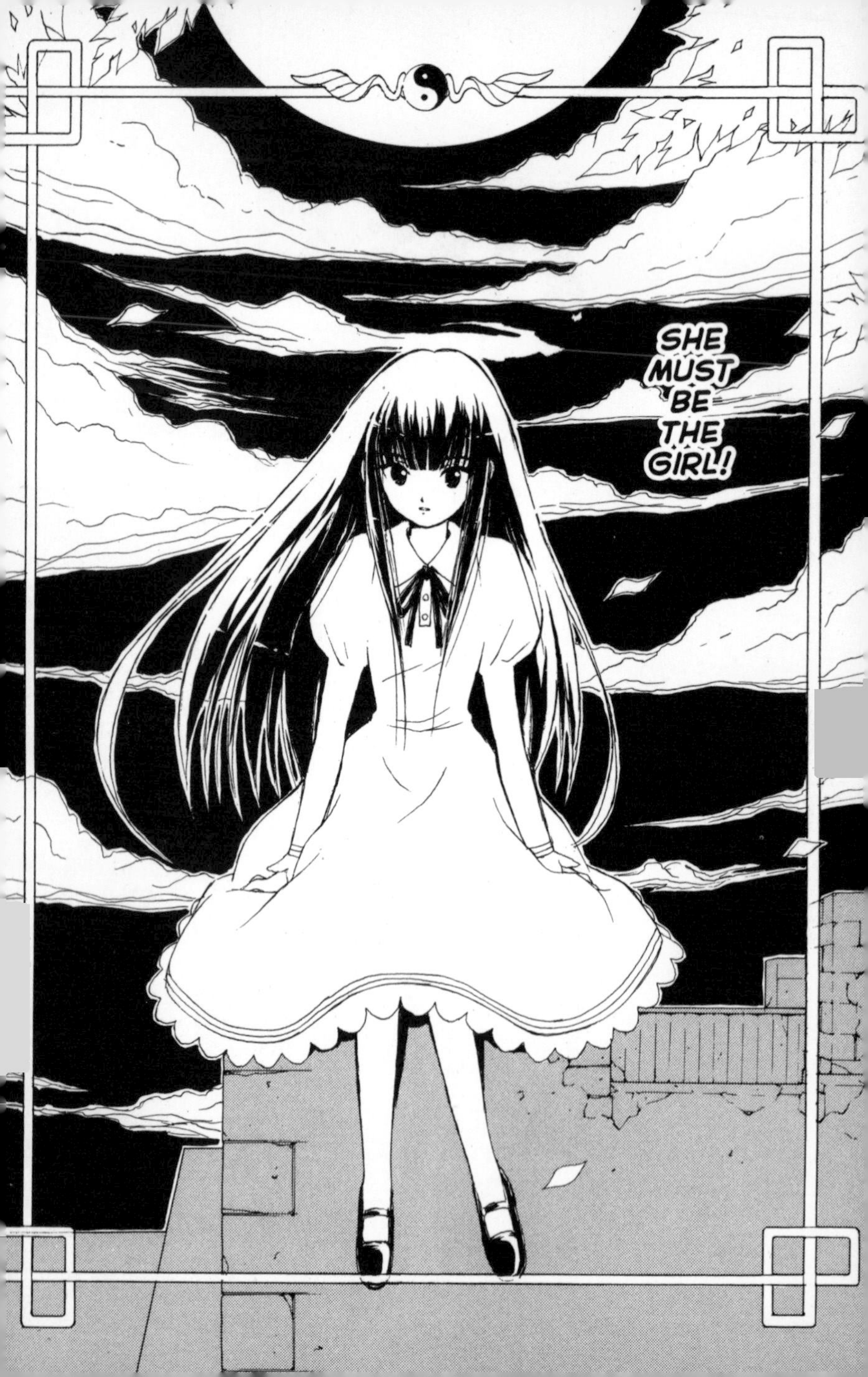
SHE MUST BE THE GIRL!

MOON 月詠 PHASE

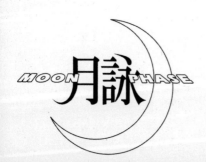

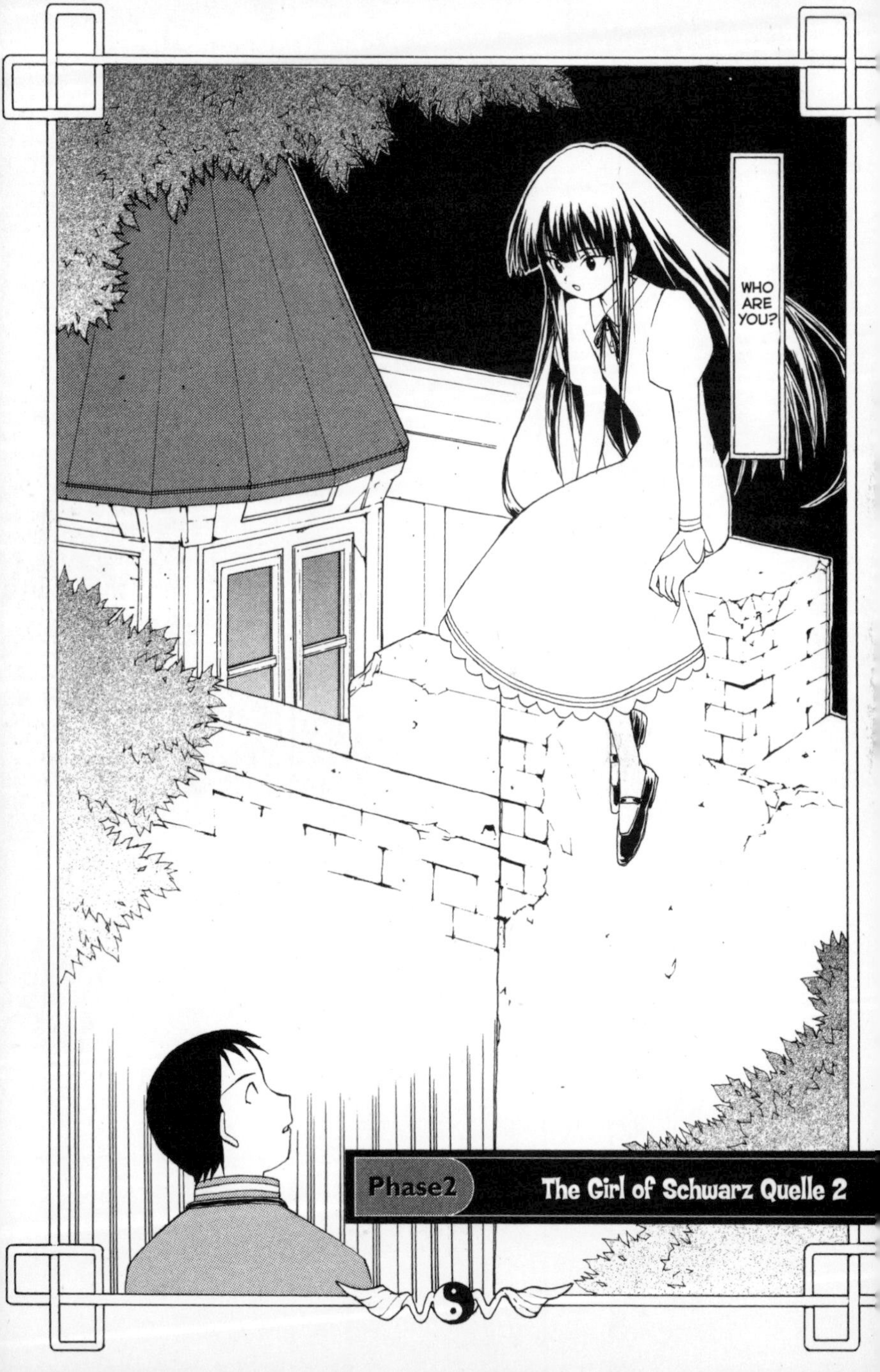
WHO ARE YOU?
Phase2
The Girl of Schwarz Quelle 2

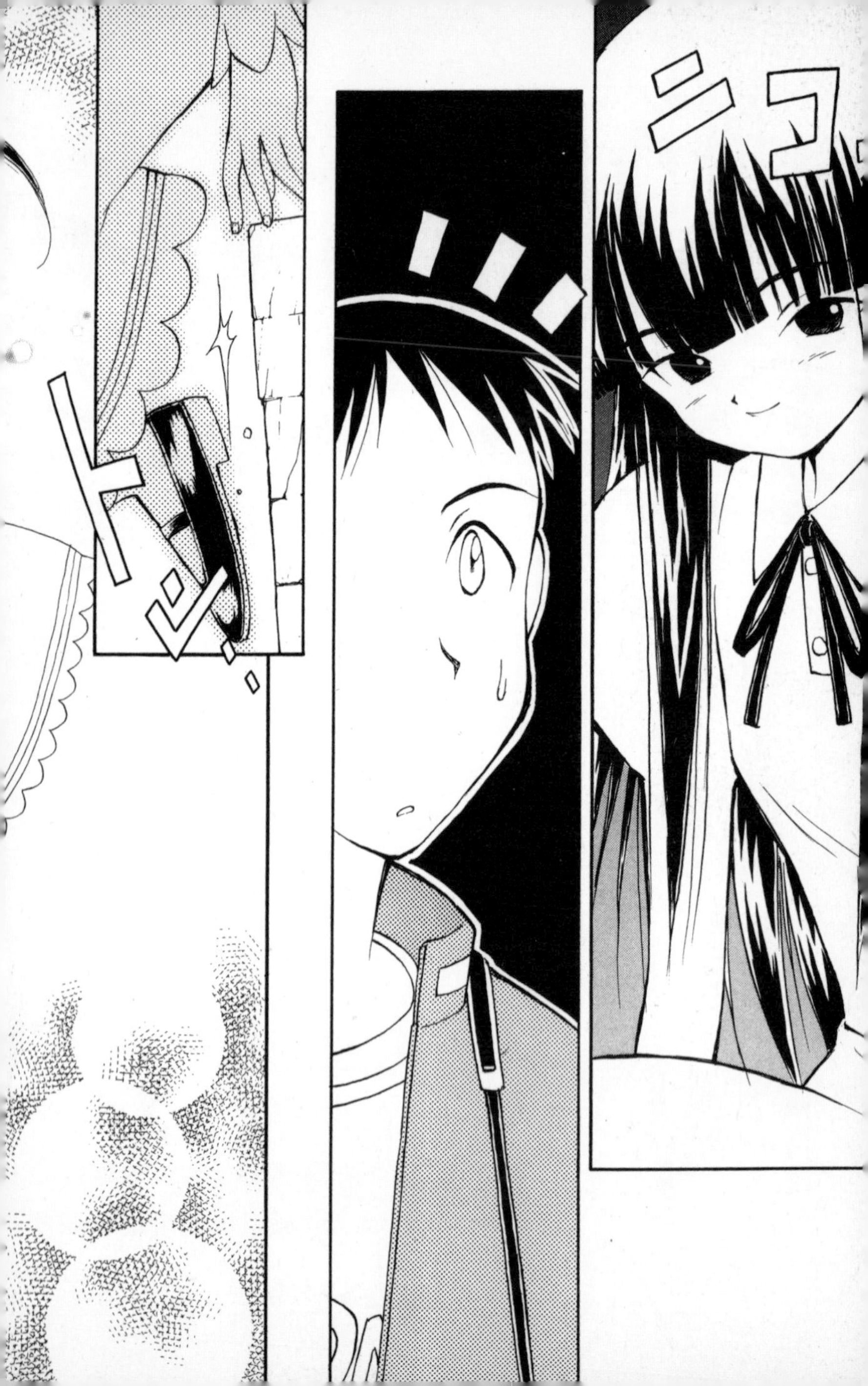
ニコ
…
トン

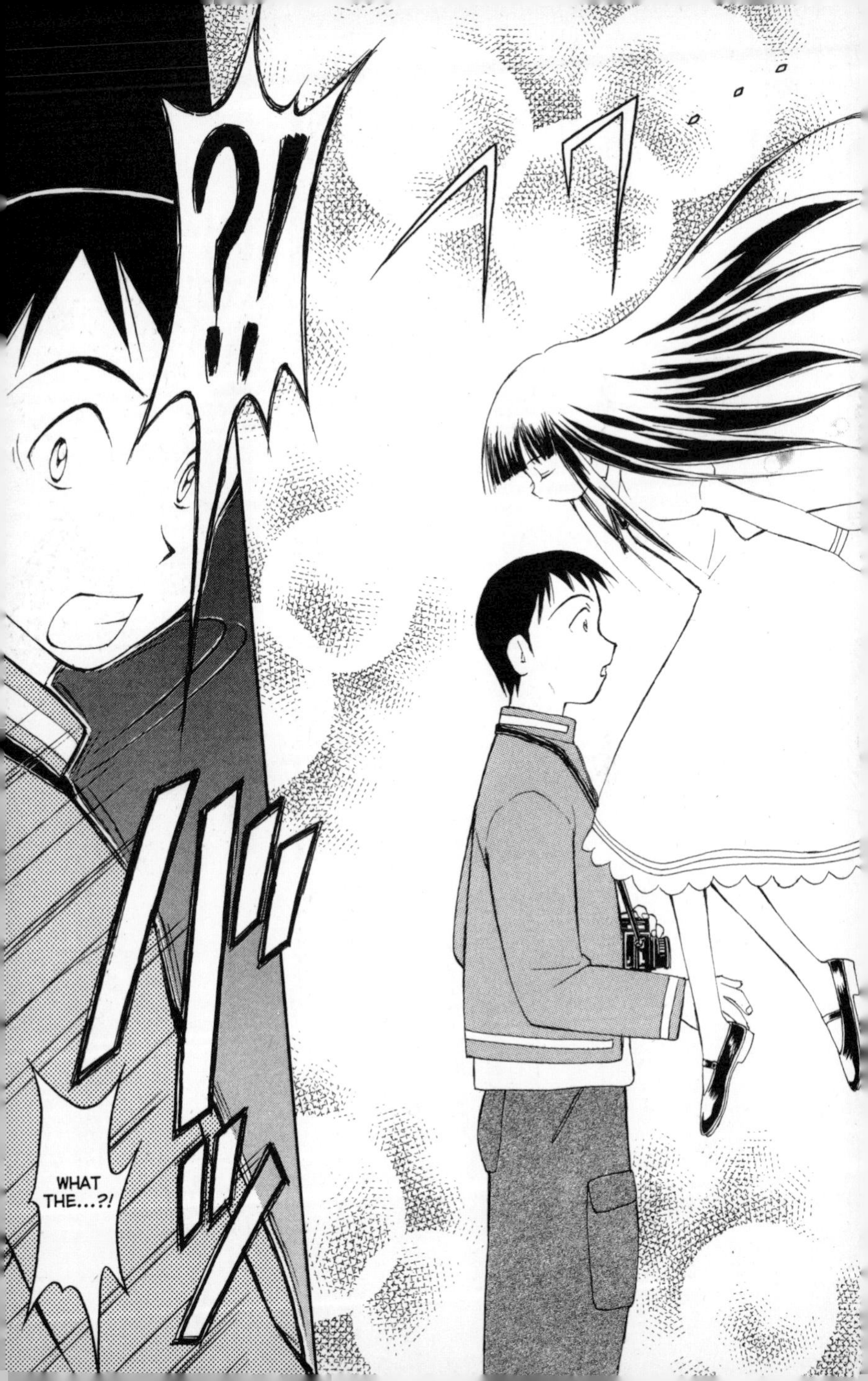
?!
WHAT THE...?!

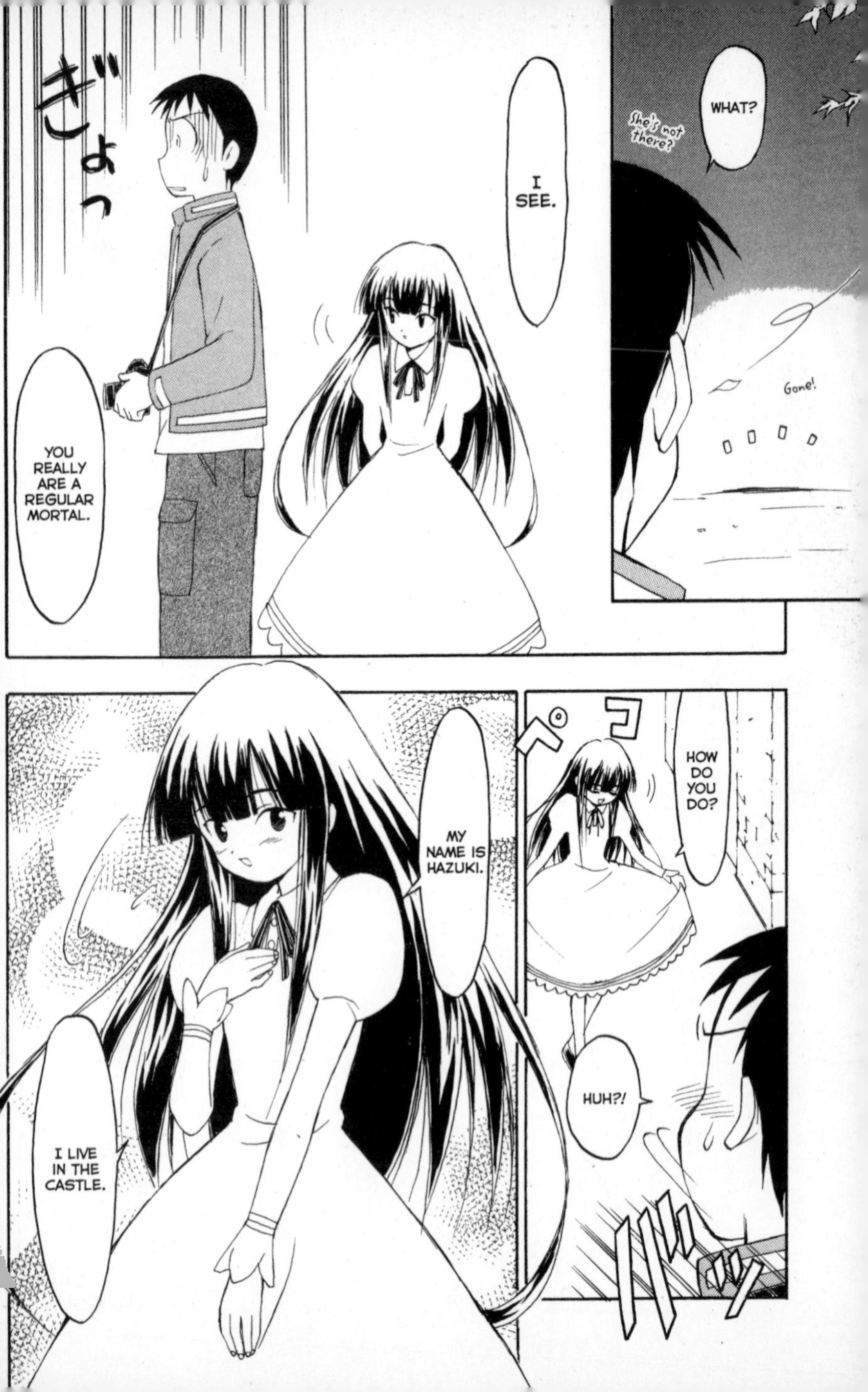
WHAT?
She's not there?
Gone!
I SEE.
ぎょっ
YOU REALLY ARE A REGULAR MORTAL.
HOW DO YOU DO?
ペコ
HUH?!
MY NAME IS HAZUKI.
I LIVE IN THE CASTLE.

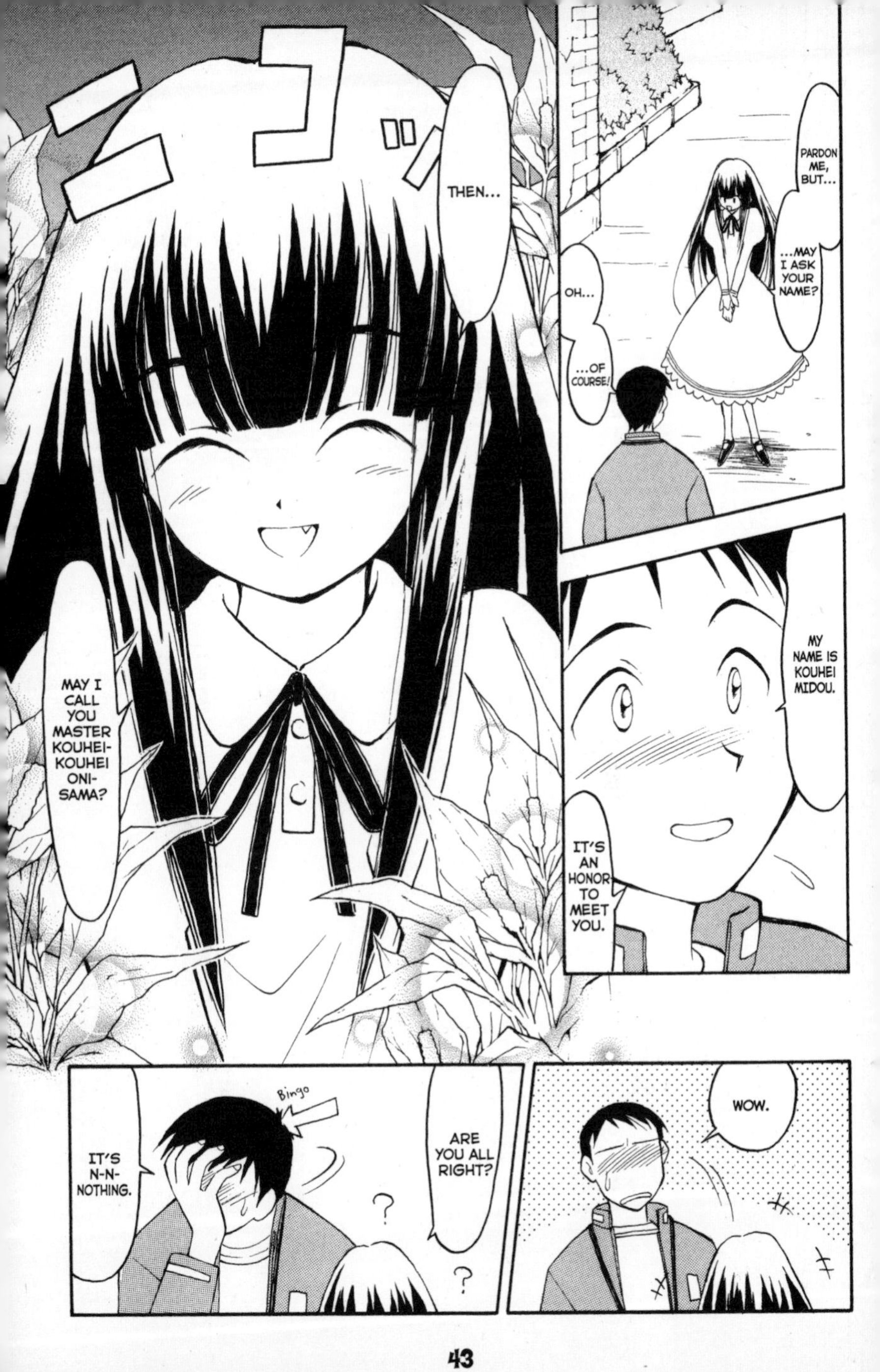
PARDON ME, BUT...
...MAY I ASK YOUR NAME?
OH...
...OF COURSE!
MY NAME IS KOUHEI MIDOU.
IT'S AN HONOR TO MEET YOU.
ニコッ
THEN...
MAY I CALL YOU MASTER KOUHEI-KOUHEI ONI-SAMA?
WOW.
ARE YOU ALL RIGHT?
Bingo
IT'S N-N-NOTHING.

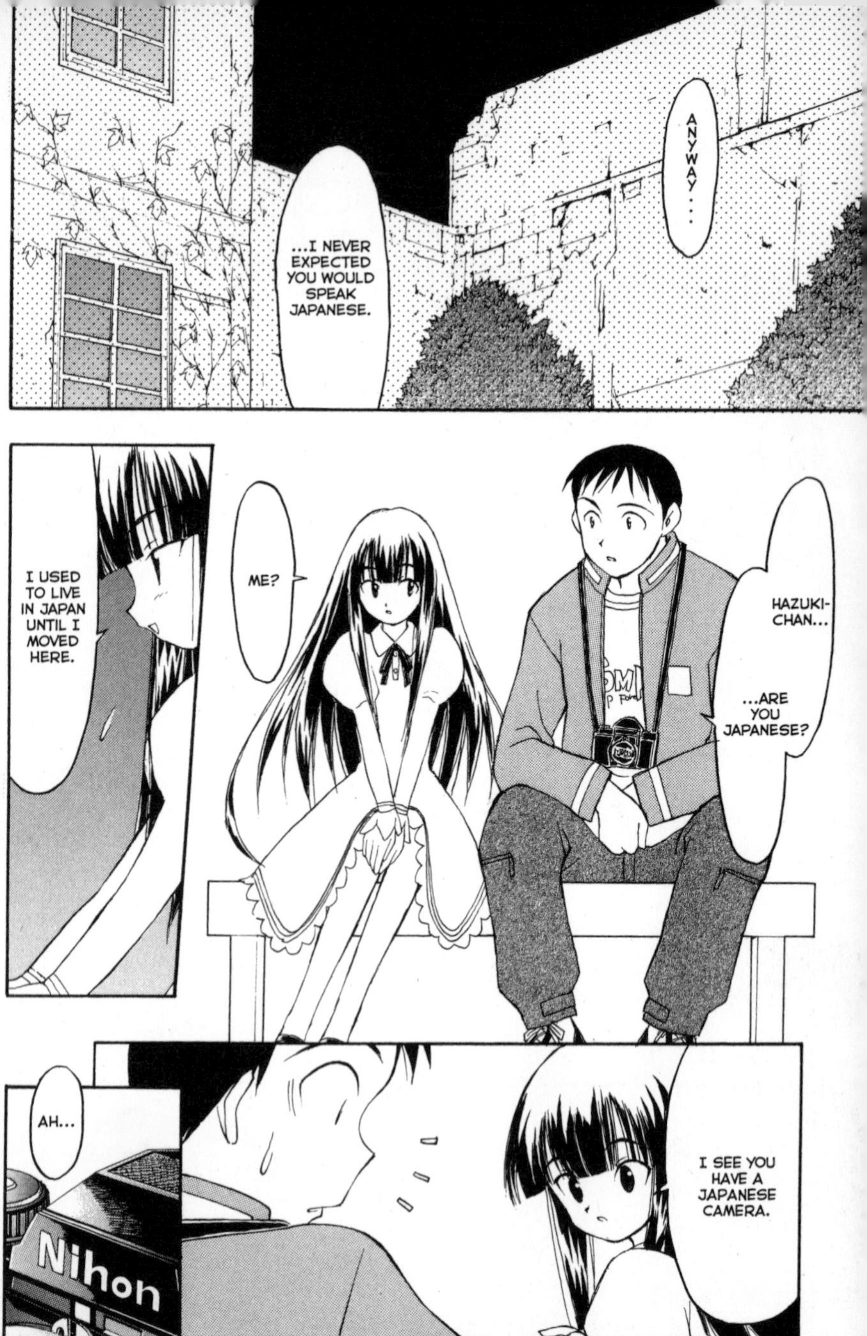
ANYWAY...
...I NEVER EXPECTED YOU WOULD SPEAK JAPANESE.
HAZUKI-CHAN...
...ARE YOU JAPANESE?
ME?
I USED TO LIVE IN JAPAN UNTIL I MOVED HERE.
I SEE YOU HAVE A JAPANESE CAMERA.
AH...
Nihon

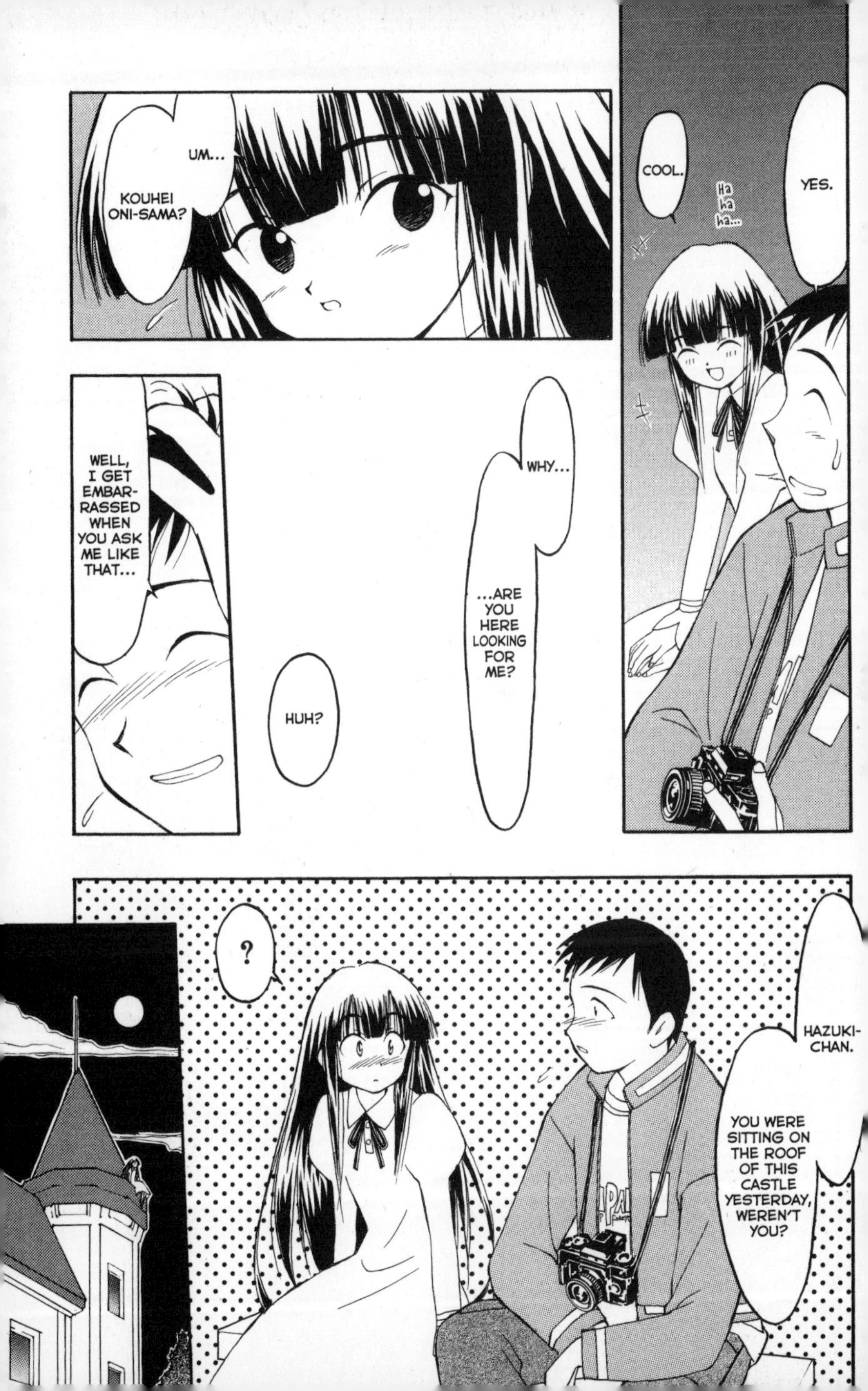
YES.
COOL.
Ha ha ha...
UM... KOUHEI ONI-SAMA?
WHY...
...ARE YOU HERE LOOKING FOR ME?
HUH?
WELL, I GET EMBARRASSED WHEN YOU ASK ME LIKE THAT...
HAZUKI-CHAN.
YOU WERE SITTING ON THE ROOF OF THIS CASTLE YESTERDAY, WEREN'T YOU?
?

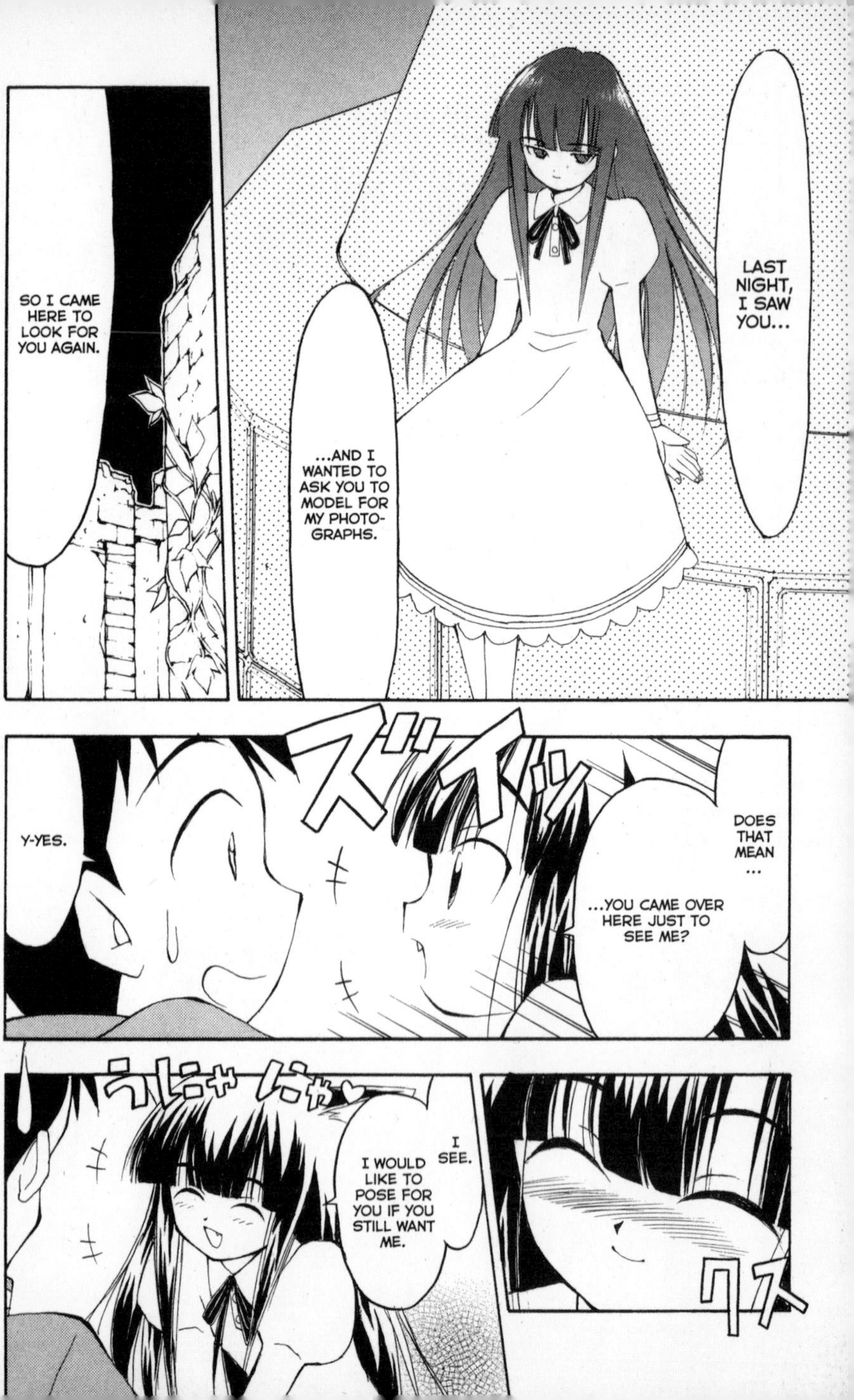
LAST NIGHT, I SAW YOU...
...AND I WANTED TO ASK YOU TO MODEL FOR MY PHOTOGRAPHS.
SO I CAME HERE TO LOOK FOR YOU AGAIN.
ズイッ
DOES THAT MEAN ...
...YOU CAME OVER HERE JUST TO SEE ME?
Y-YES.
クス
I SEE.
I WOULD LIKE TO POSE FOR YOU IF YOU STILL WANT ME.

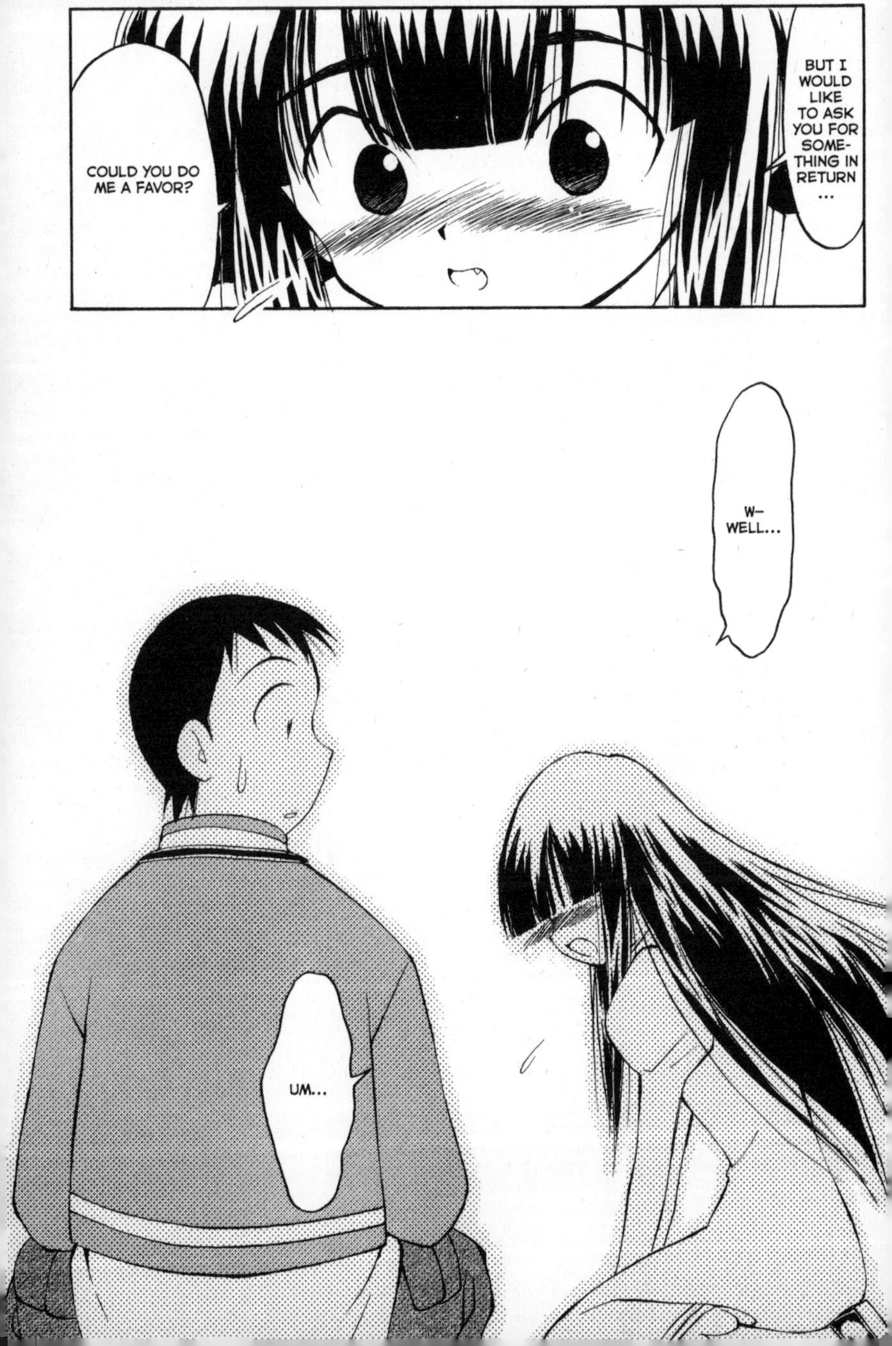
BUT I WOULD LIKE TO ASK YOU FOR SOME-THING IN RETURN ...
COULD YOU DO ME A FAVOR?
W— WELL...
UM...

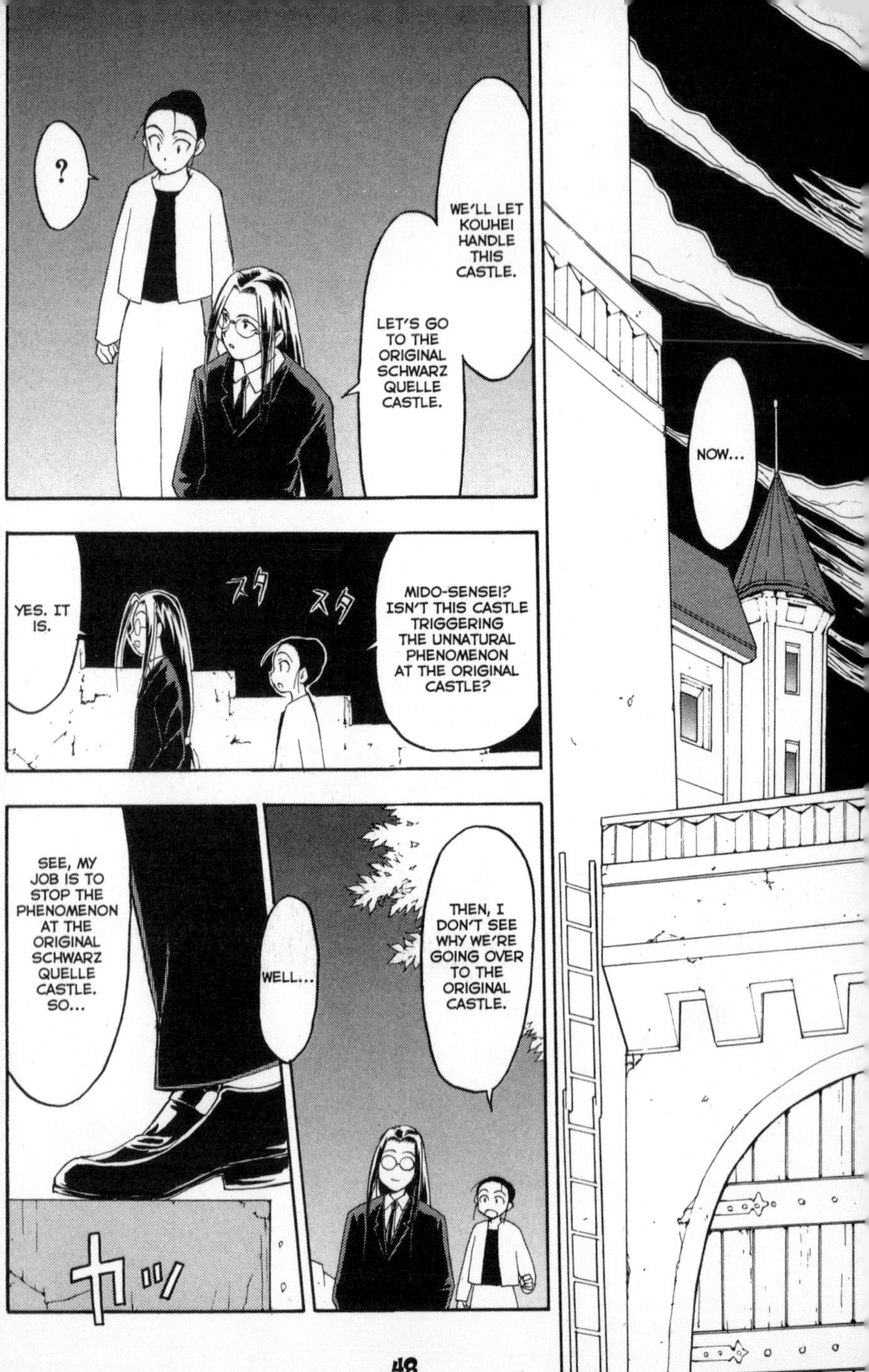
NOW...
WE'LL LET KOUHEI HANDLE THIS CASTLE.
LET'S GO TO THE ORIGINAL SCHWARZ QUELLE CASTLE.
?
MIDO-SENSEI? ISN'T THIS CASTLE TRIGGERING THE UNNATURAL PHENOMENON AT THE ORIGINAL CASTLE?
スタ スタ
YES. IT IS.
THEN, I DON'T SEE WHY WE'RE GOING OVER TO THE ORIGINAL CASTLE.
WELL...
SEE, MY JOB IS TO STOP THE PHENOMENON AT THE ORIGINAL SCHWARZ QUELLE CASTLE. SO...
ヤッ

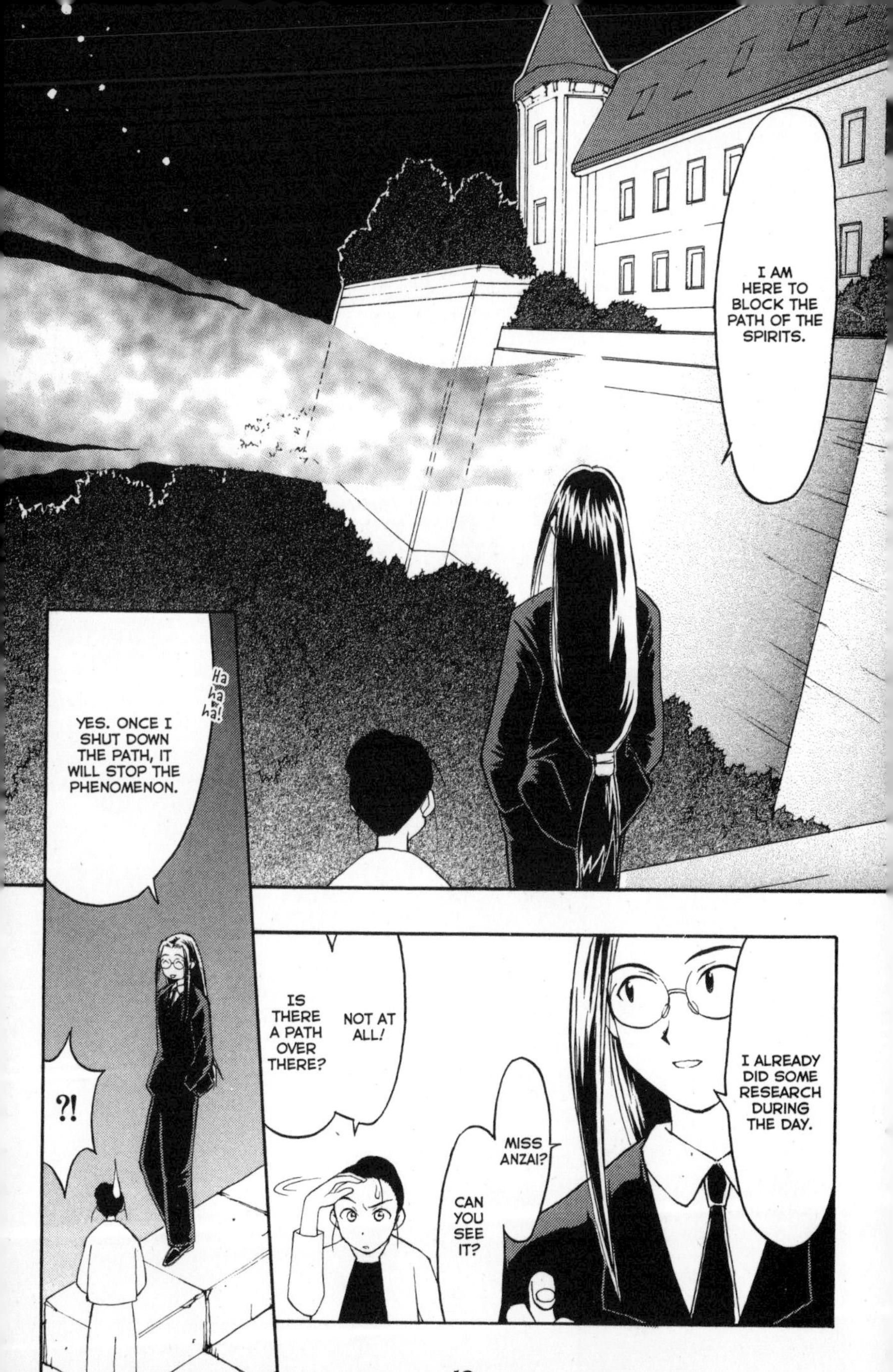
I AM HERE TO BLOCK THE PATH OF THE SPIRITS.
YES. ONCE I SHUT DOWN THE PATH, IT WILL STOP THE PHENOMENON.
Ha ha ha!
?!
I ALREADY DID SOME RESEARCH DURING THE DAY.
NOT AT ALL!
IS THERE A PATH OVER THERE?
MISS ANZAI?
CAN YOU SEE IT?

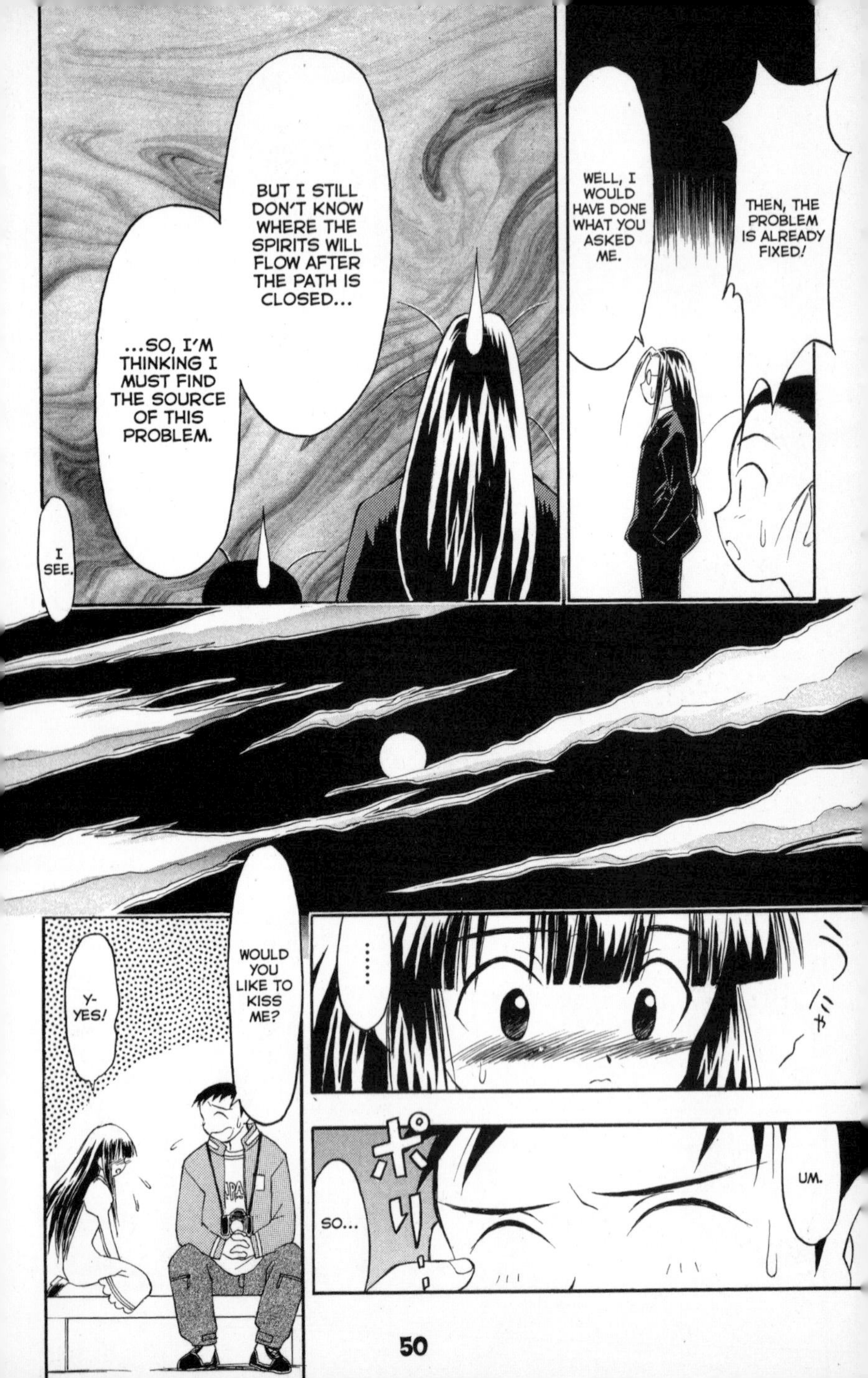
THEN, THE PROBLEM IS ALREADY FIXED!
WELL, I WOULD HAVE DONE WHAT YOU ASKED ME.
BUT I STILL DON'T KNOW WHERE THE SPIRITS WILL FLOW AFTER THE PATH IS CLOSED...
...SO, I'M THINKING I MUST FIND THE SOURCE OF THIS PROBLEM.
I SEE.
......
UM.
SO...
WOULD YOU LIKE TO KISS ME?
Y-YES!

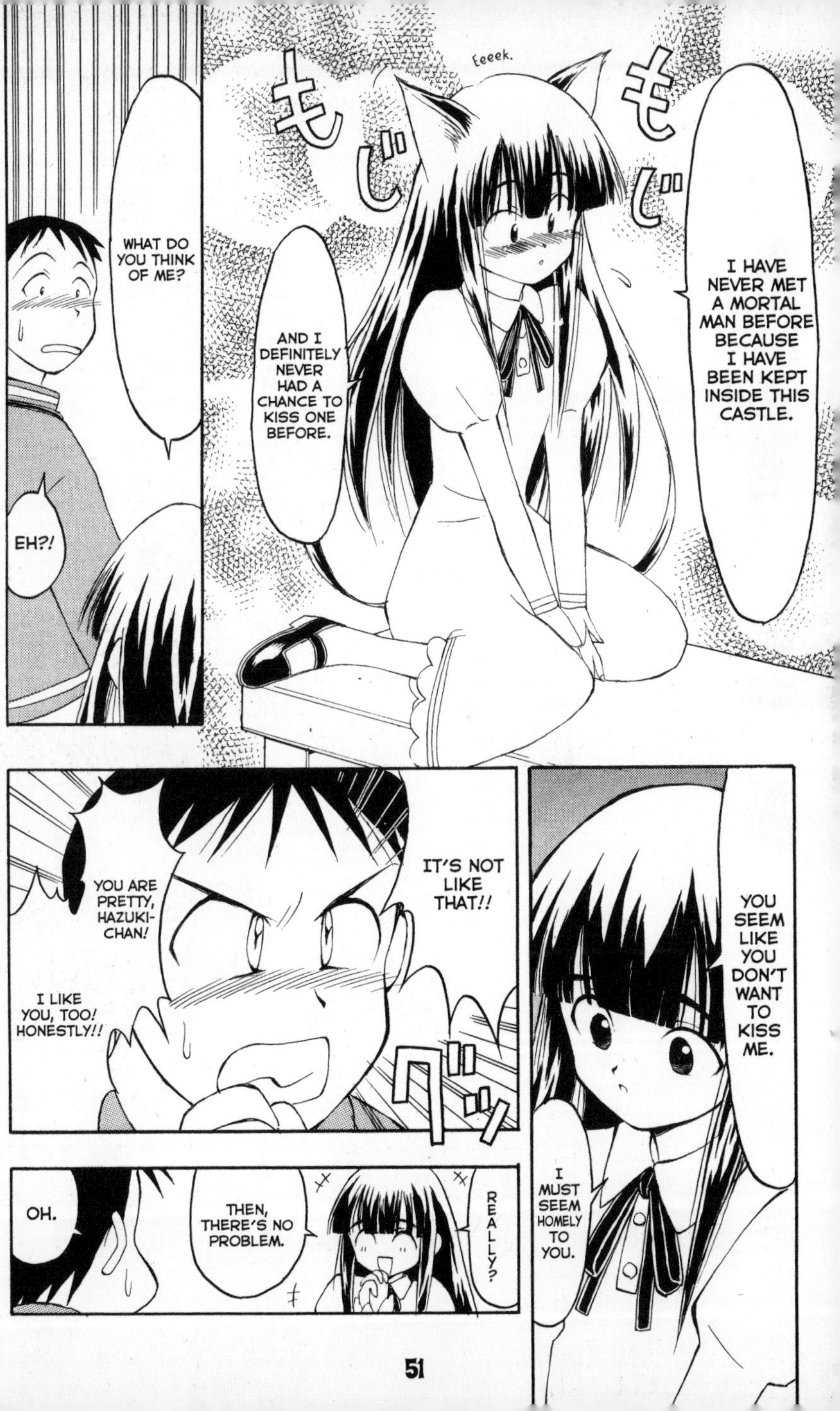

もじもじ
Eeeek.
I HAVE NEVER MET A MORTAL MAN BEFORE BECAUSE I HAVE BEEN KEPT INSIDE THIS CASTLE.
AND I DEFINITELY NEVER HAD A CHANCE TO KISS ONE BEFORE.
WHAT DO YOU THINK OF ME?
EH?!
YOU SEEM LIKE YOU DON'T WANT TO KISS ME.
I MUST SEEM HOMELY TO YOU.
IT'S NOT LIKE THAT!!
YOU ARE PRETTY, HAZUKI-CHAN!
I LIKE YOU, TOO! HONESTLY!!
グッ
REALLY?
THEN, THERE'S NO PROBLEM.
OH.

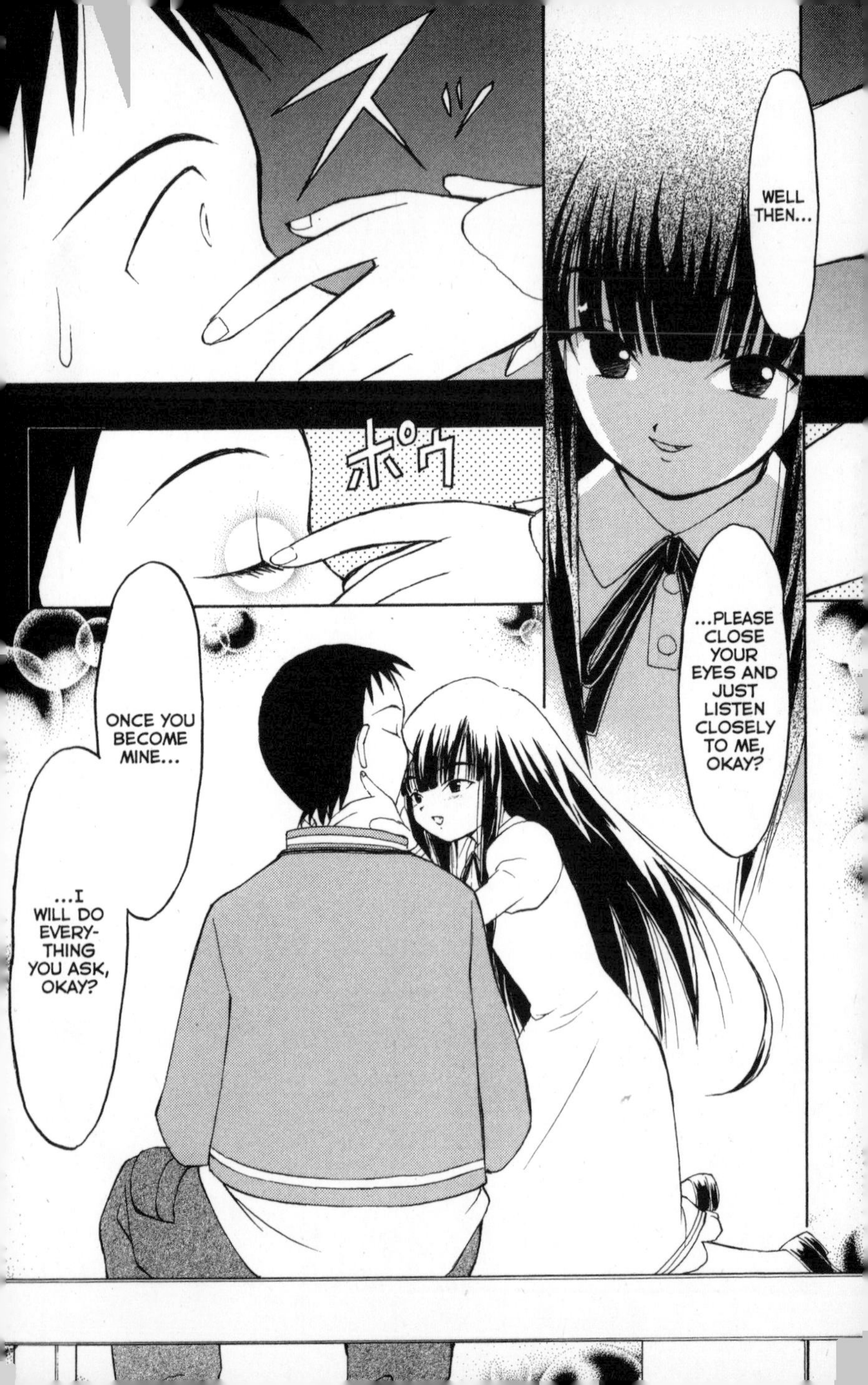
WELL THEN...
...PLEASE CLOSE YOUR EYES AND JUST LISTEN CLOSELY TO ME, OKAY?
スッ
ポウ
ONCE YOU BECOME MINE...
...I WILL DO EVERY-THING YOU ASK, OKAY?

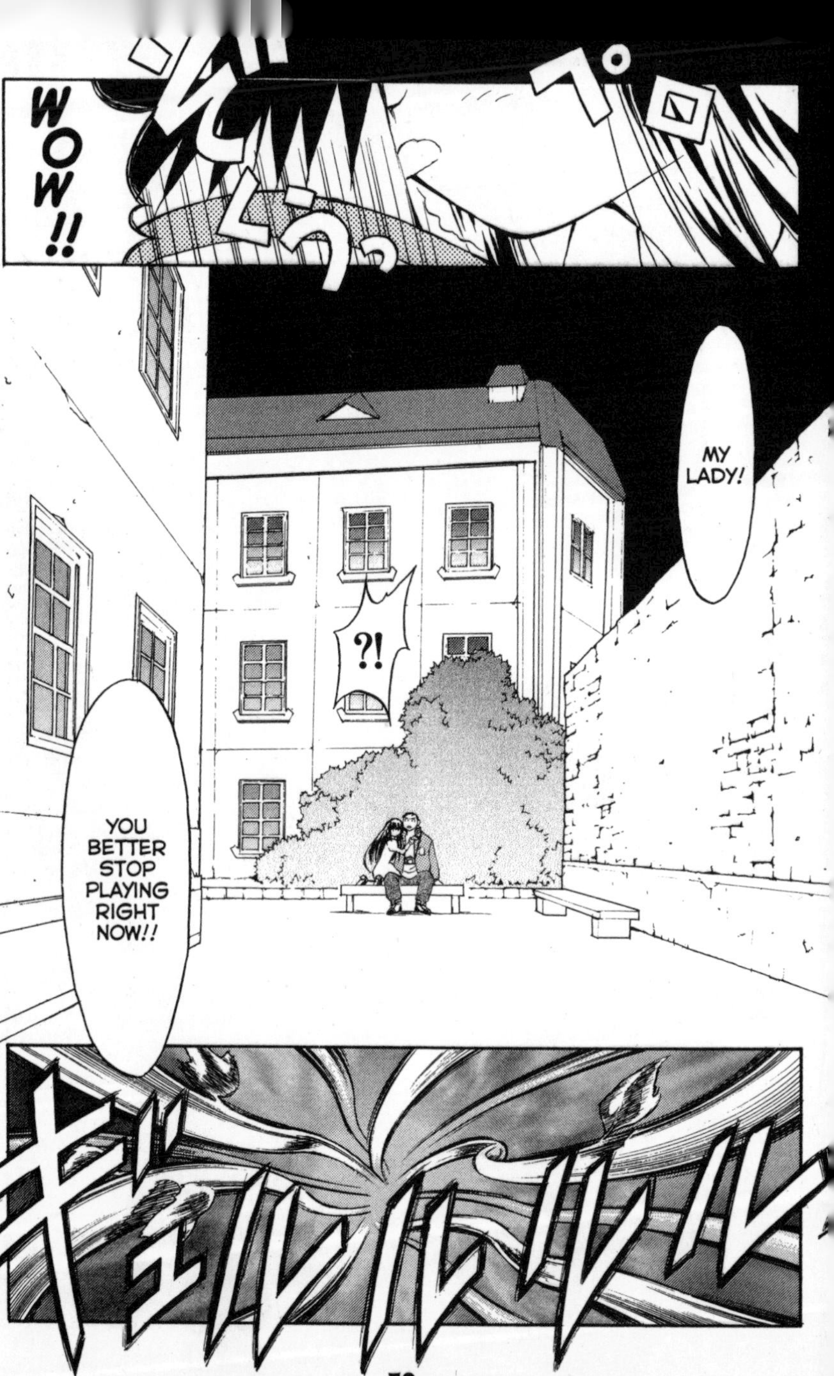
WOW!!
MY LADY!
?!
YOU BETTER STOP PLAYING RIGHT NOW!!

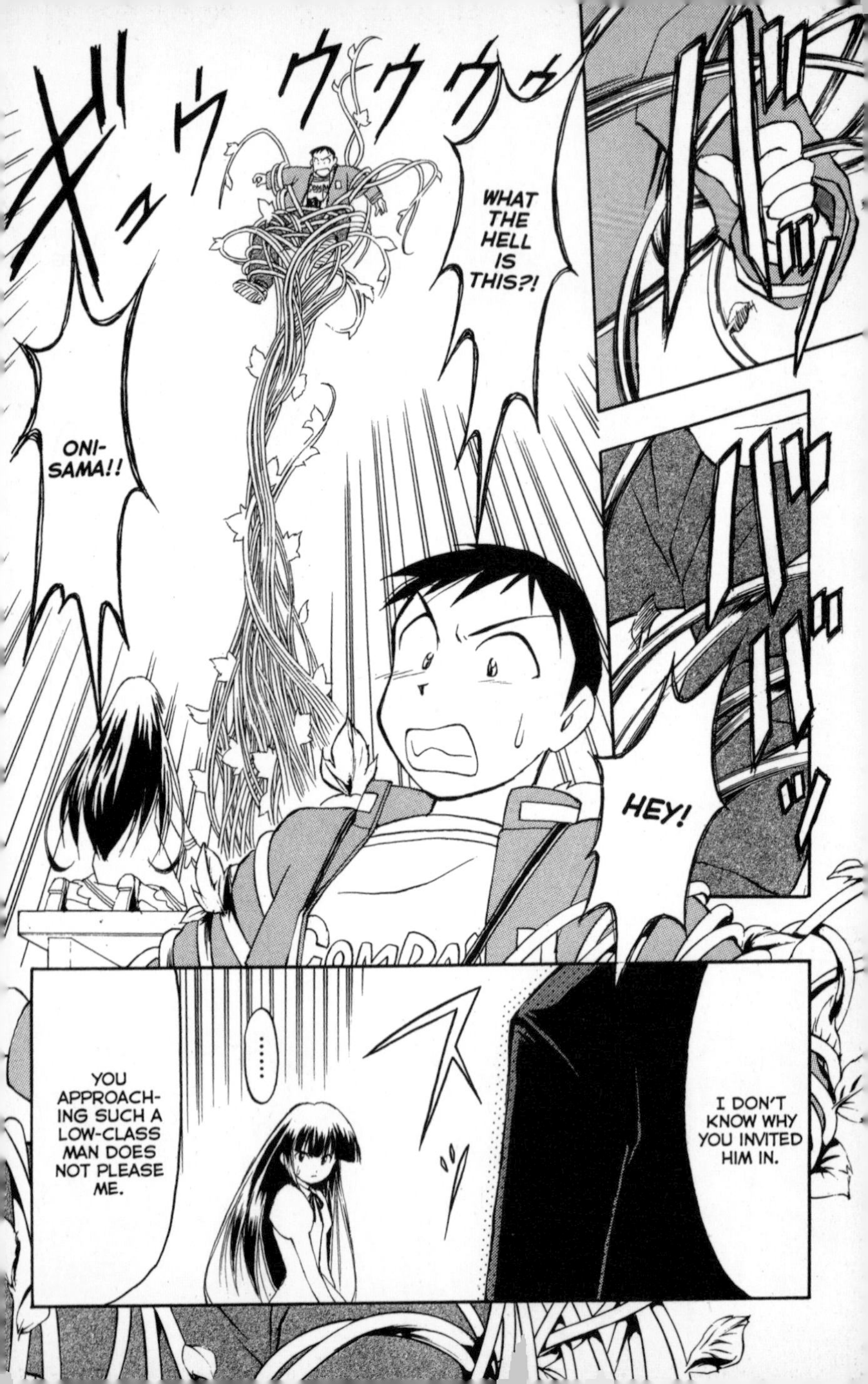
HEY!
ギュウウウウゥ
WHAT THE HELL IS THIS?!
ONI-SAMA!!
I DON'T KNOW WHY YOU INVITED HIM IN.
ス
......
YOU APPROACHING SUCH A LOW-CLASS MAN DOES NOT PLEASE ME.

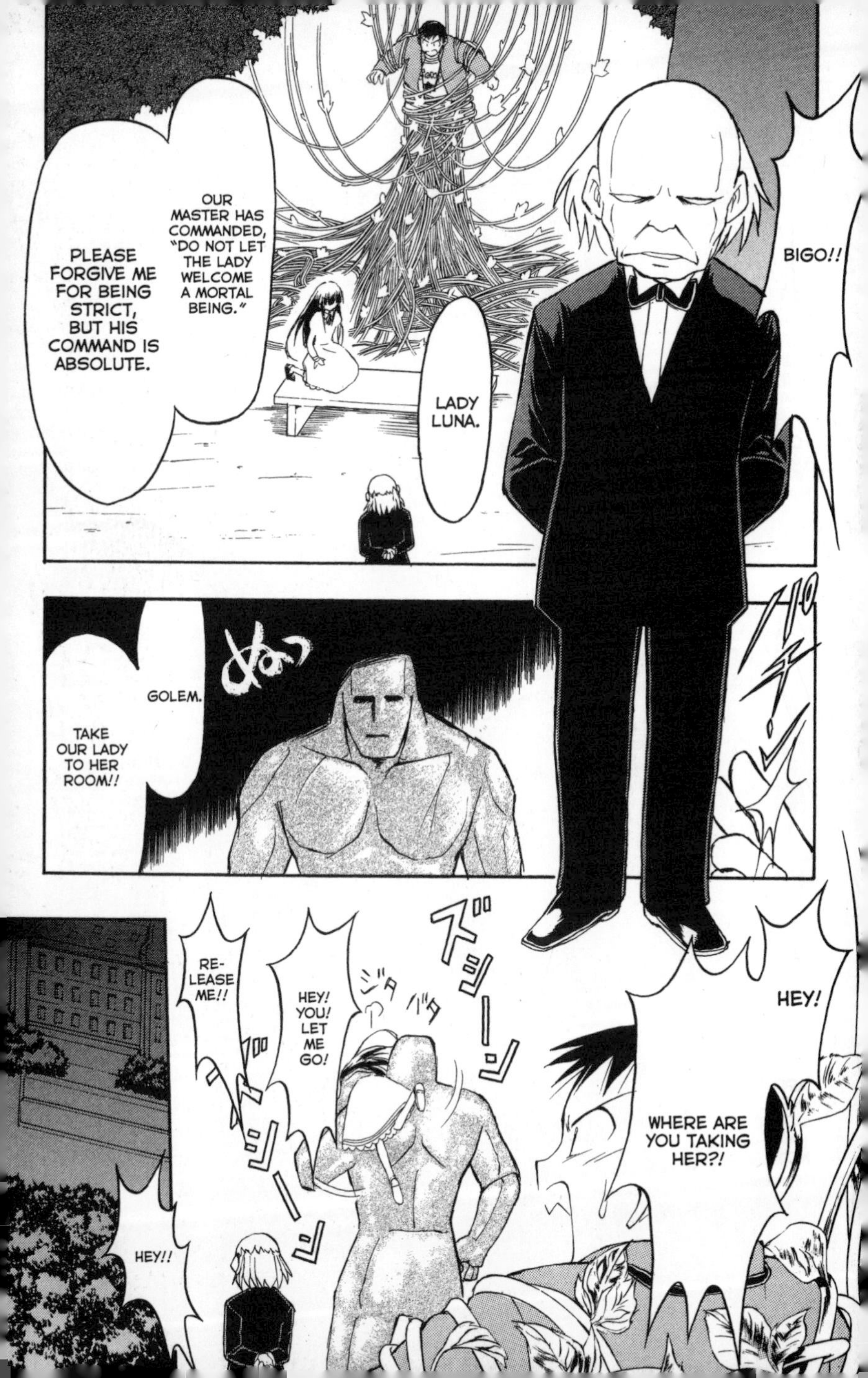

BIGO!!
LADY LUNA.
OUR MASTER HAS COMMANDED, "DO NOT LET THE LADY WELCOME A MORTAL BEING."
PLEASE FORGIVE ME FOR BEING STRICT, BUT HIS COMMAND IS ABSOLUTE.
GOLEM.
TAKE OUR LADY TO HER ROOM!!
HEY!
WHERE ARE YOU TAKING HER?!
HEY! YOU! LET ME GO!
RE-LEASE ME!!
HEY!!

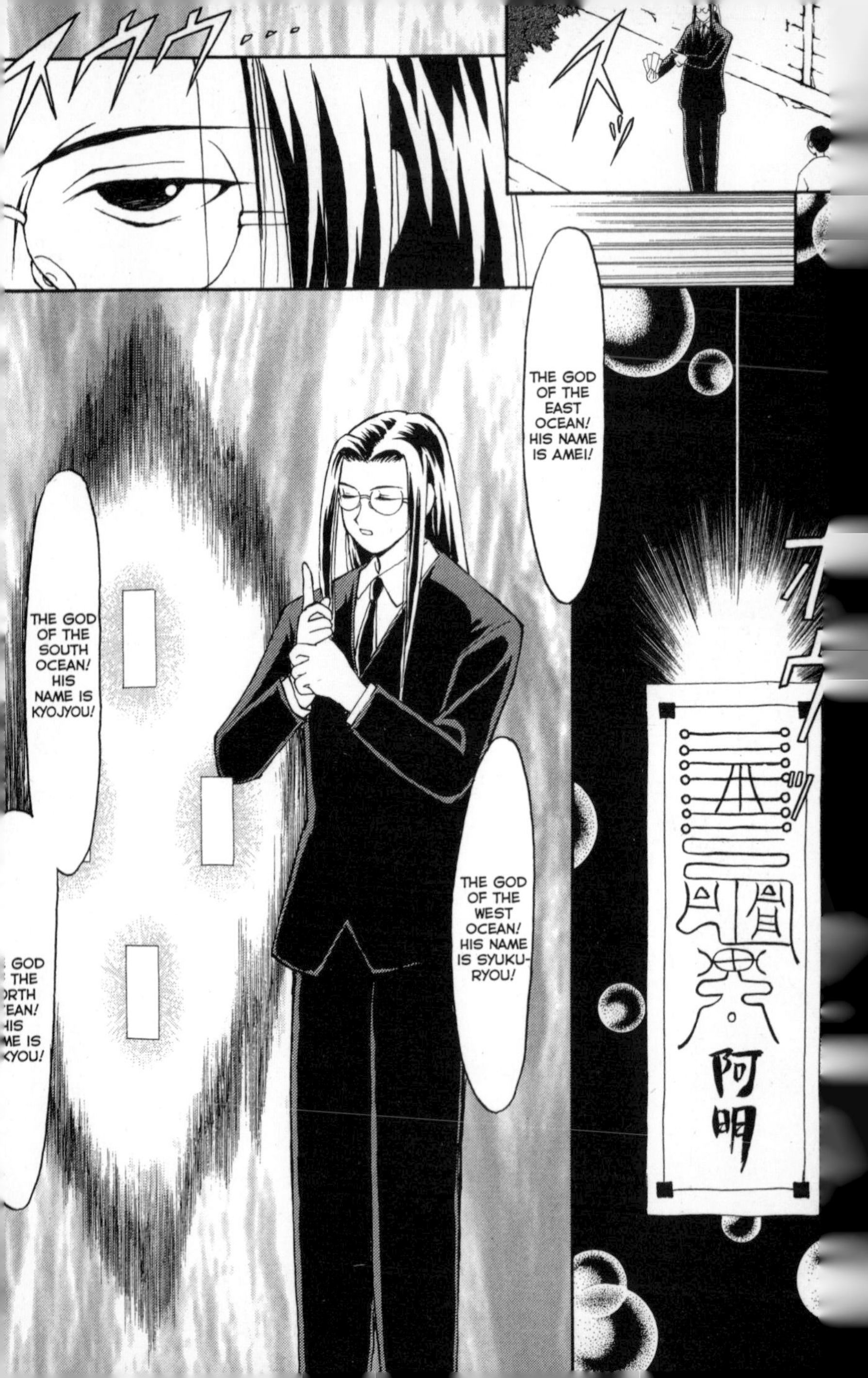
スッ
スウウ…
THE GOD OF THE EAST OCEAN! HIS NAME IS AMEI!
阿明
THE GOD OF THE WEST OCEAN! HIS NAME IS SYUKU-RYOU!
THE GOD OF THE SOUTH OCEAN! HIS NAME IS KYOJYOU!
GOD THE RTH EAN! HIS ME IS KYOU!

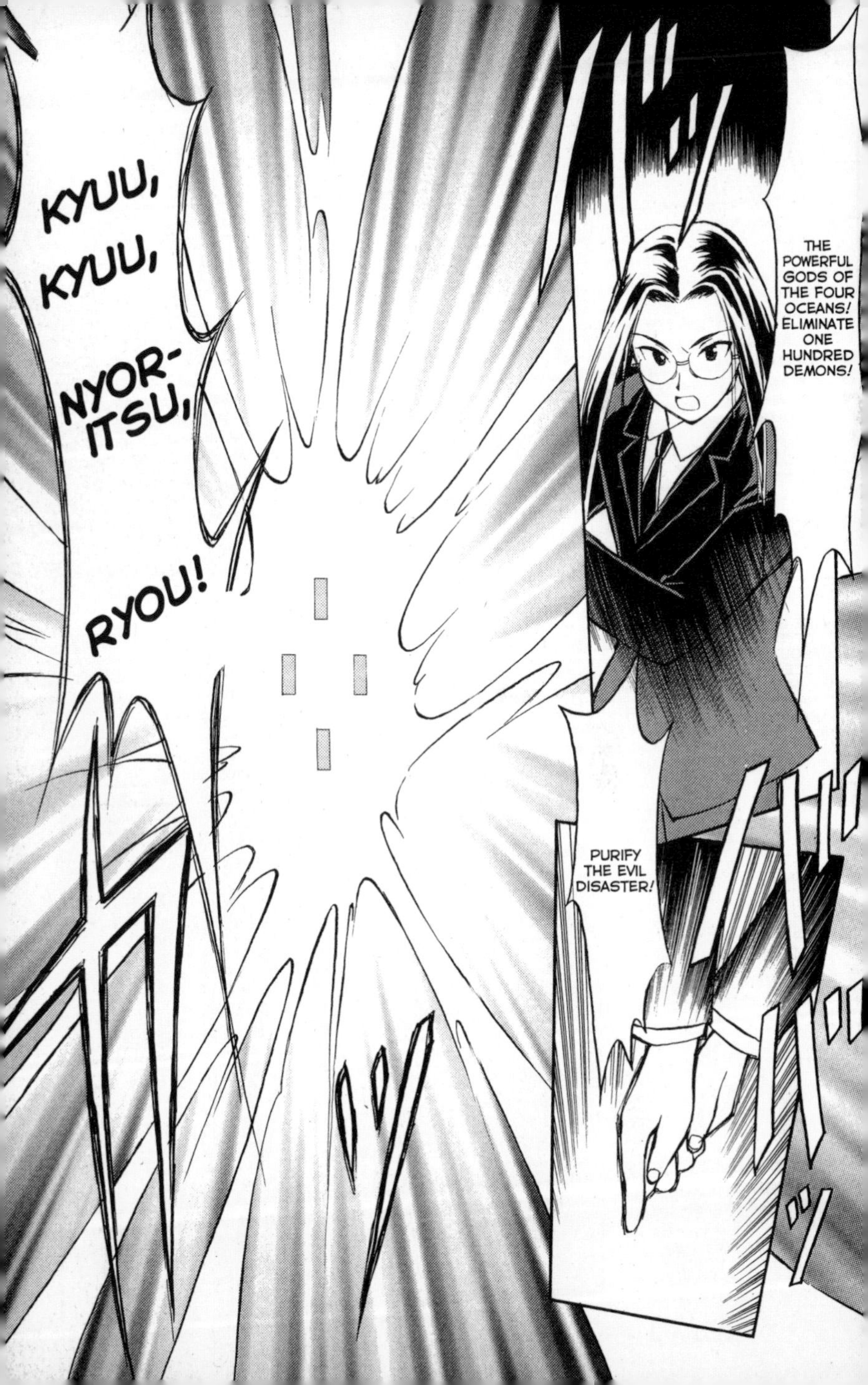
THE POWERFUL GODS OF THE FOUR OCEANS! ELIMINATE ONE HUNDRED DEMONS!
PURIFY THE EVIL DISASTER!
KYUU, KYUU,
NYOR-ITSU,
RYOU!

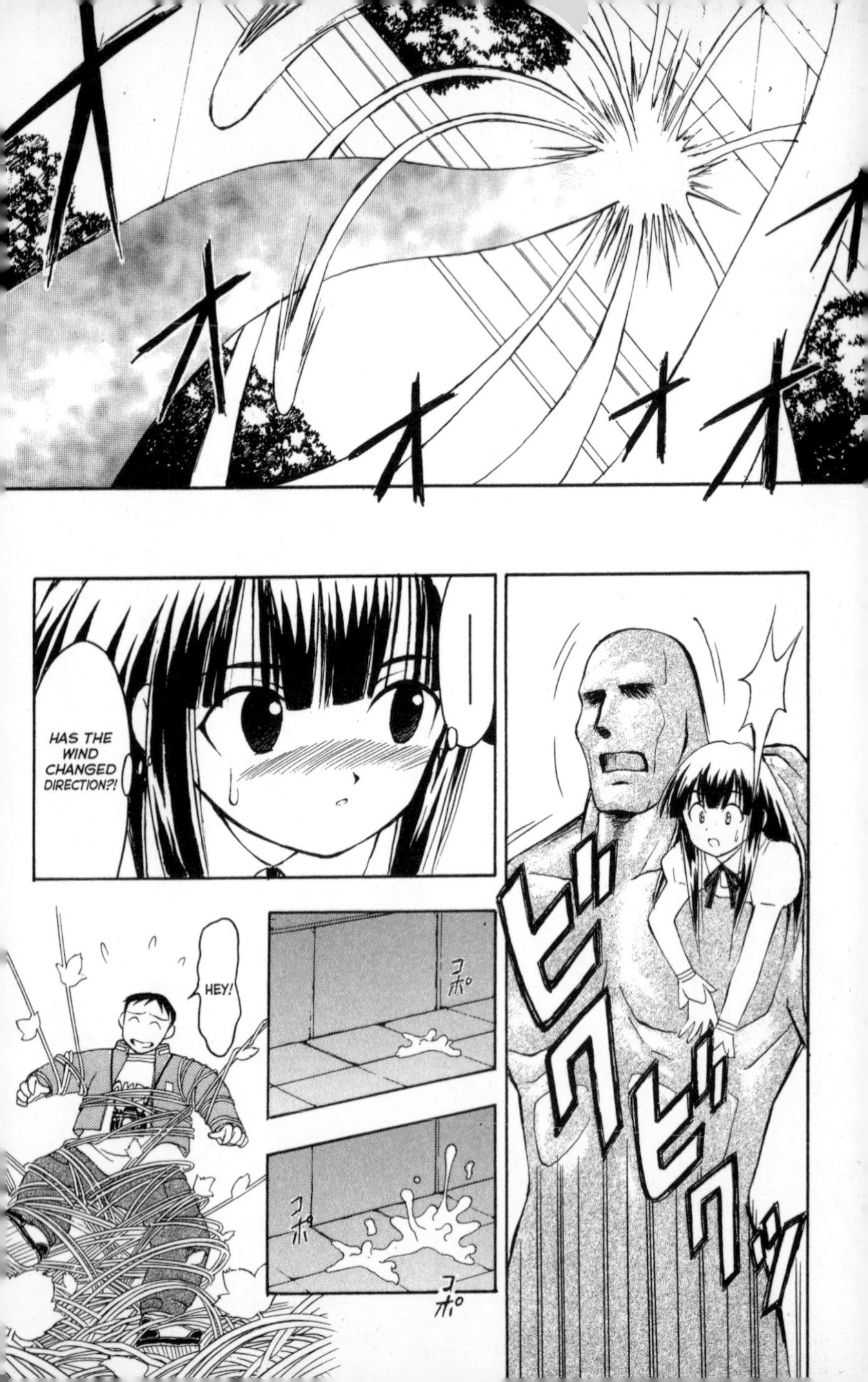
オオオオオ
ビクビクッ
HAS THE WIND CHANGED DIRECTION?!
コポ
コポ
コポ
HEY!

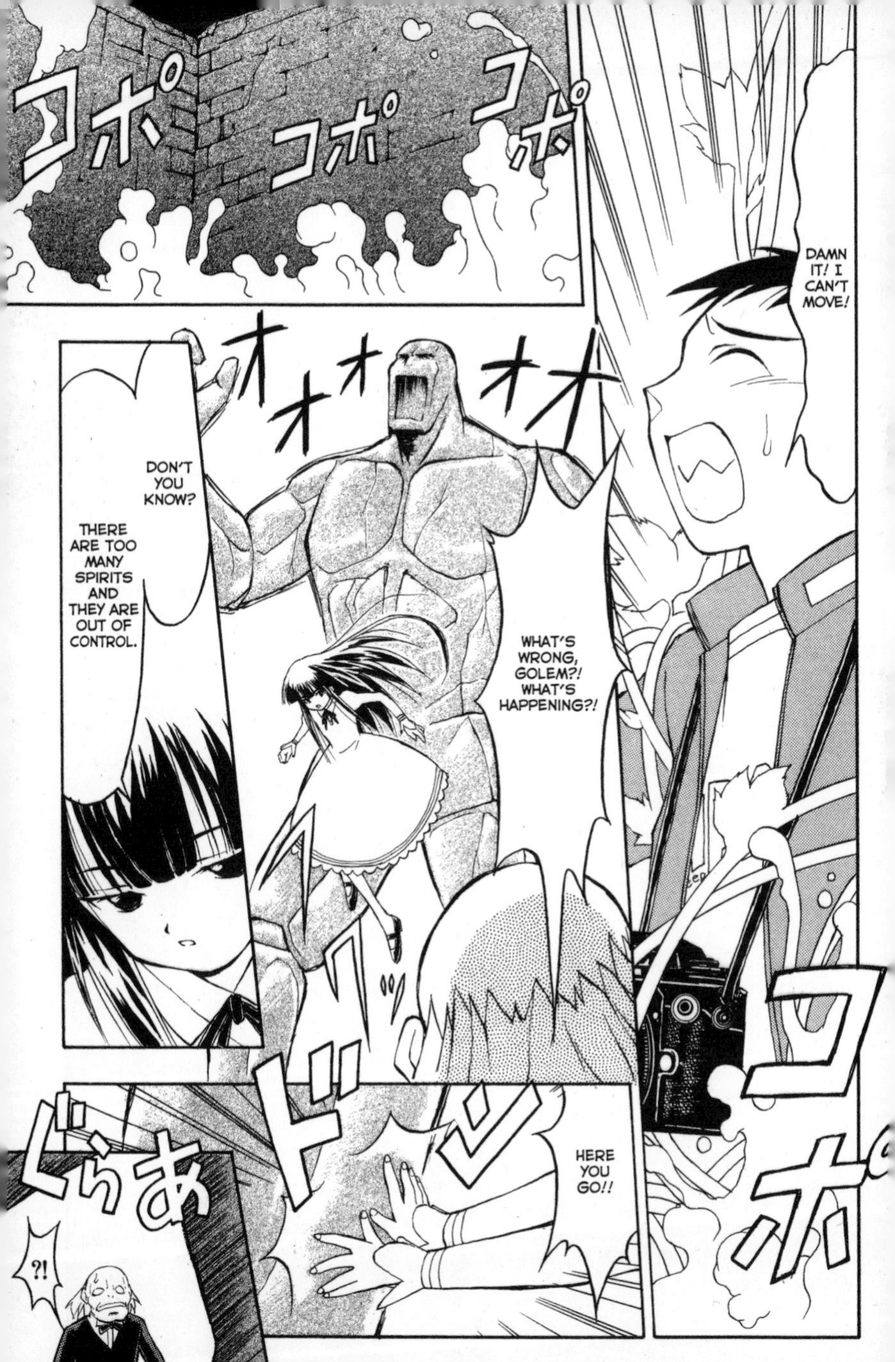
DAMN IT! I CAN'T MOVE!
WHAT'S WRONG, GOLEM?! WHAT'S HAPPENING?!
DON'T YOU KNOW?
THERE ARE TOO MANY SPIRITS AND THEY ARE OUT OF CONTROL.
HERE YOU GO!!
?!

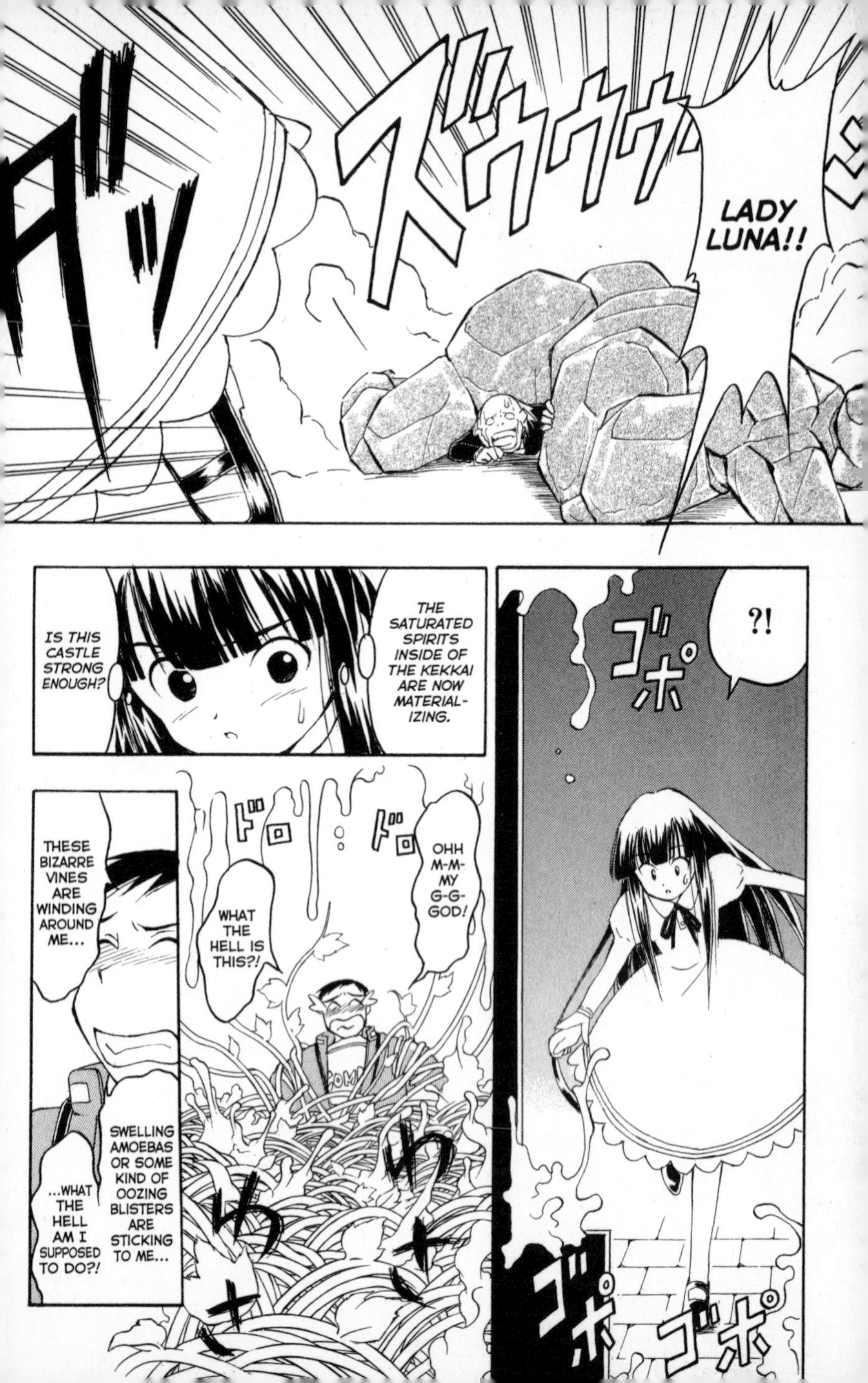
LADY LUNA!!
ズゥウウウ
ダッ
?!
ゴポ
ゴポ ゴポ
THE SATURATED SPIRITS INSIDE OF THE KEKKAI ARE NOW MATERIAL-IZING.
IS THIS CASTLE STRONG ENOUGH?
ドロ ドロ
OHH M-M-MY G-G-GOD!
WHAT THE HELL IS THIS?!
THESE BIZARRE VINES ARE WINDING AROUND ME...
SWELLING AMOEBAS OR SOME KIND OF OOZING BLISTERS ARE STICKING TO ME...
...WHAT THE HELL AM I SUPPOSED TO DO?!

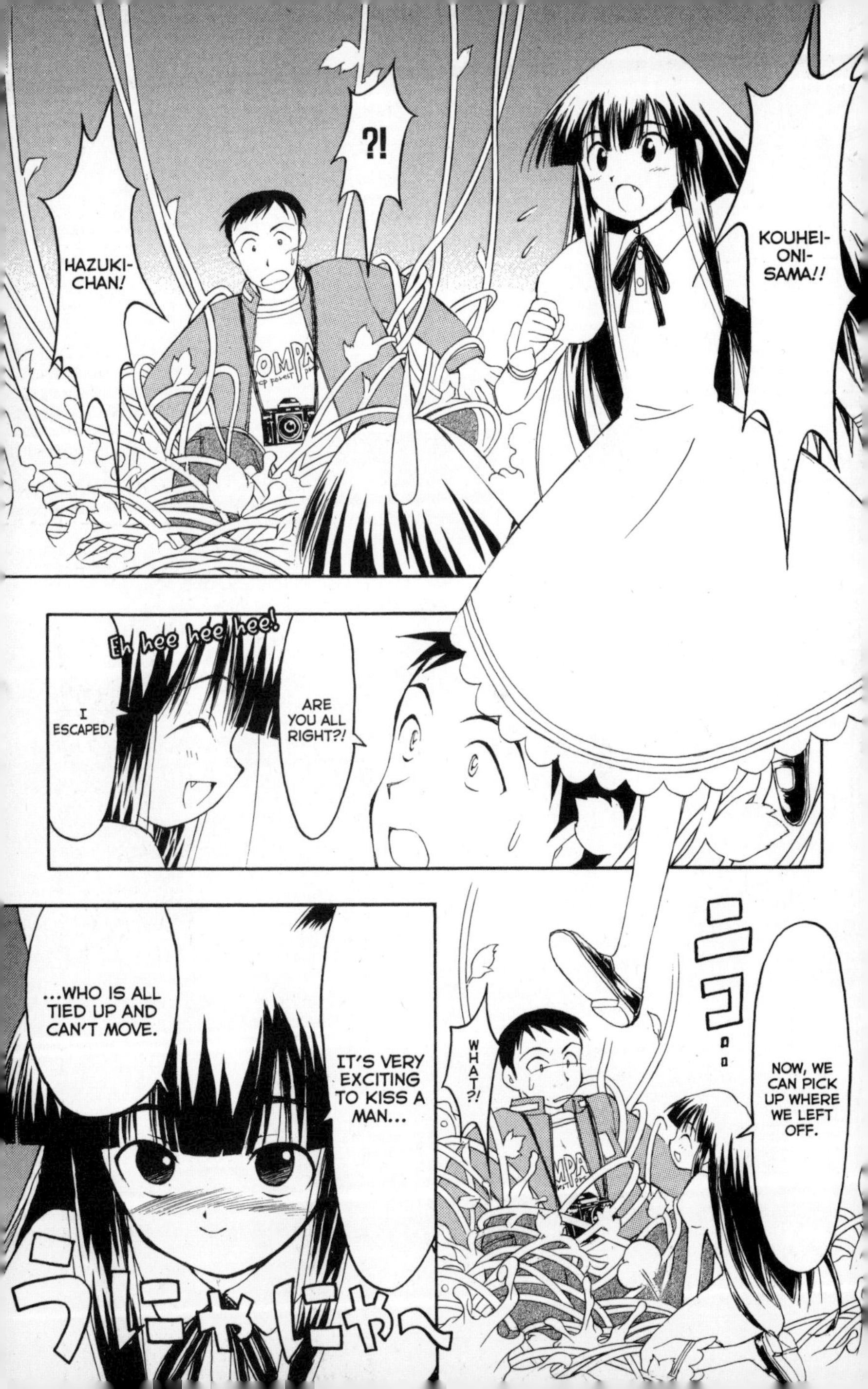
KOUHEI-ONI-SAMA!!
?!
HAZUKI-CHAN!
ARE YOU ALL RIGHT?!
Eh hee hee hee!
I ESCAPED!
NOW, WE CAN PICK UP WHERE WE LEFT OFF.
WHAT?!
IT'S VERY EXCITING TO KISS A MAN...
...WHO IS ALL TIED UP AND CAN'T MOVE.

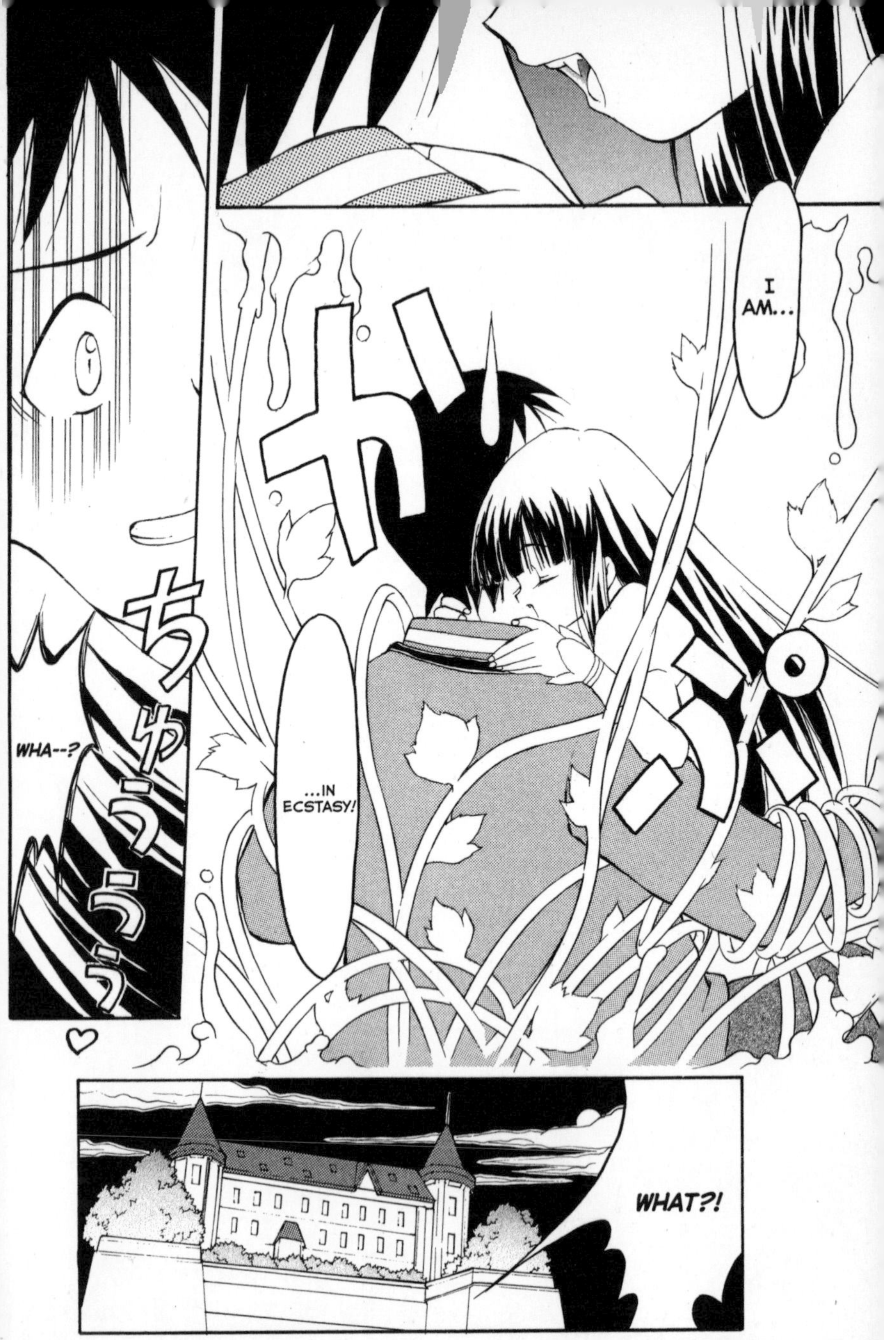

I AM...
ガ
...IN ECSTASY!
WHA--?
ちゅううう
WHAT?!

MOON 月詠 PHASE

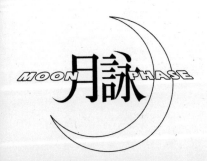

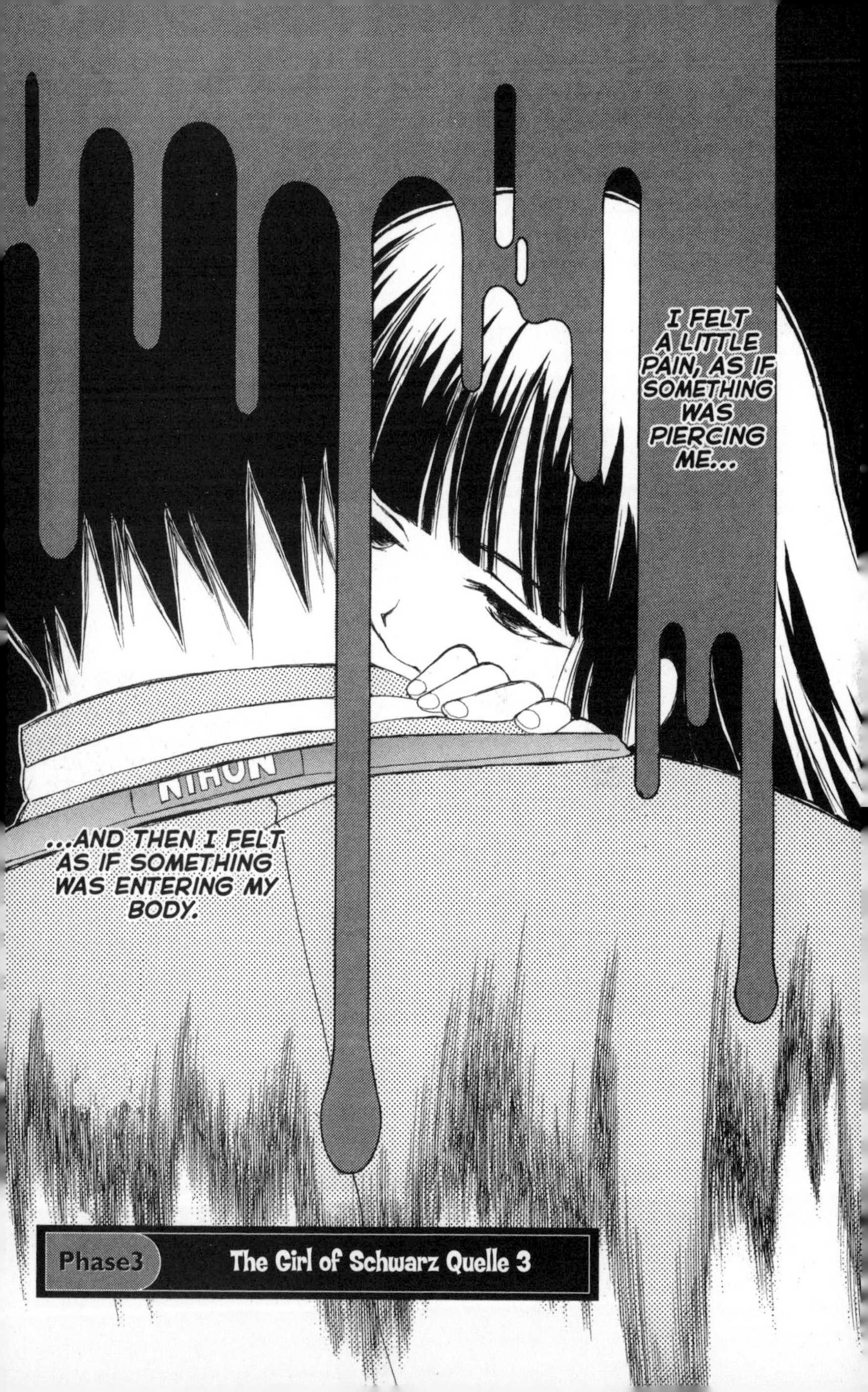

Phase3 The Girl of Schwarz Quelle 3

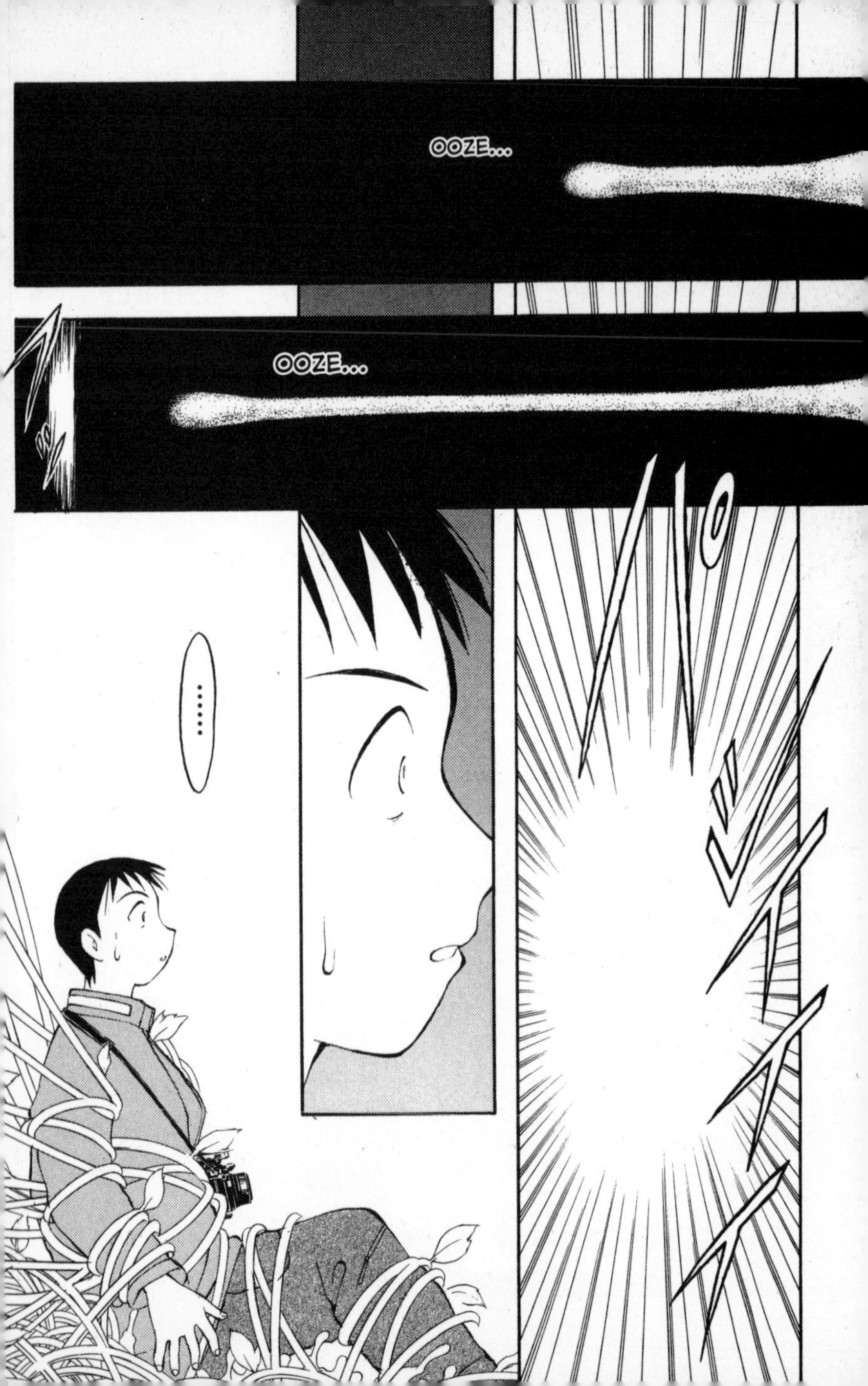
OOZE...
OOZE...
......

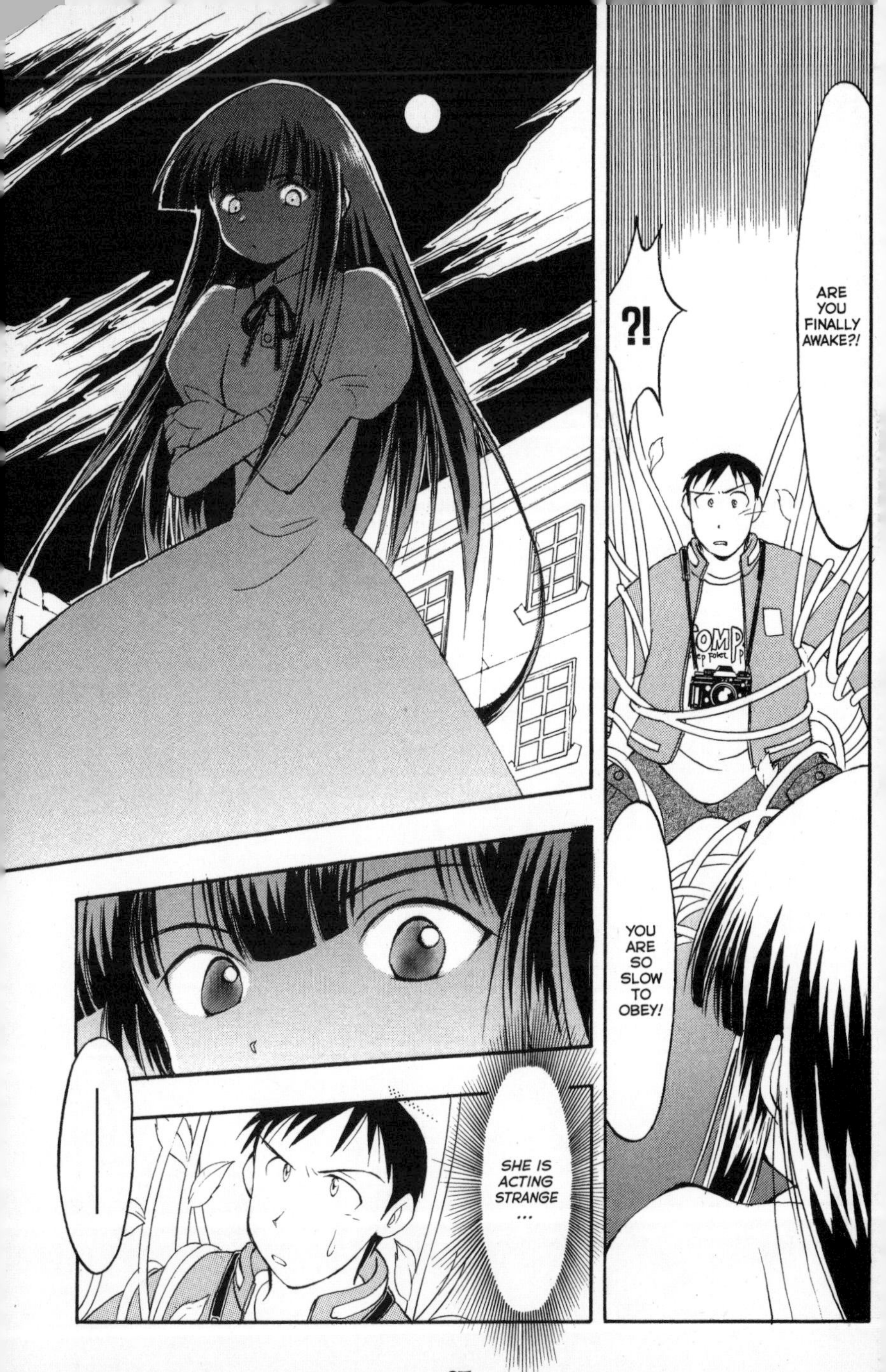
ARE YOU FINALLY AWAKE?!
?!
YOU ARE SO SLOW TO OBEY!
SHE IS ACTING STRANGE ...

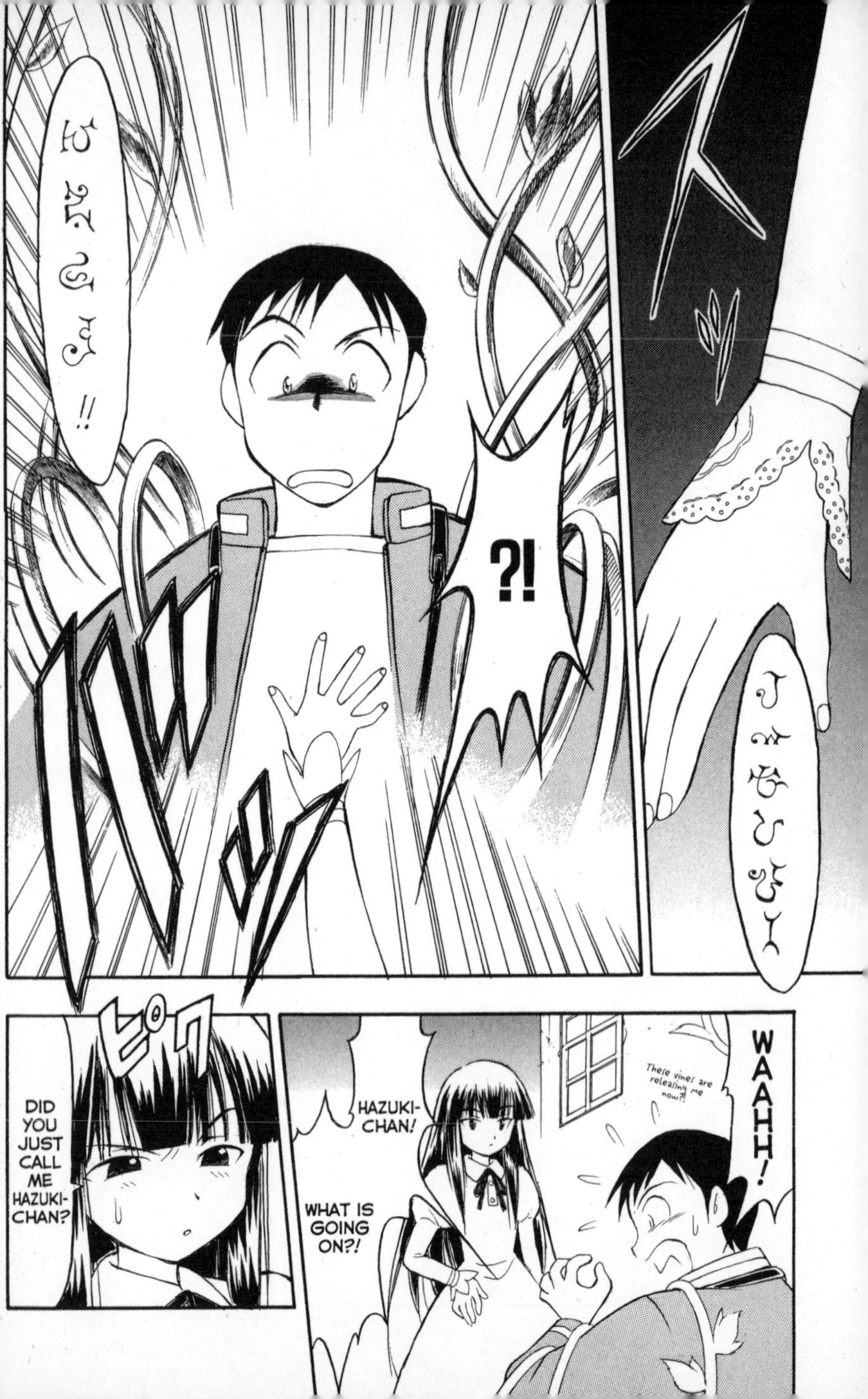
?!
WAAHH!
These vines are releasing me now?!
HAZUKI-CHAN!
WHAT IS GOING ON?!
DID YOU JUST CALL ME HAZUKI-CHAN?

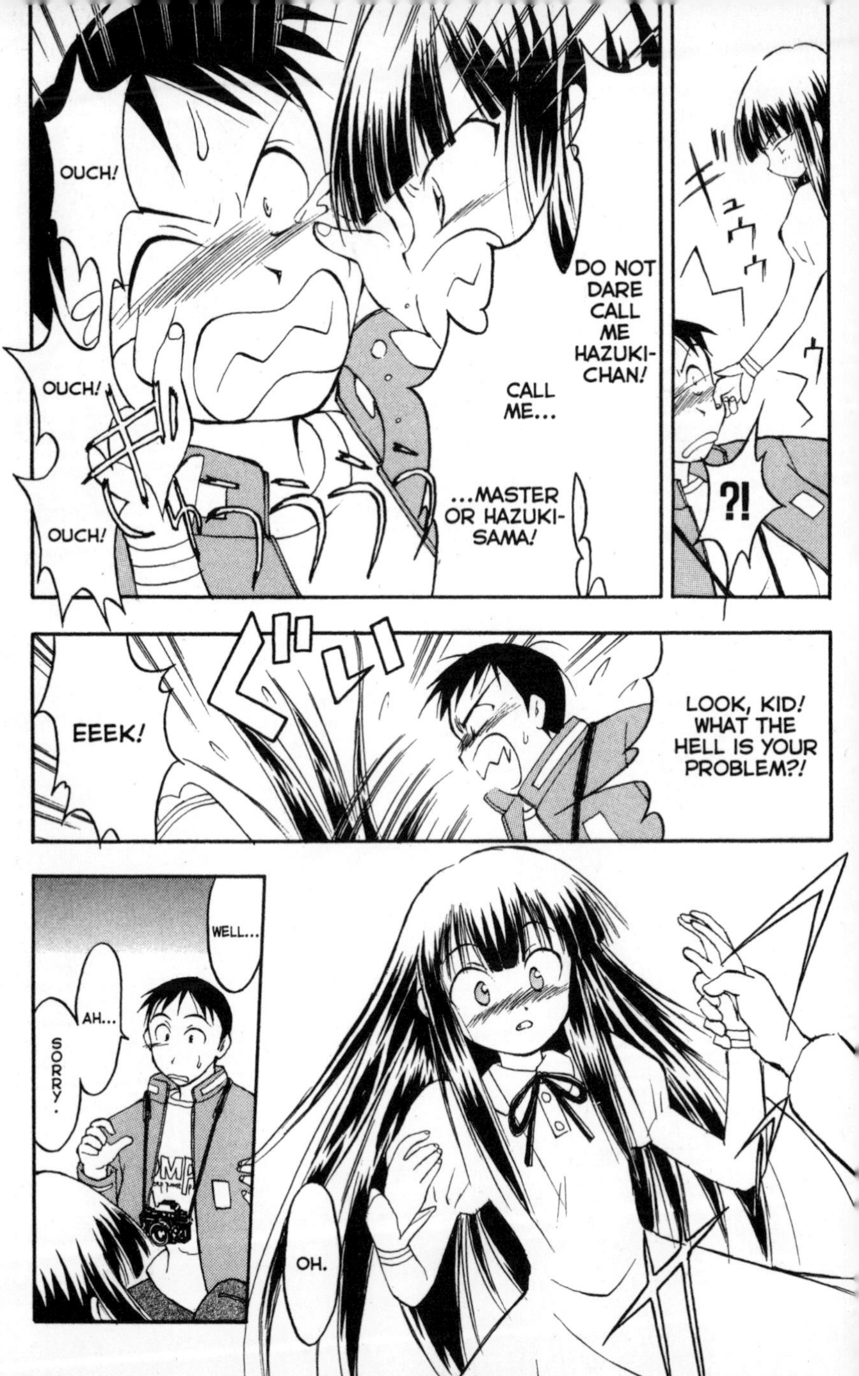
?!
DO NOT DARE CALL ME HAZUKI-CHAN!
CALL ME...
...MASTER OR HAZUKI-SAMA!
OUCH!
OUCH!
OUCH!
LOOK, KID! WHAT THE HELL IS YOUR PROBLEM?!
EEEK!
OH.
WELL...
AH...
SORRY.

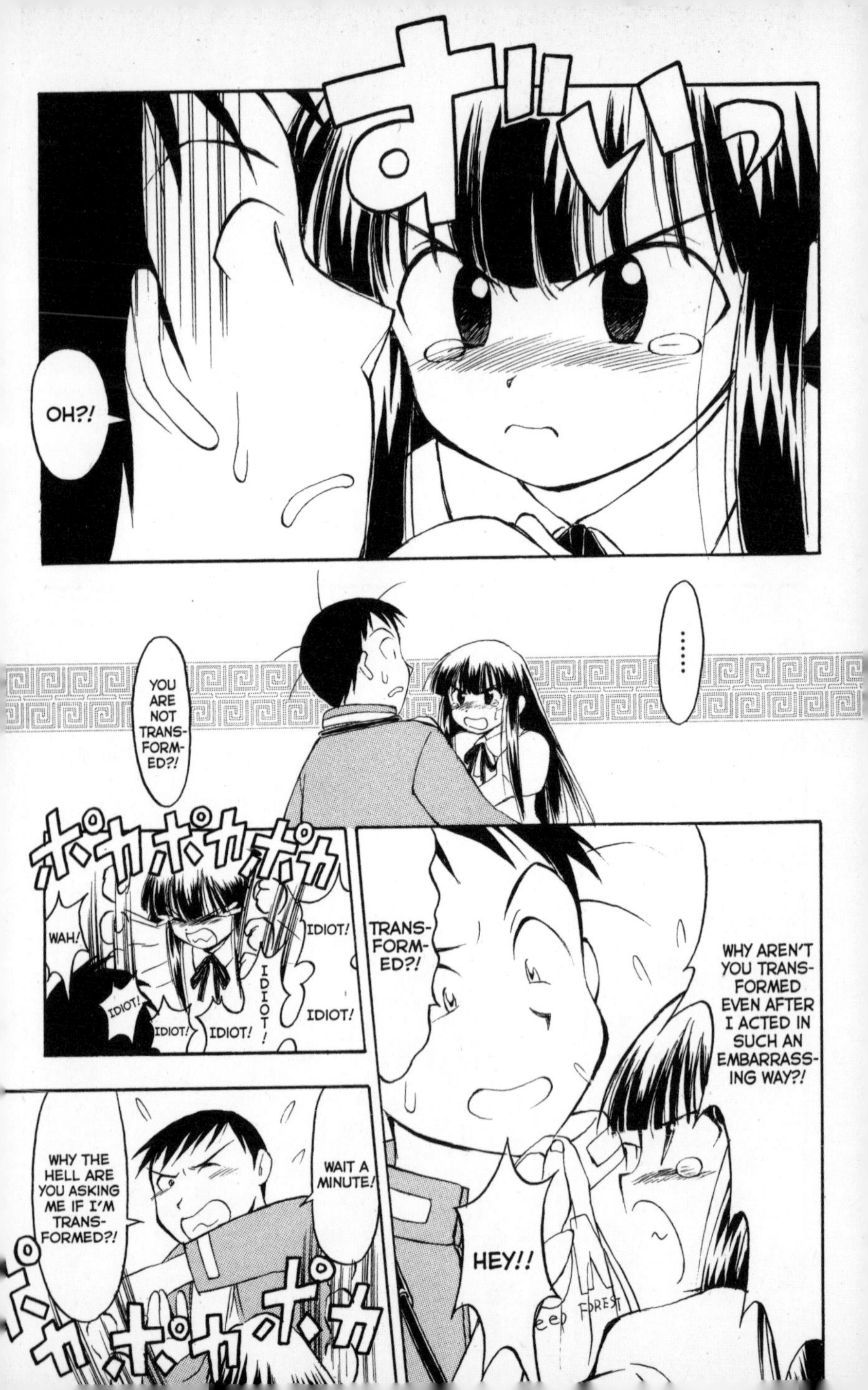
OH?!
......
YOU ARE NOT TRANSFORMED?!
WHY AREN'T YOU TRANSFORMED EVEN AFTER I ACTED IN SUCH AN EMBARRASSING WAY?!
TRANSFORMED?!
ポカポカポカ
IDIOT!
WAH!
IDIOT!
IDIOT!
IDIOT!
IDIOT!
IDIOT!
IDIOT!
HEY!!
WAIT A MINUTE!
WHY THE HELL ARE YOU ASKING ME IF I'M TRANSFORMED?!
ポカポカポカ

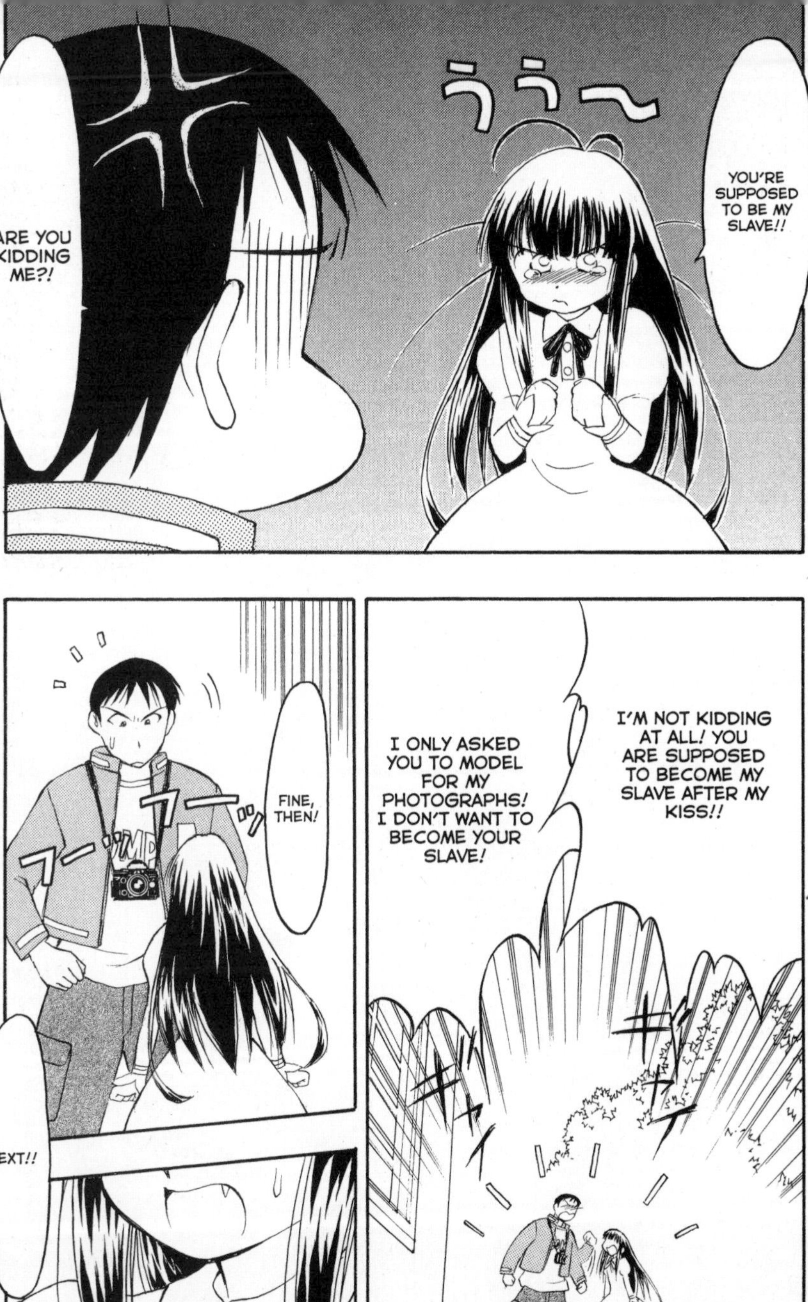
YOU'RE SUPPOSED TO BE MY SLAVE!!
うう〜
ARE YOU KIDDING ME?!
I'M NOT KIDDING AT ALL! YOU ARE SUPPOSED TO BECOME MY SLAVE AFTER MY KISS!!
I ONLY ASKED YOU TO MODEL FOR MY PHOTOGRAPHS! I DON'T WANT TO BECOME YOUR SLAVE!
FINE, THEN!
NEXT!!

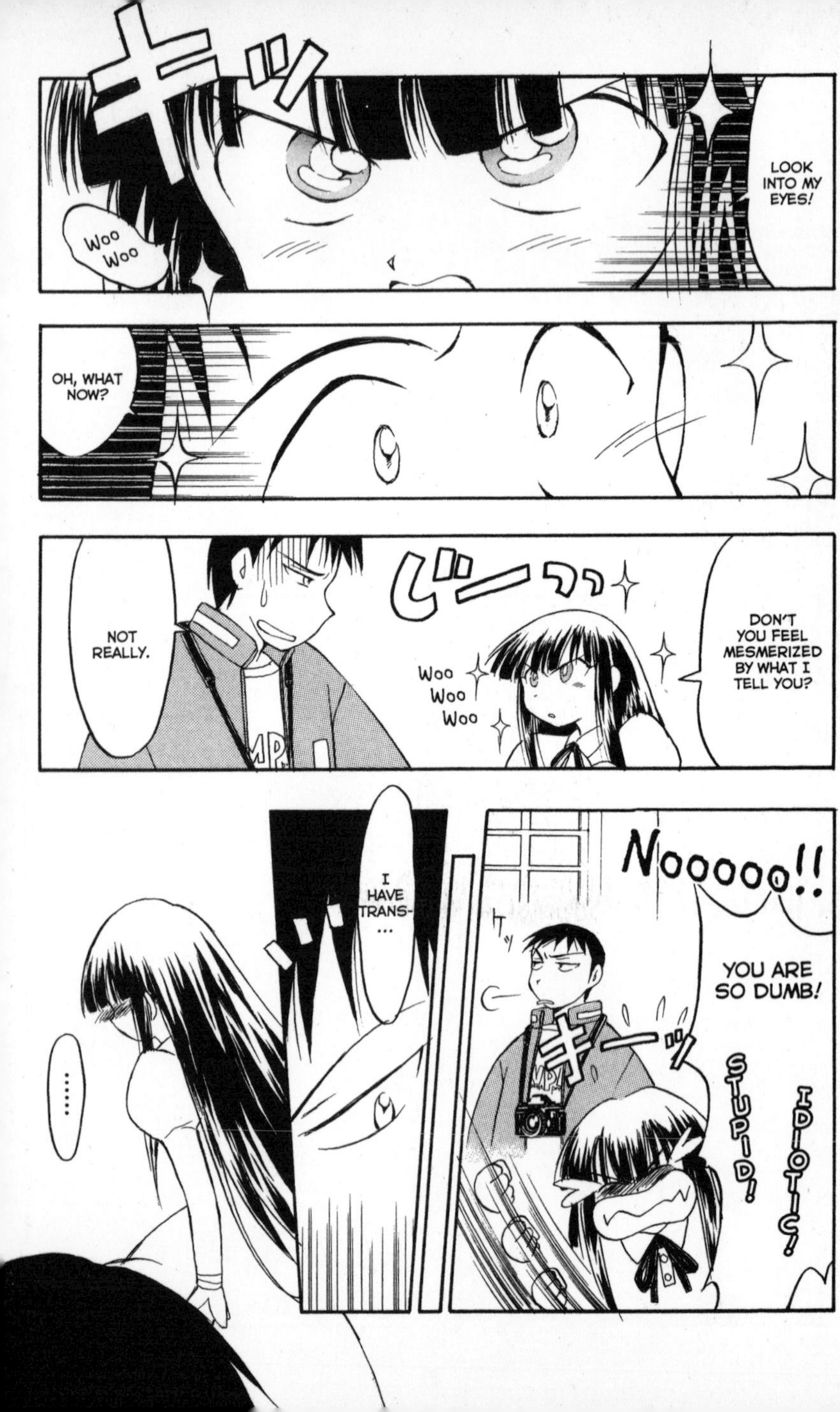
LOOK INTO MY EYES!
Woo Woo
OH, WHAT NOW?
DON'T YOU FEEL MESMERIZED BY WHAT I TELL YOU?
Woo Woo Woo
NOT REALLY.
Nooooo!!
YOU ARE SO DUMB!
IDIOTIC!
STUPID!
I HAVE TRANS-...
......

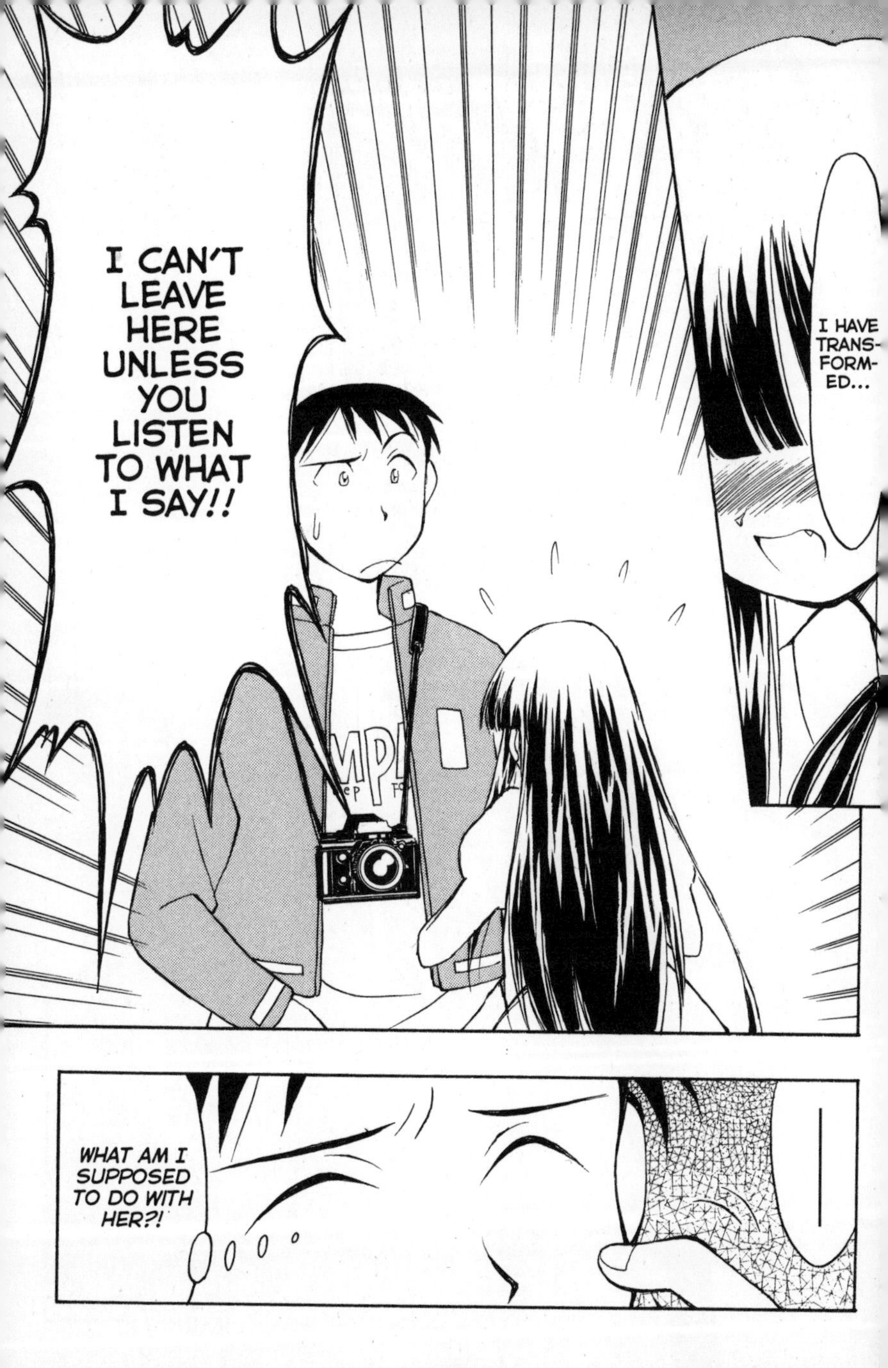
I HAVE TRANSFORMED...
I CAN'T LEAVE HERE UNLESS YOU LISTEN TO WHAT I SAY!!
WHAT AM I SUPPOSED TO DO WITH HER?!

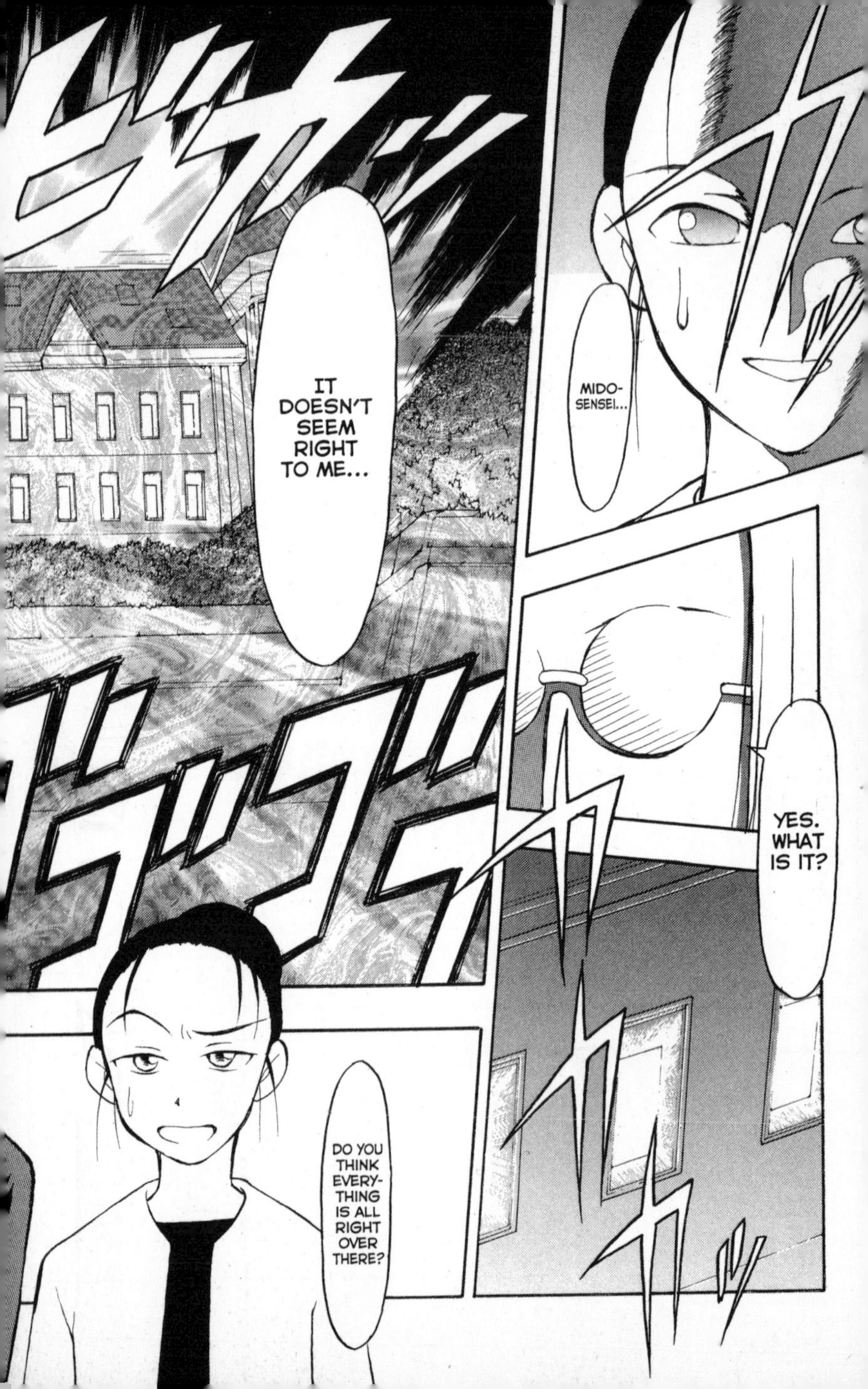
MIDO-SENSEI...
YES. WHAT IS IT?
IT DOESN'T SEEM RIGHT TO ME...
DO YOU THINK EVERYTHING IS ALL RIGHT OVER THERE?

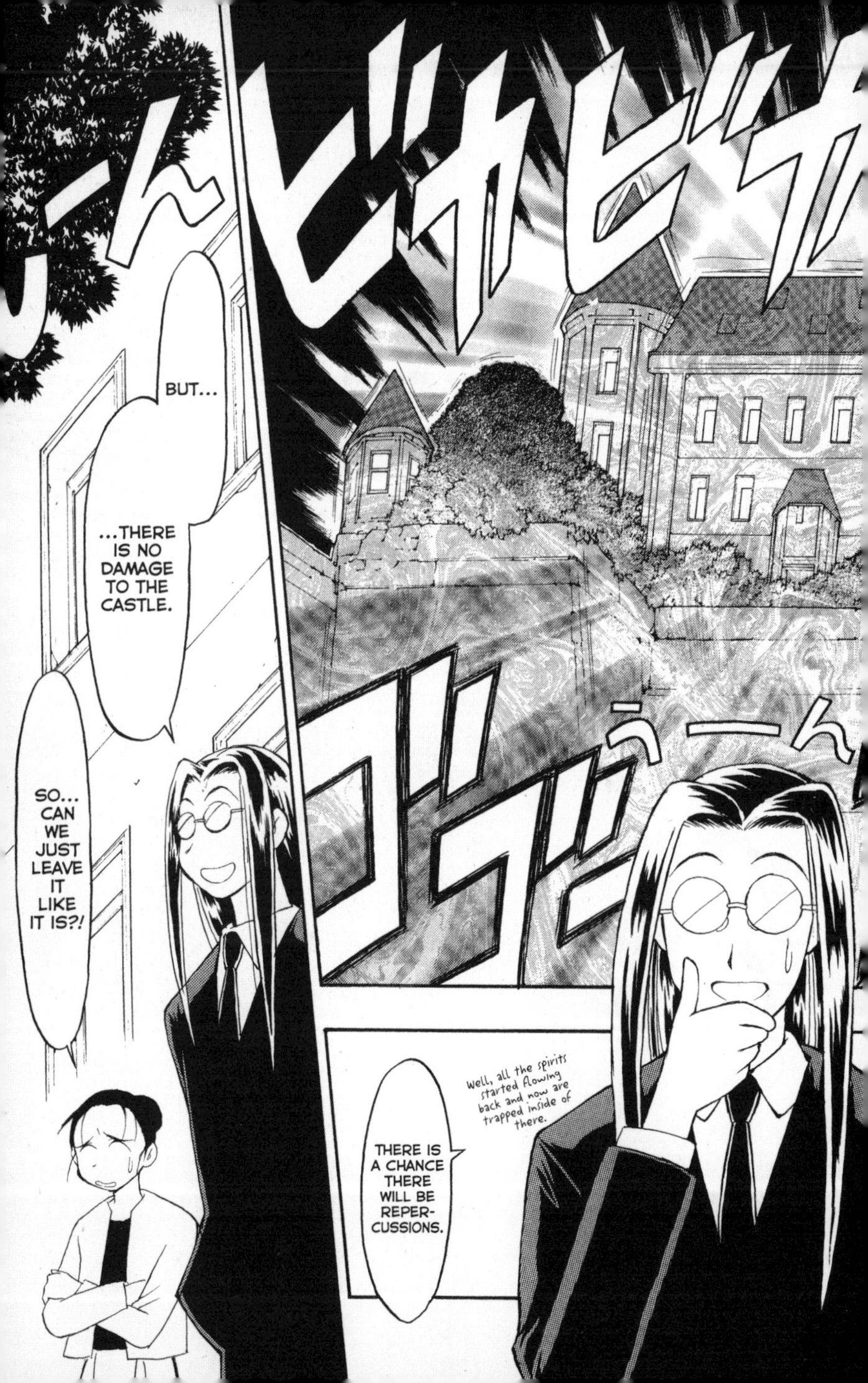
うーん
THERE IS A CHANCE THERE WILL BE REPER-CUSSIONS.
Well, all the spirits started flowing back and now are trapped inside of there.
BUT...
...THERE IS NO DAMAGE TO THE CASTLE.
SO... CAN WE JUST LEAVE IT LIKE IT IS?!

YES. MOST LIKELY THERE WON'T BE A PROBLEM.

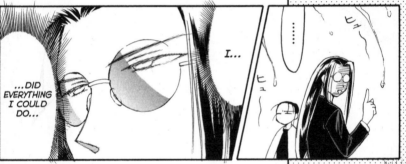

...DID EVERYTHING I COULD DO...

I...

.....

PLEASE TAKE CARE OF...

...THAT CASTLE, KOU-KUN!

KEKKAI?

WHAT THE HELL IS THAT?

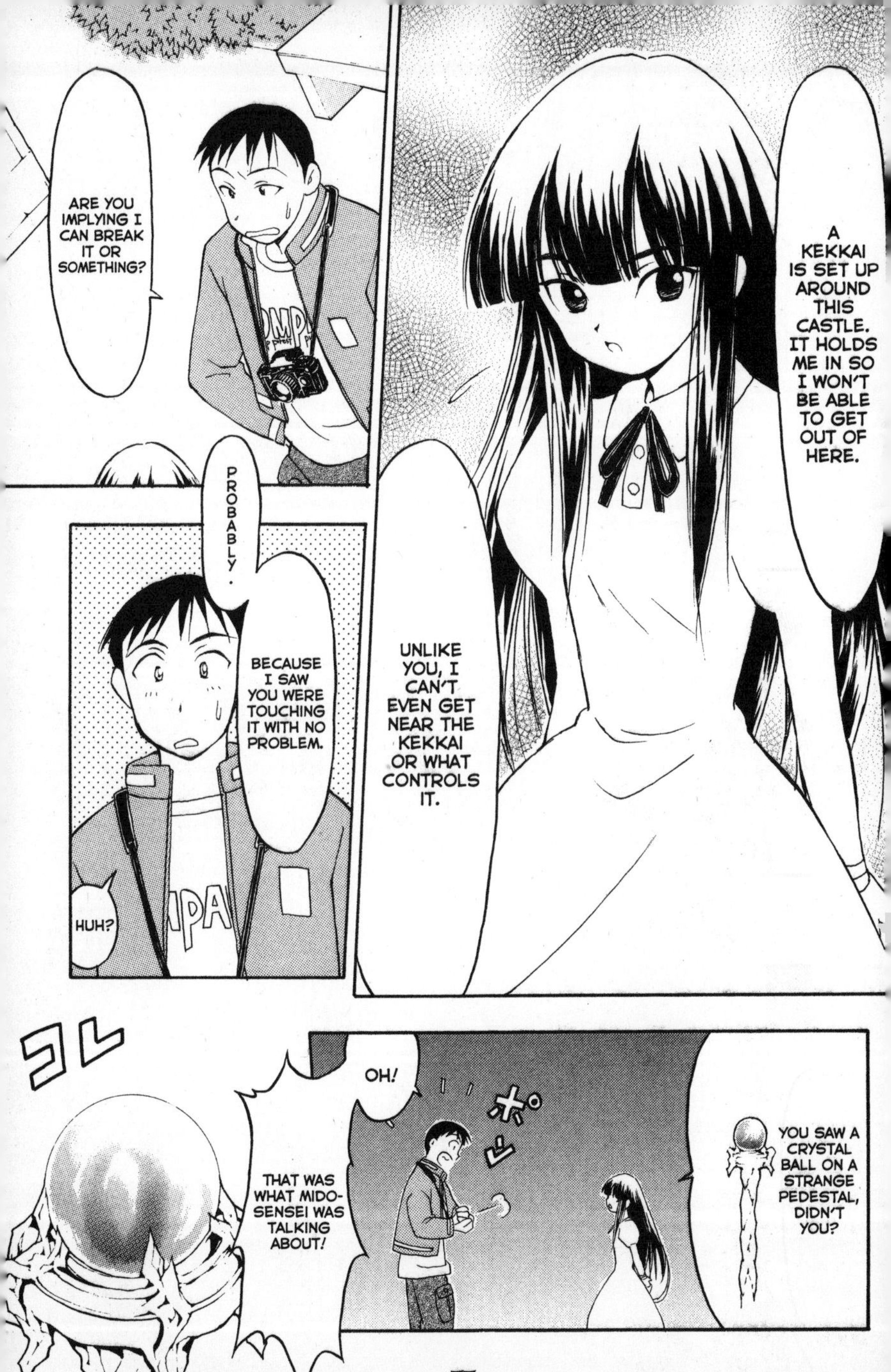
A KEKKAI IS SET UP AROUND THIS CASTLE. IT HOLDS ME IN SO I WON'T BE ABLE TO GET OUT OF HERE.
UNLIKE YOU, I CAN'T EVEN GET NEAR THE KEKKAI OR WHAT CONTROLS IT.
ARE YOU IMPLYING I CAN BREAK IT OR SOMETHING?
PROBABLY.
BECAUSE I SAW YOU WERE TOUCHING IT WITH NO PROBLEM.
HUH?
YOU SAW A CRYSTAL BALL ON A STRANGE PEDESTAL, DIDN'T YOU?
OH!
コレ
THAT WAS WHAT MIDO-SENSEI WAS TALKING ABOUT!

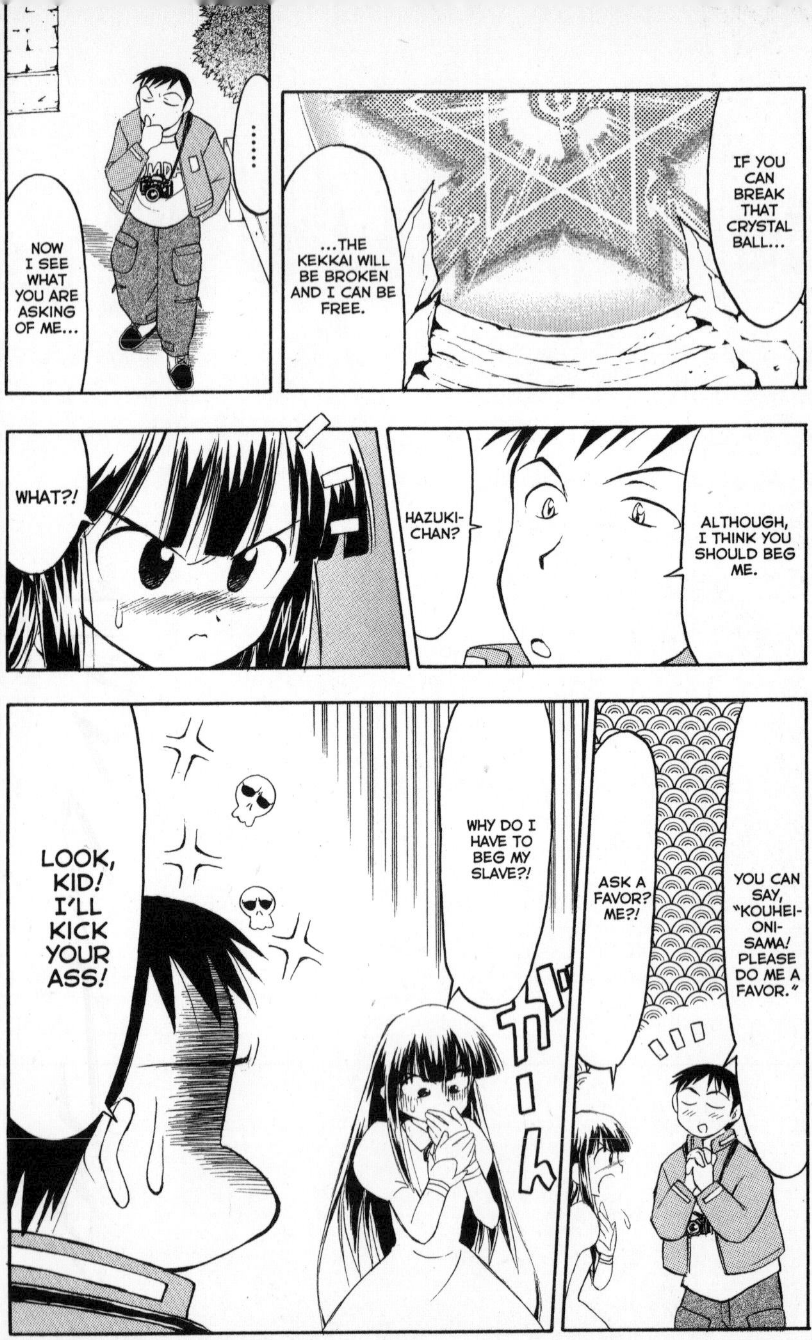
IF YOU CAN BREAK THAT CRYSTAL BALL...
...THE KEKKAI WILL BE BROKEN AND I CAN BE FREE.
......
NOW I SEE WHAT YOU ARE ASKING OF ME...
ALTHOUGH, I THINK YOU SHOULD BEG ME.
HAZUKI-CHAN?
WHAT?!
YOU CAN SAY, "KOUHEI-ONI-SAMA! PLEASE DO ME A FAVOR."
ASK A FAVOR? ME?!
WHY DO I HAVE TO BEG MY SLAVE?!
LOOK, KID! I'LL KICK YOUR ASS!

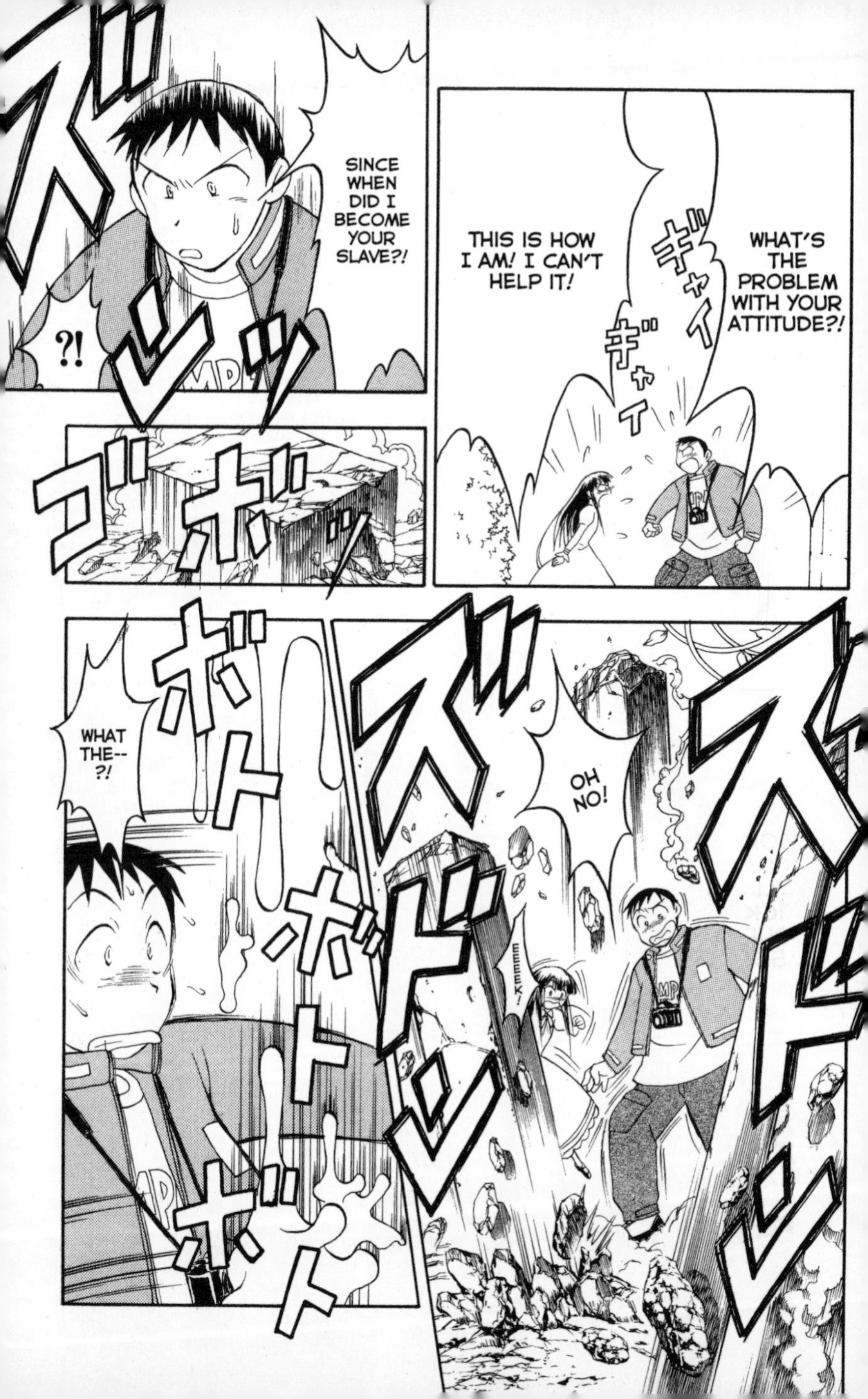
WHAT'S THE PROBLEM WITH YOUR ATTITUDE?!
ギャイ
ギャイ
THIS IS HOW I AM! I CAN'T HELP IT!
SINCE WHEN DID I BECOME YOUR SLAVE?!
?!
OH NO!
EEEEK!
WHAT THE-- ?!
ボト
ボト
ボト

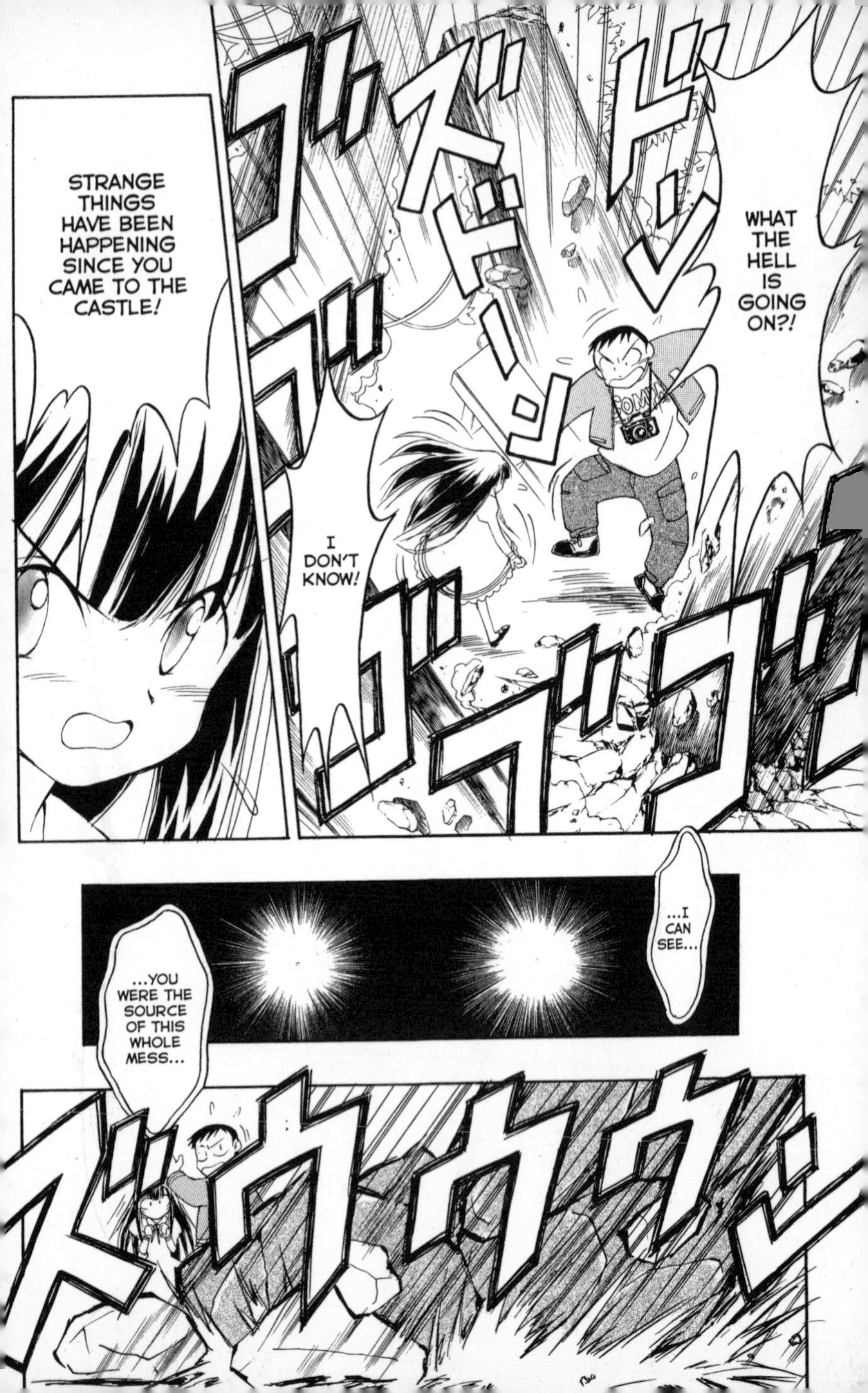
WHAT THE HELL IS GOING ON?!
I DON'T KNOW!
STRANGE THINGS HAVE BEEN HAPPENING SINCE YOU CAME TO THE CASTLE!
...I CAN SEE...
...YOU WERE THE SOURCE OF THIS WHOLE MESS...

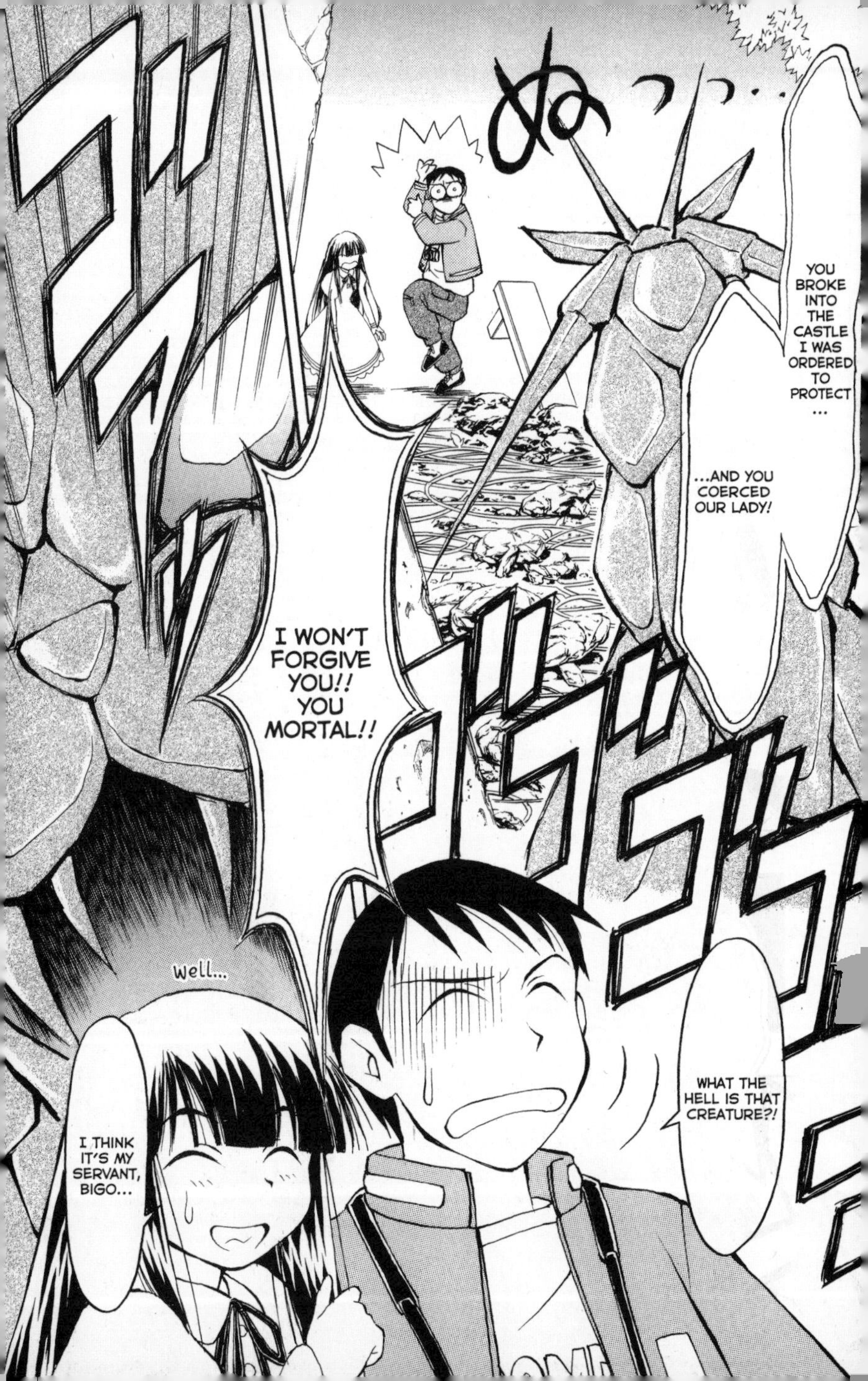
YOU BROKE INTO THE CASTLE I WAS ORDERED TO PROTECT...
...AND YOU COERCED OUR LADY!
I WON'T FORGIVE YOU!! YOU MORTAL!!
WHAT THE HELL IS THAT CREATURE?!
Well...
I THINK IT'S MY SERVANT, BIGO...

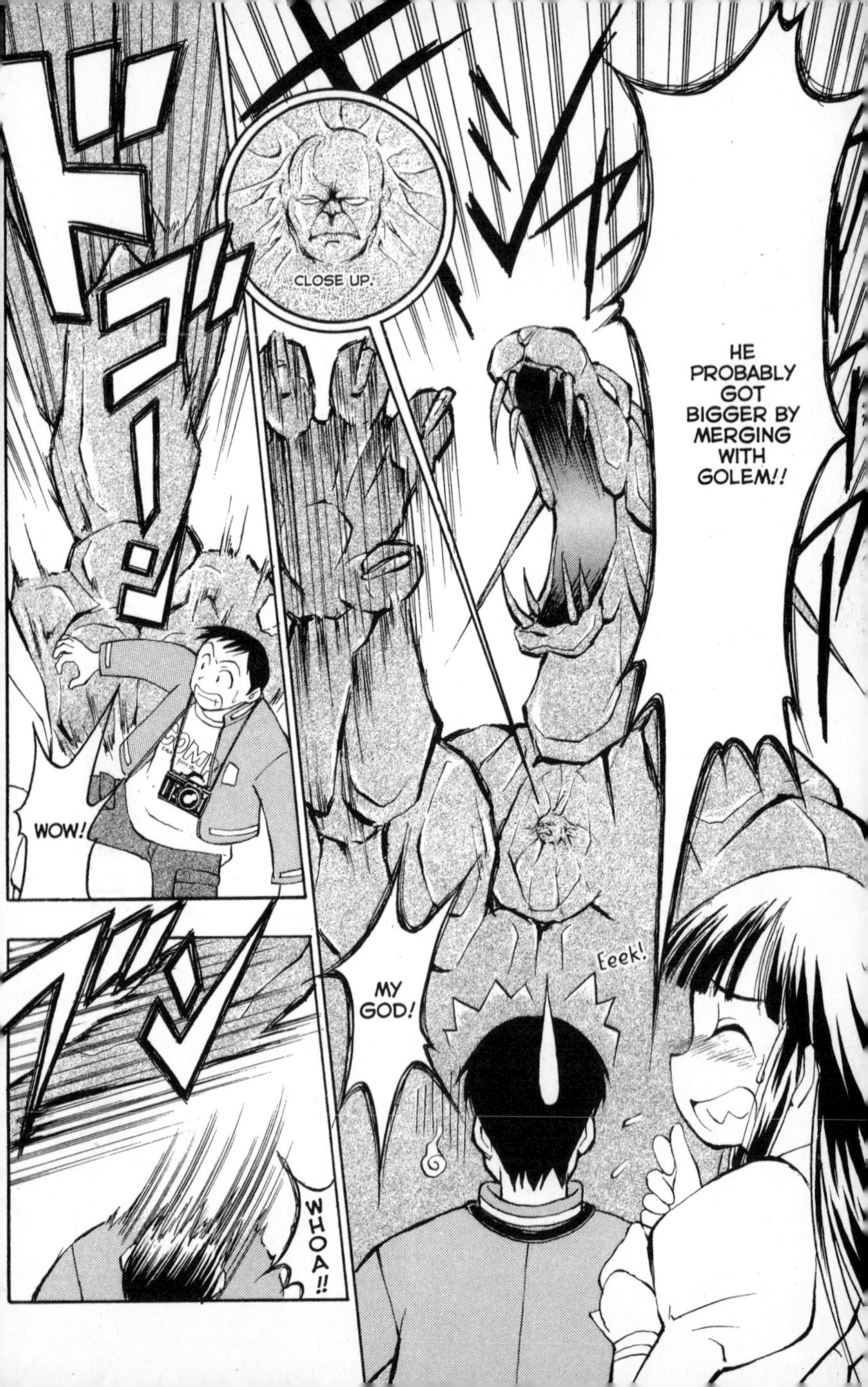
HE PROBABLY GOT BIGGER BY MERGING WITH GOLEM!!
CLOSE UP.
Eeek!
MY GOD!
WOW!
WHOA!!

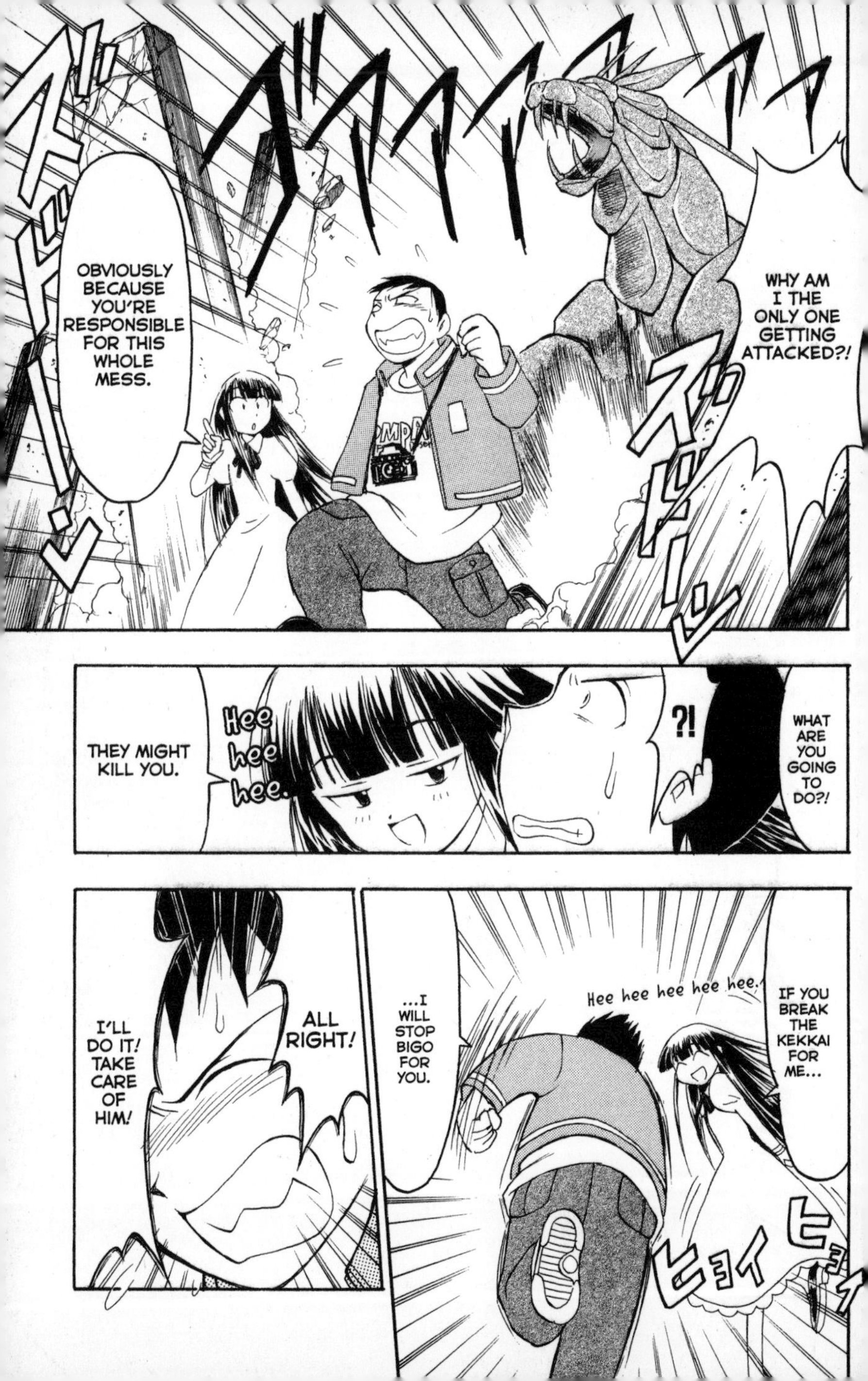
WHY AM I THE ONLY ONE GETTING ATTACKED?!
OBVIOUSLY BECAUSE YOU'RE RESPONSIBLE FOR THIS WHOLE MESS.
WHAT ARE YOU GOING TO DO?!
?!
Hee hee hee.
THEY MIGHT KILL YOU.
IF YOU BREAK THE KEKKAI FOR ME...
Hee hee hee hee hee.
...I WILL STOP BIGO FOR YOU.
ALL RIGHT!
I'LL DO IT! TAKE CARE OF HIM!

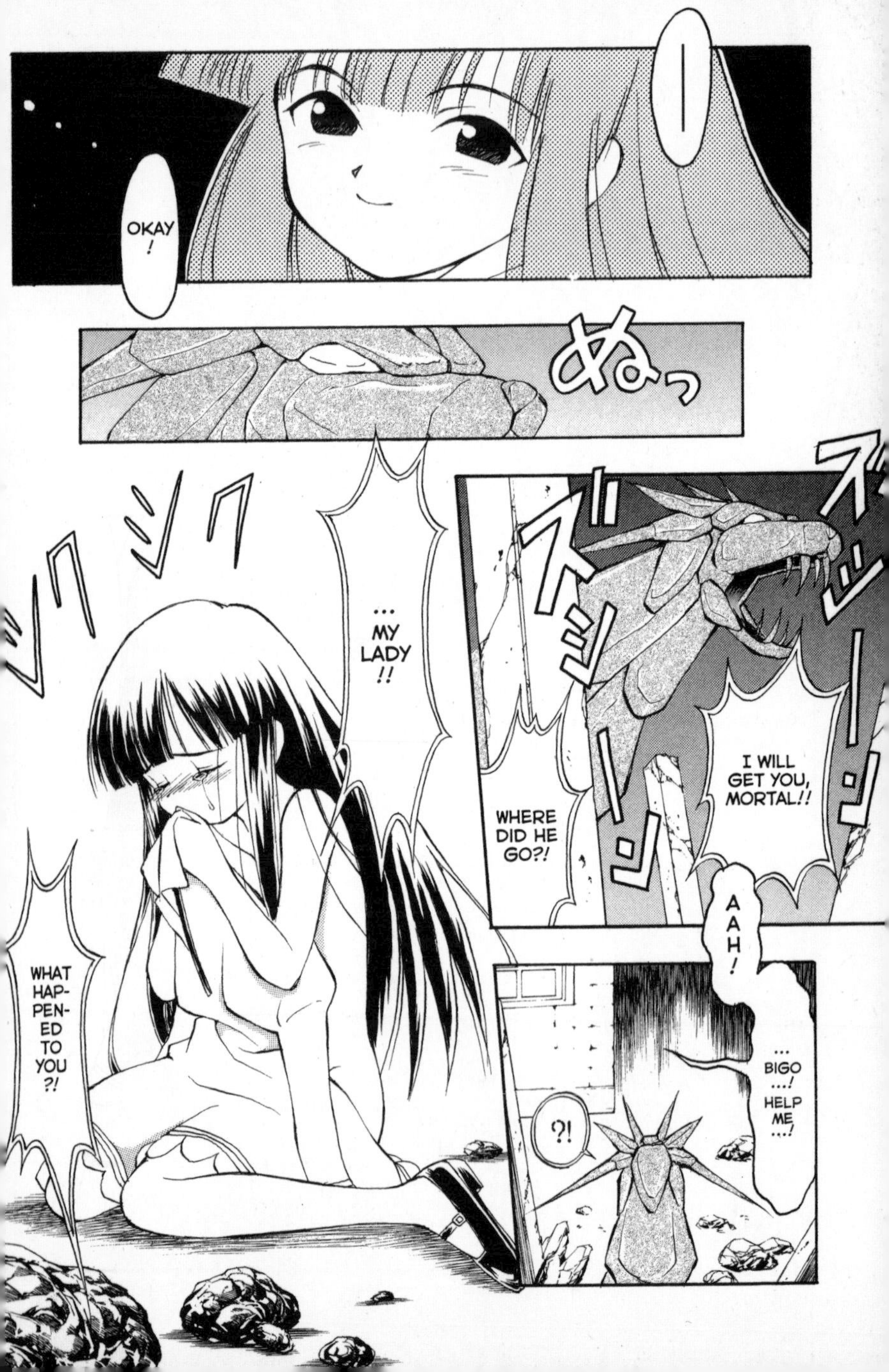
OKAY!
ぬっ
ズシーン
ズシーン
I WILL GET YOU, MORTAL!!
WHERE DID HE GO?!
AAH!
... BIGO...! HELP ME...!
?!
... MY LADY!!
シクシク
WHAT HAP-PEN-ED TO YOU?!

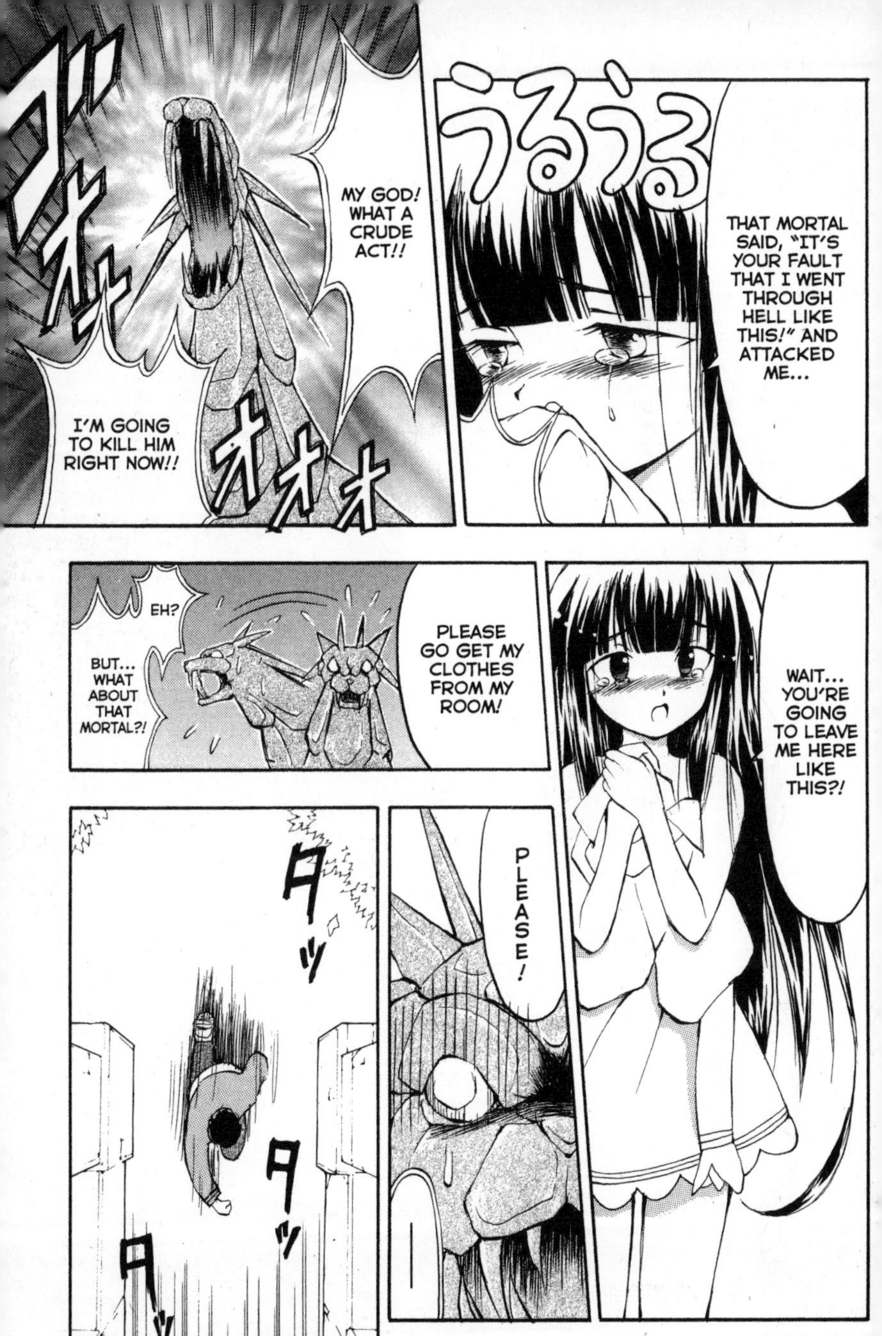
うるうる
THAT MORTAL SAID, "IT'S YOUR FAULT THAT I WENT THROUGH HELL LIKE THIS!" AND ATTACKED ME...
MY GOD! WHAT A CRUDE ACT!!
ゴォォ
オオオ
I'M GOING TO KILL HIM RIGHT NOW!!
WAIT... YOU'RE GOING TO LEAVE ME HERE LIKE THIS?!
PLEASE GO GET MY CLOTHES FROM MY ROOM!
EH?
BUT... WHAT ABOUT THAT MORTAL?!
PLEASE!
タッ
タッ
タッ

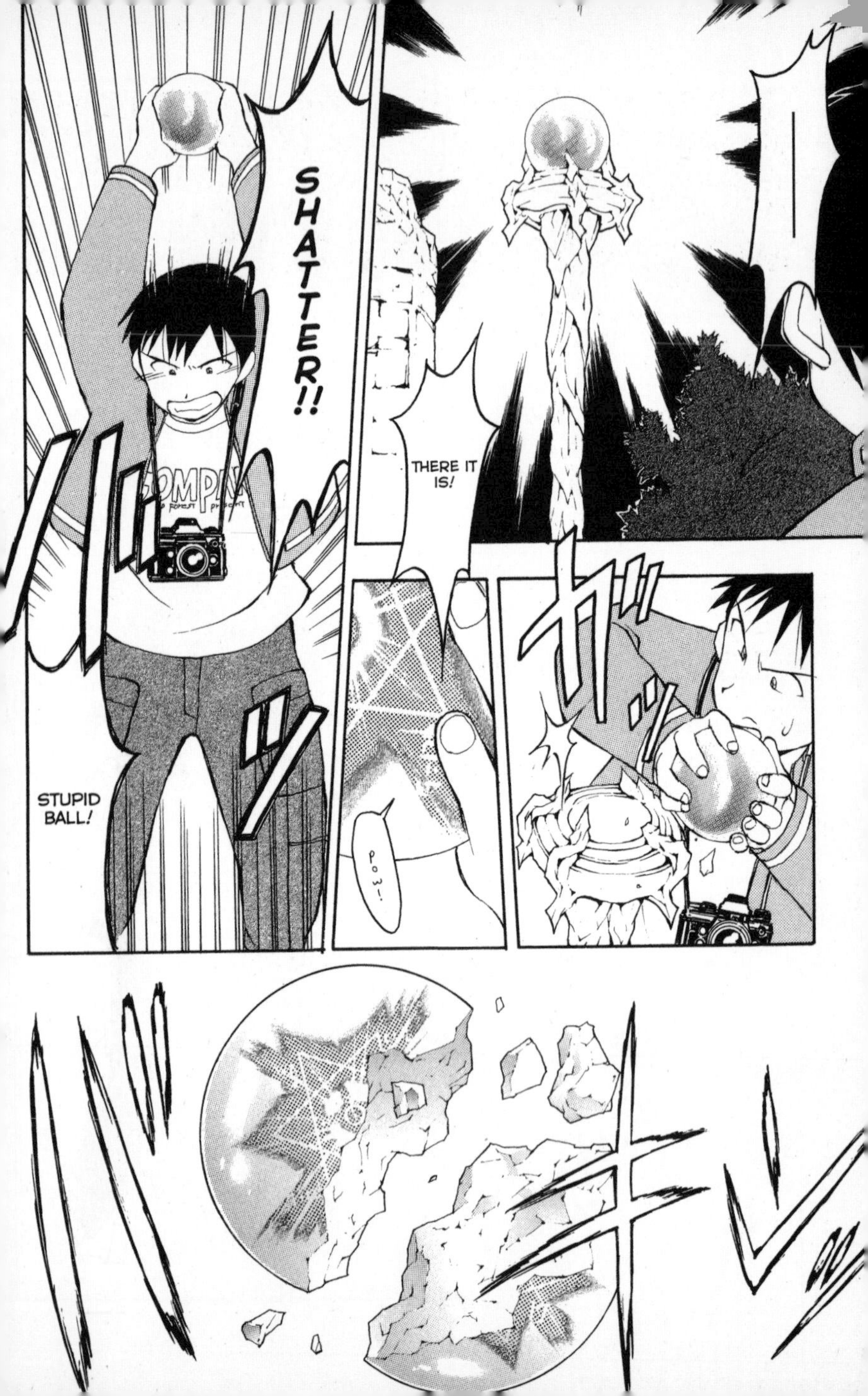
THERE IT IS!
pow!
SHATTER!!
STUPID BALL!

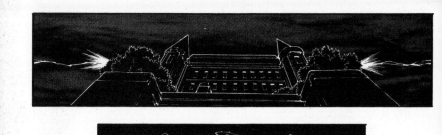

BIGO.
DID YOU
KNOW?

?!

THE
KEKKAI
...

I HAVE
ALREADY
KISSED
KOUHEI.

...IS
VANISH-
ING?!

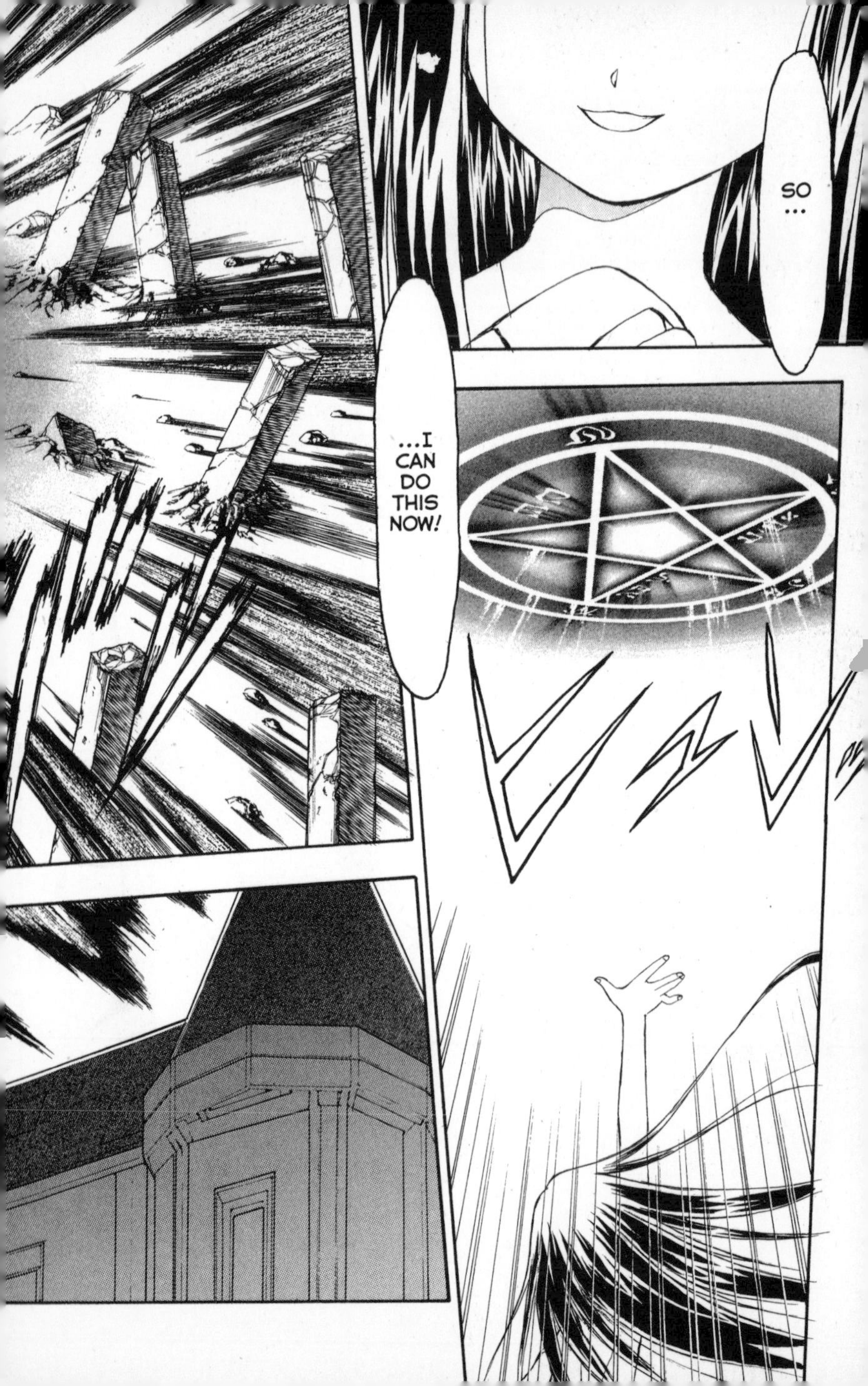
SO ...
...I CAN DO THIS NOW!

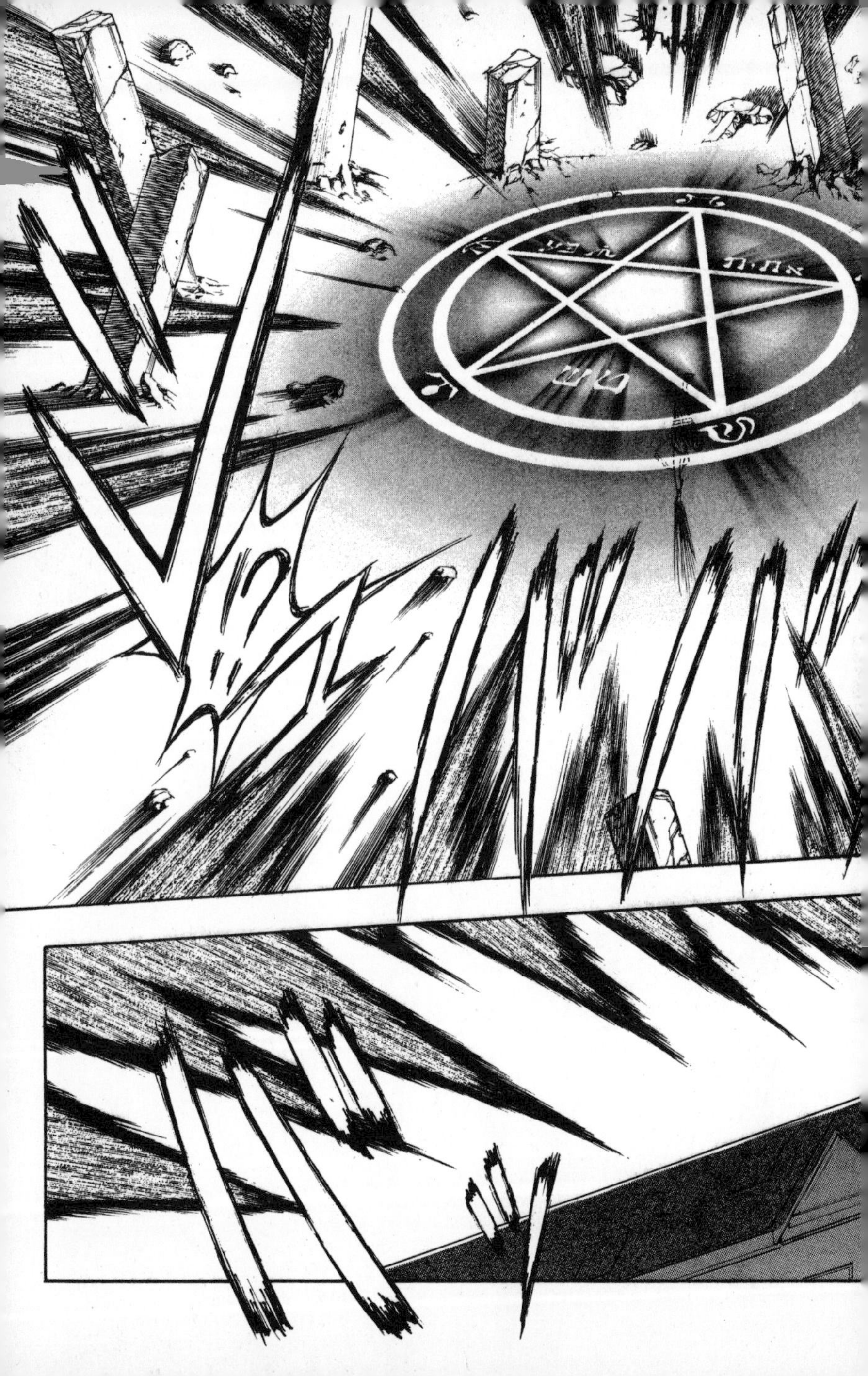

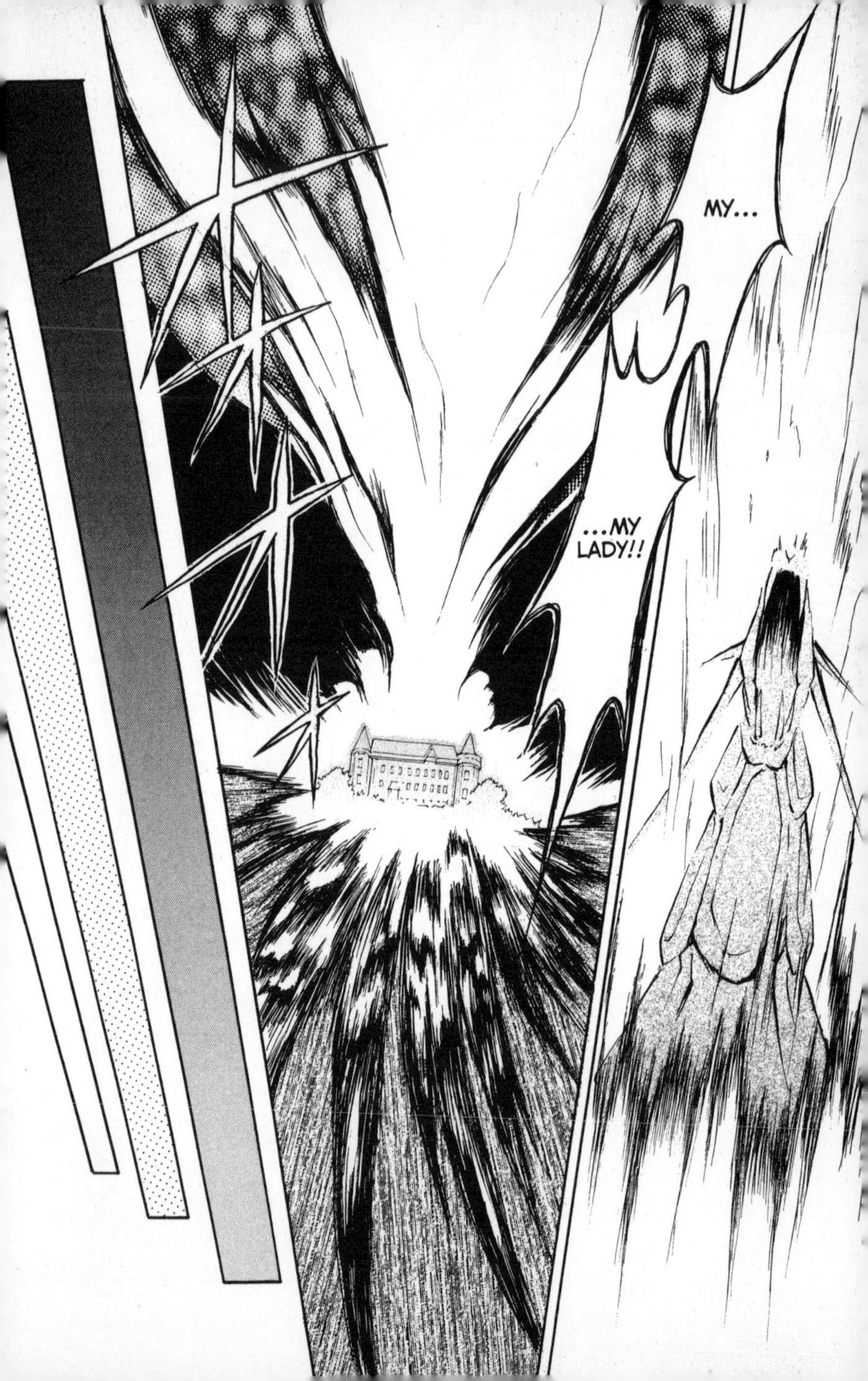
MY...
...MY LADY!!

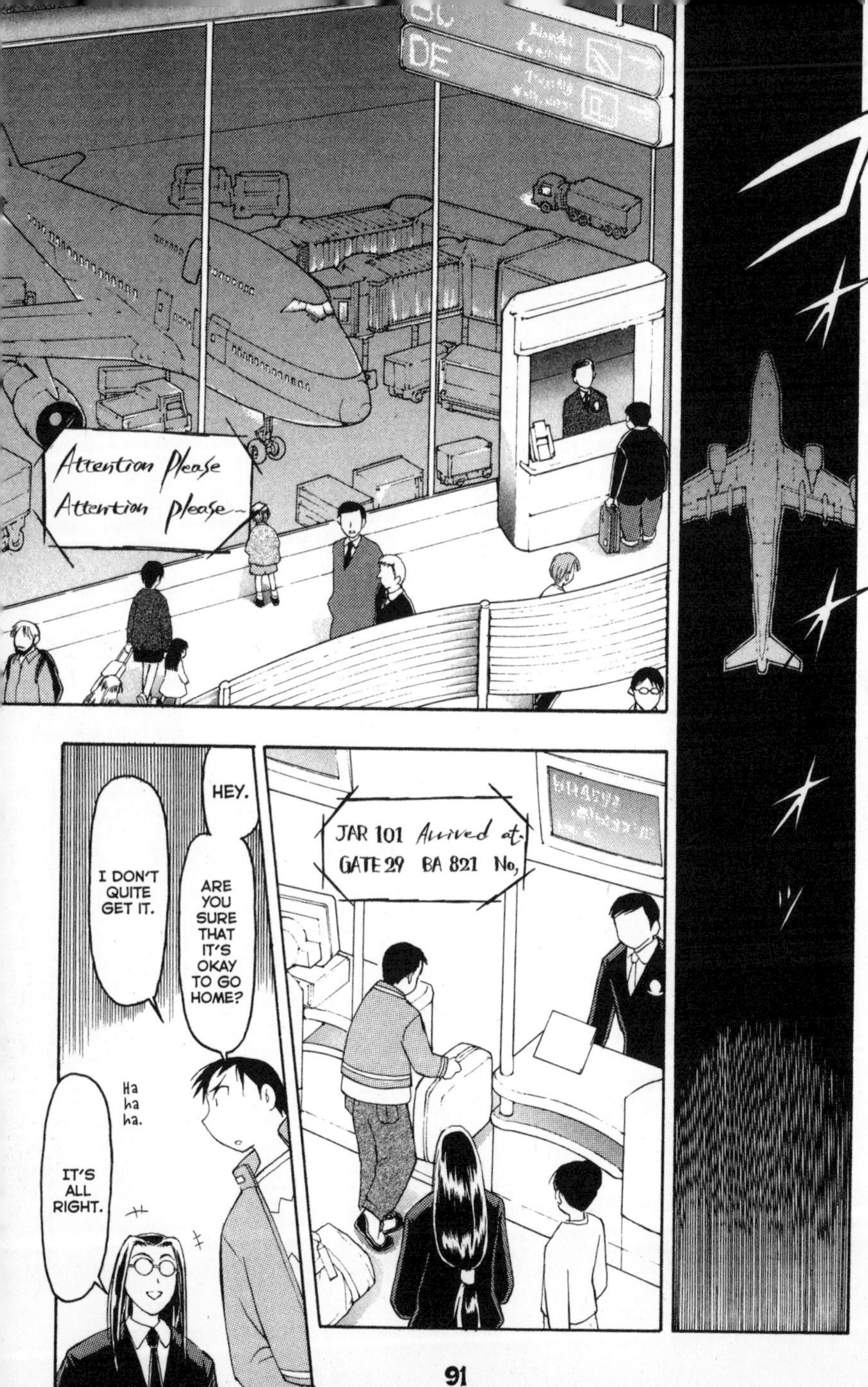
Attention Please
Attention please~
JAR 101 Arrived at GATE 29 BA 821 No,
HEY.
ARE YOU SURE THAT IT'S OKAY TO GO HOME?
I DON'T QUITE GET IT.
Ha ha ha.
IT'S ALL RIGHT.

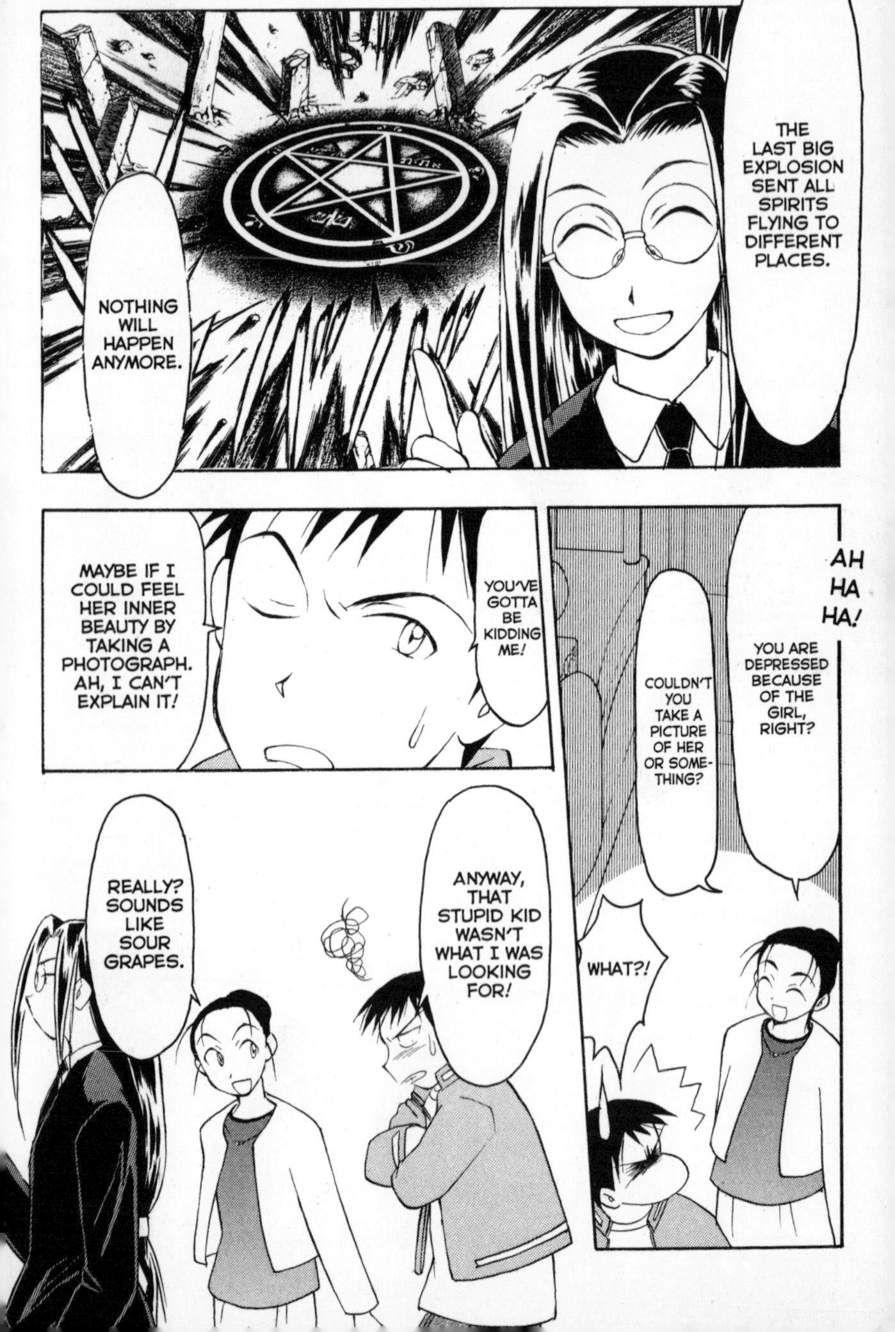
THE LAST BIG EXPLOSION SENT ALL SPIRITS FLYING TO DIFFERENT PLACES.
NOTHING WILL HAPPEN ANYMORE.
AH HA HA!
YOU ARE DEPRESSED BECAUSE OF THE GIRL, RIGHT?
COULDN'T YOU TAKE A PICTURE OF HER OR SOME-THING?
WHAT?!
YOU'VE GOTTA BE KIDDING ME!
MAYBE IF I COULD FEEL HER INNER BEAUTY BY TAKING A PHOTOGRAPH. AH, I CAN'T EXPLAIN IT!
ANYWAY, THAT STUPID KID WASN'T WHAT I WAS LOOKING FOR!
REALLY? SOUNDS LIKE SOUR GRAPES.

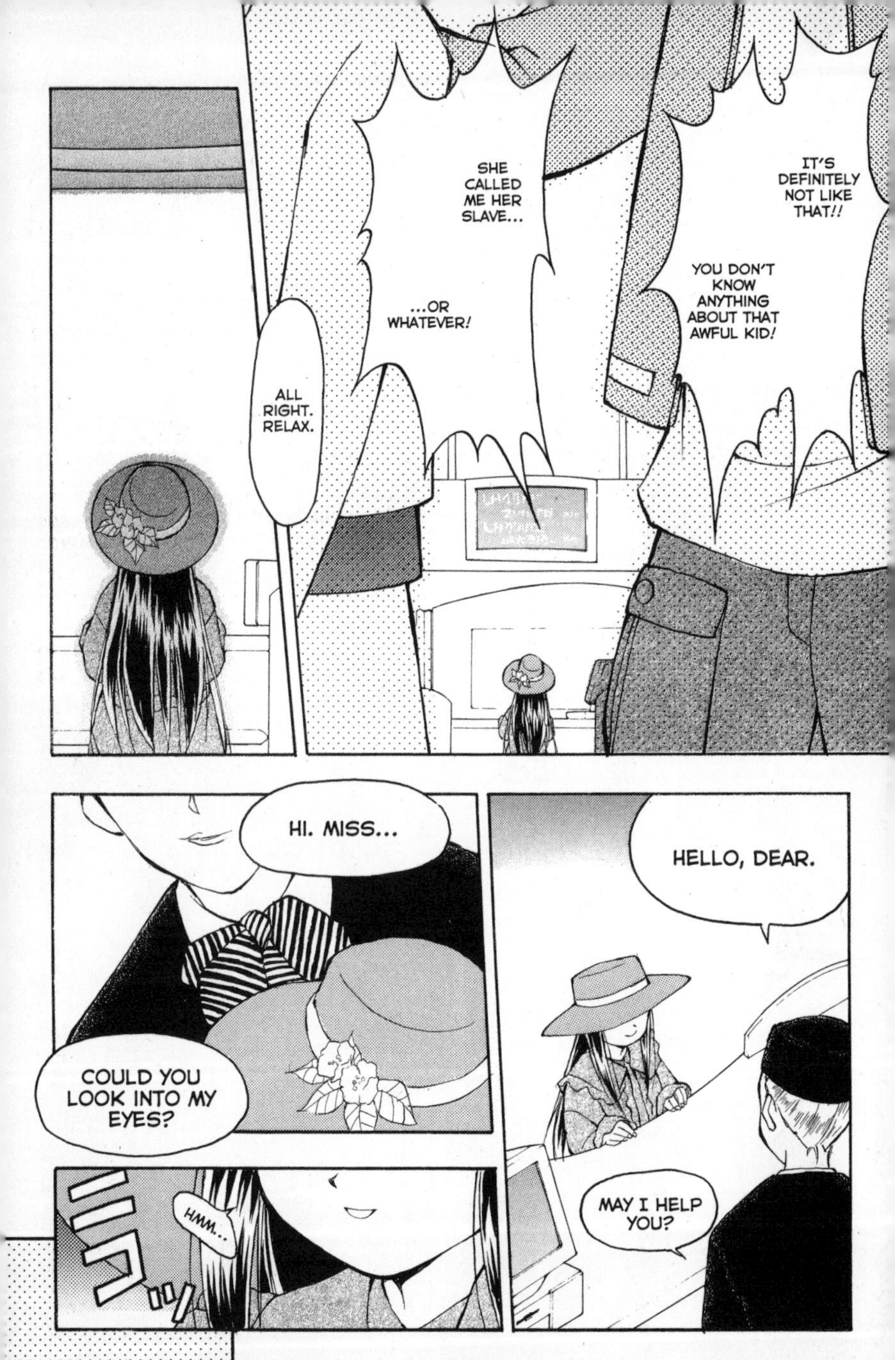
IT'S DEFINITELY NOT LIKE THAT!!
YOU DON'T KNOW ANYTHING ABOUT THAT AWFUL KID!
SHE CALLED ME HER SLAVE...
...OR WHATEVER!
ALL RIGHT. RELAX.
HELLO, DEAR.
MAY I HELP YOU?
HI. MISS...
COULD YOU LOOK INTO MY EYES?
HMM...

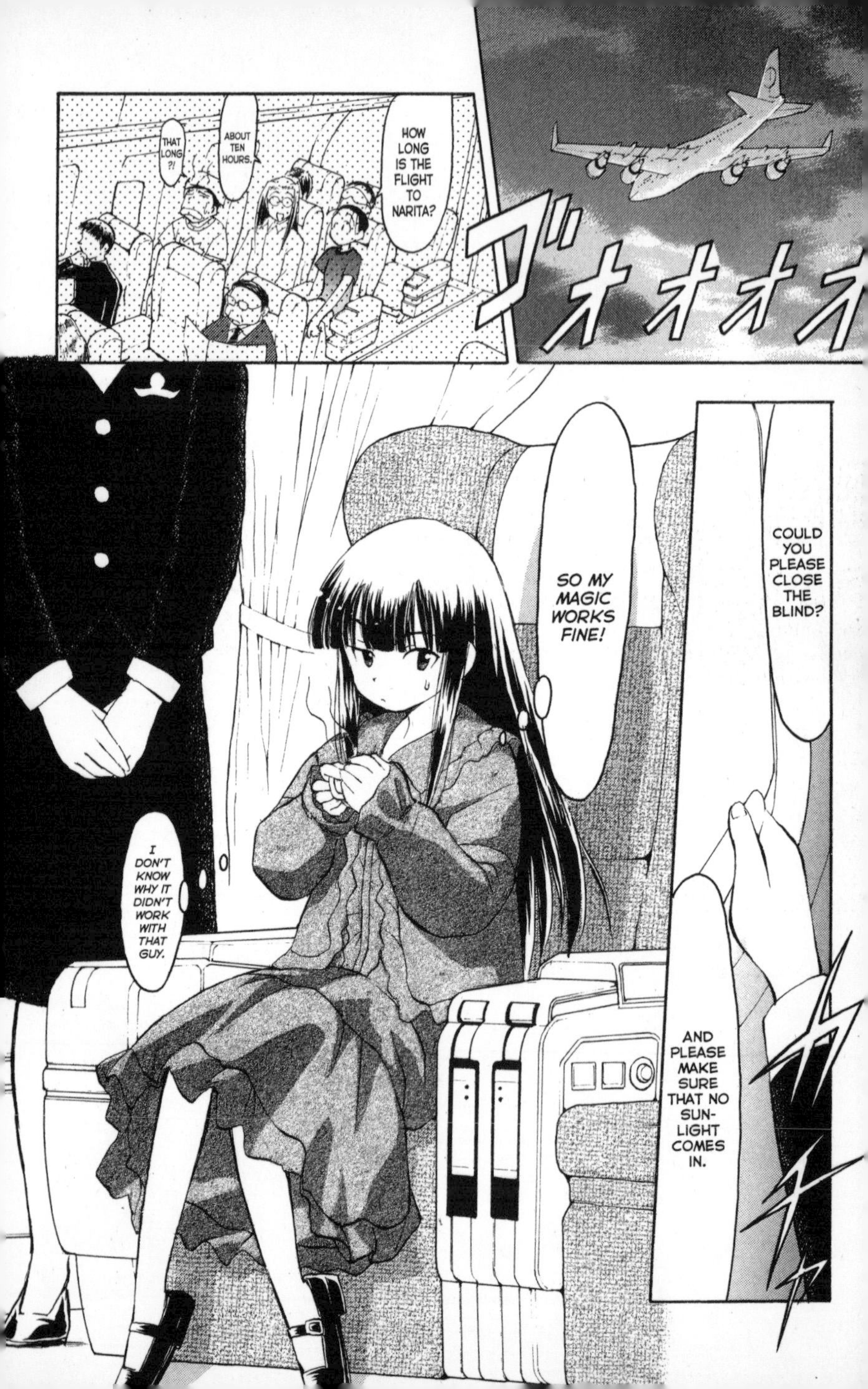
ゴオオオオ
HOW LONG IS THE FLIGHT TO NARITA?
ABOUT TEN HOURS.
THAT LONG ?!
COULD YOU PLEASE CLOSE THE BLIND?
AND PLEASE MAKE SURE THAT NO SUN-LIGHT COMES IN.
SO MY MAGIC WORKS FINE!
I DON'T KNOW WHY IT DIDN'T WORK WITH THAT GUY.

TO NEXT STAGE

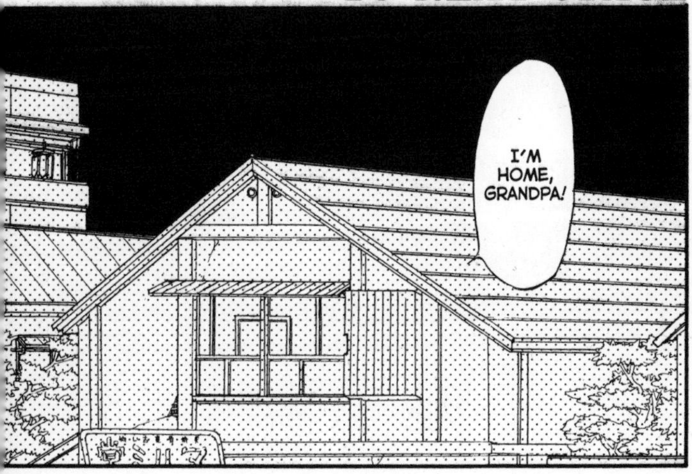
I'M HOME, GRANDPA!

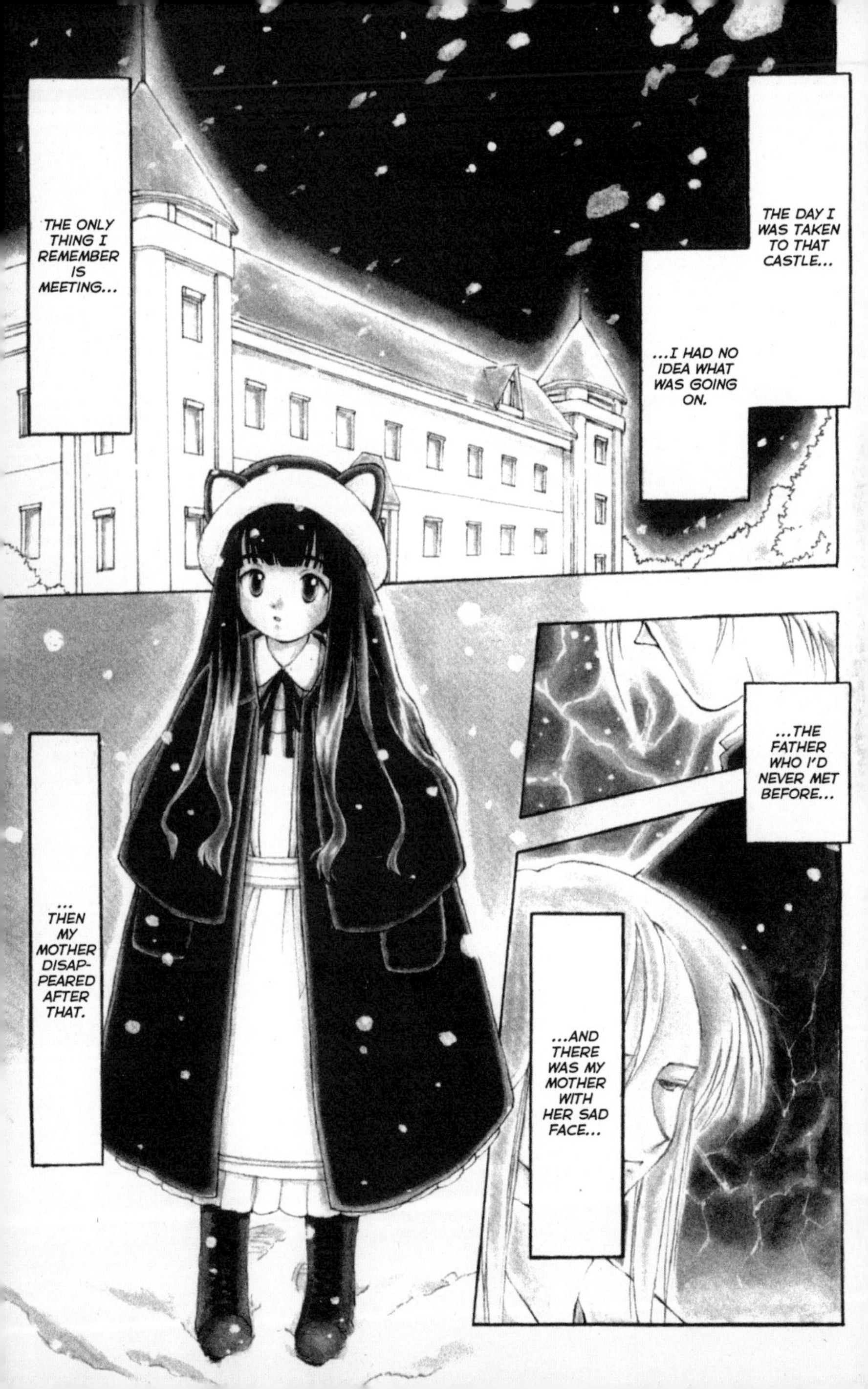
THE DAY I WAS TAKEN TO THAT CASTLE...
...I HAD NO IDEA WHAT WAS GOING ON.
THE ONLY THING I REMEMBER IS MEETING...
...THE FATHER WHO I'D NEVER MET BEFORE...
...AND THERE WAS MY MOTHER WITH HER SAD FACE...
...THEN MY MOTHER DISAP-PEARED AFTER THAT.

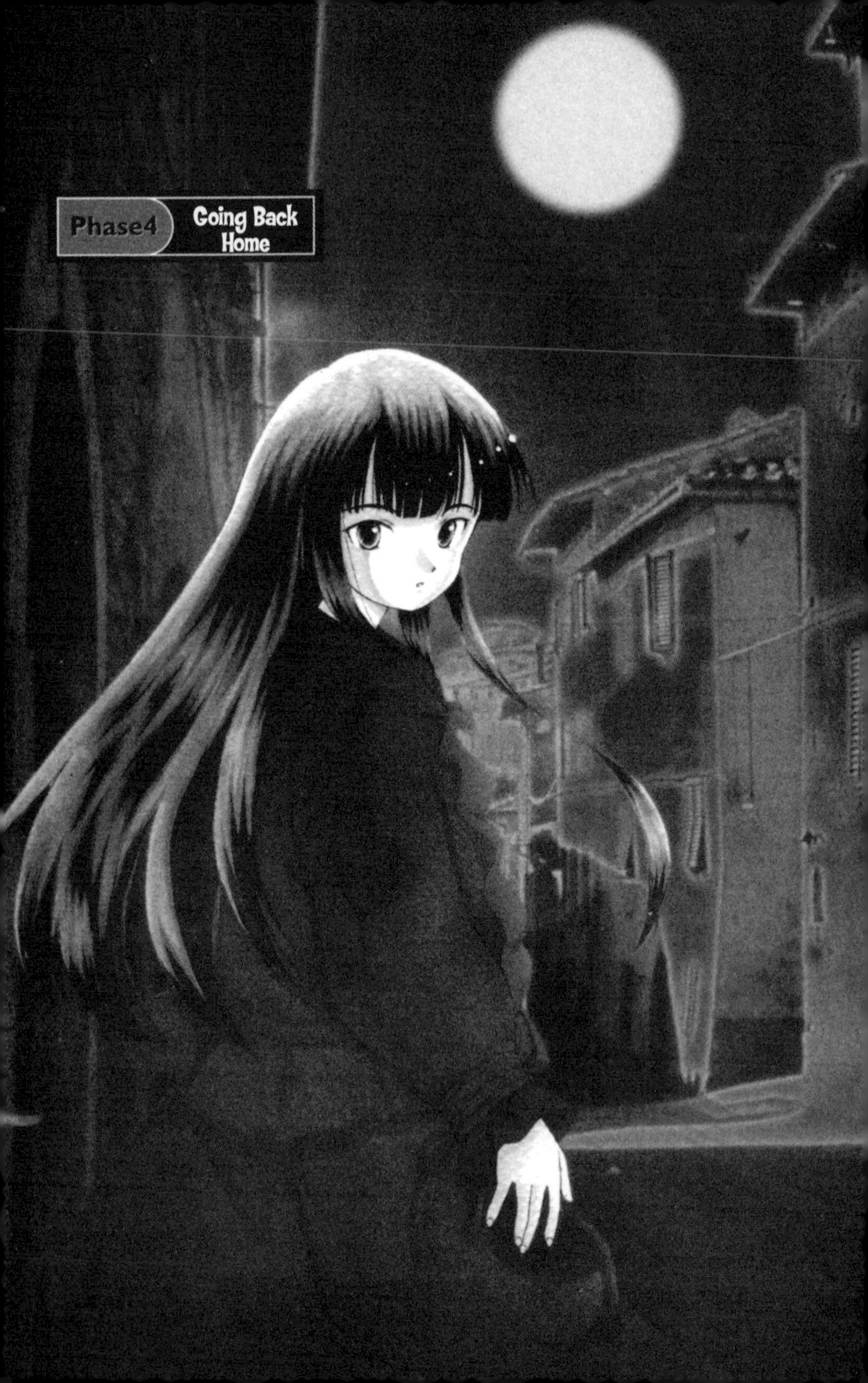
Phase4
Going Back Home

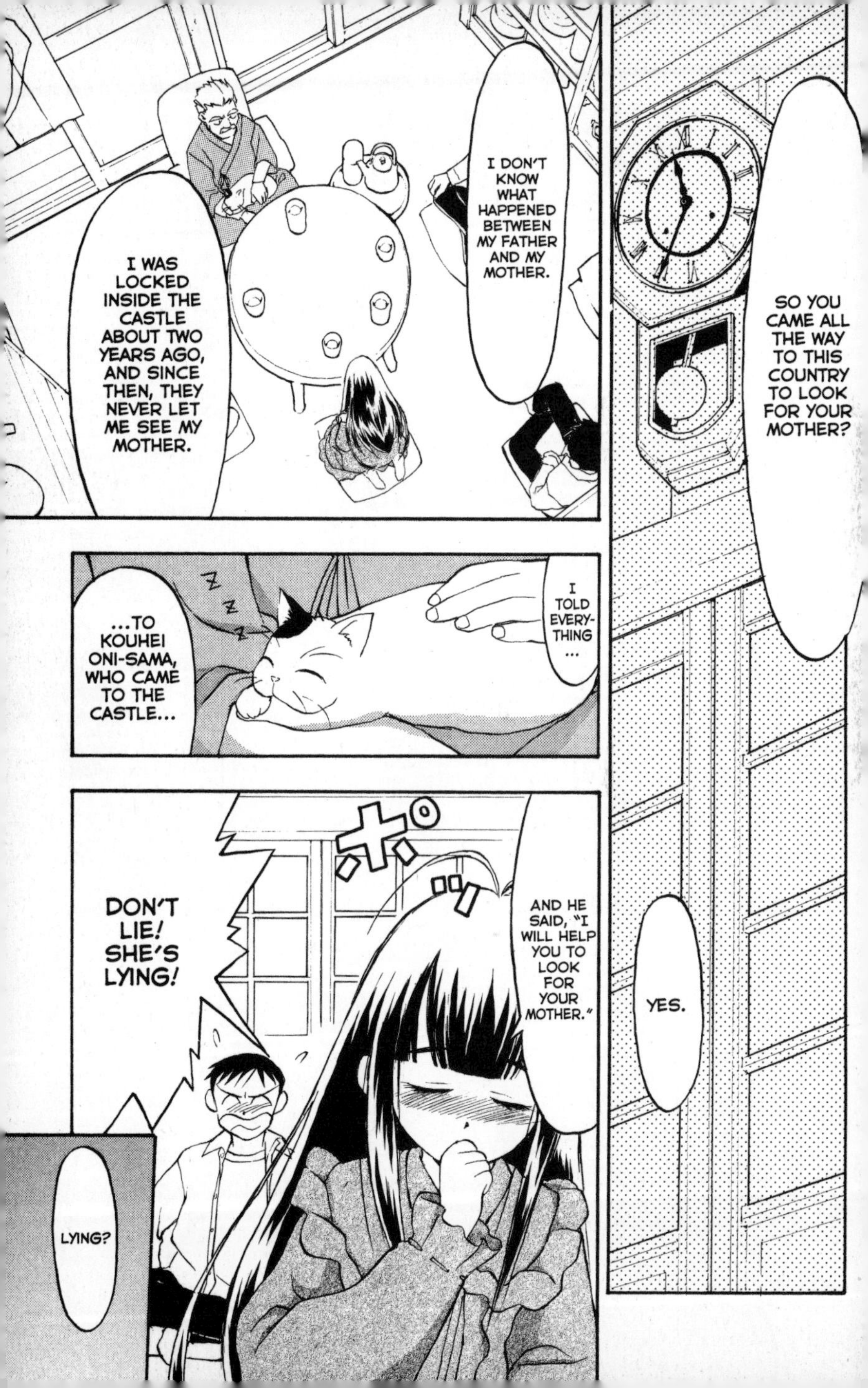
SO YOU CAME ALL THE WAY TO THIS COUNTRY TO LOOK FOR YOUR MOTHER?
YES.
I DON'T KNOW WHAT HAPPENED BETWEEN MY FATHER AND MY MOTHER.
I WAS LOCKED INSIDE THE CASTLE ABOUT TWO YEARS AGO, AND SINCE THEN, THEY NEVER LET ME SEE MY MOTHER.
I TOLD EVERY-THING...
...TO KOUHEI ONI-SAMA, WHO CAME TO THE CASTLE...
AND HE SAID, "I WILL HELP YOU TO LOOK FOR YOUR MOTHER."
DON'T LIE! SHE'S LYING!
LYING?

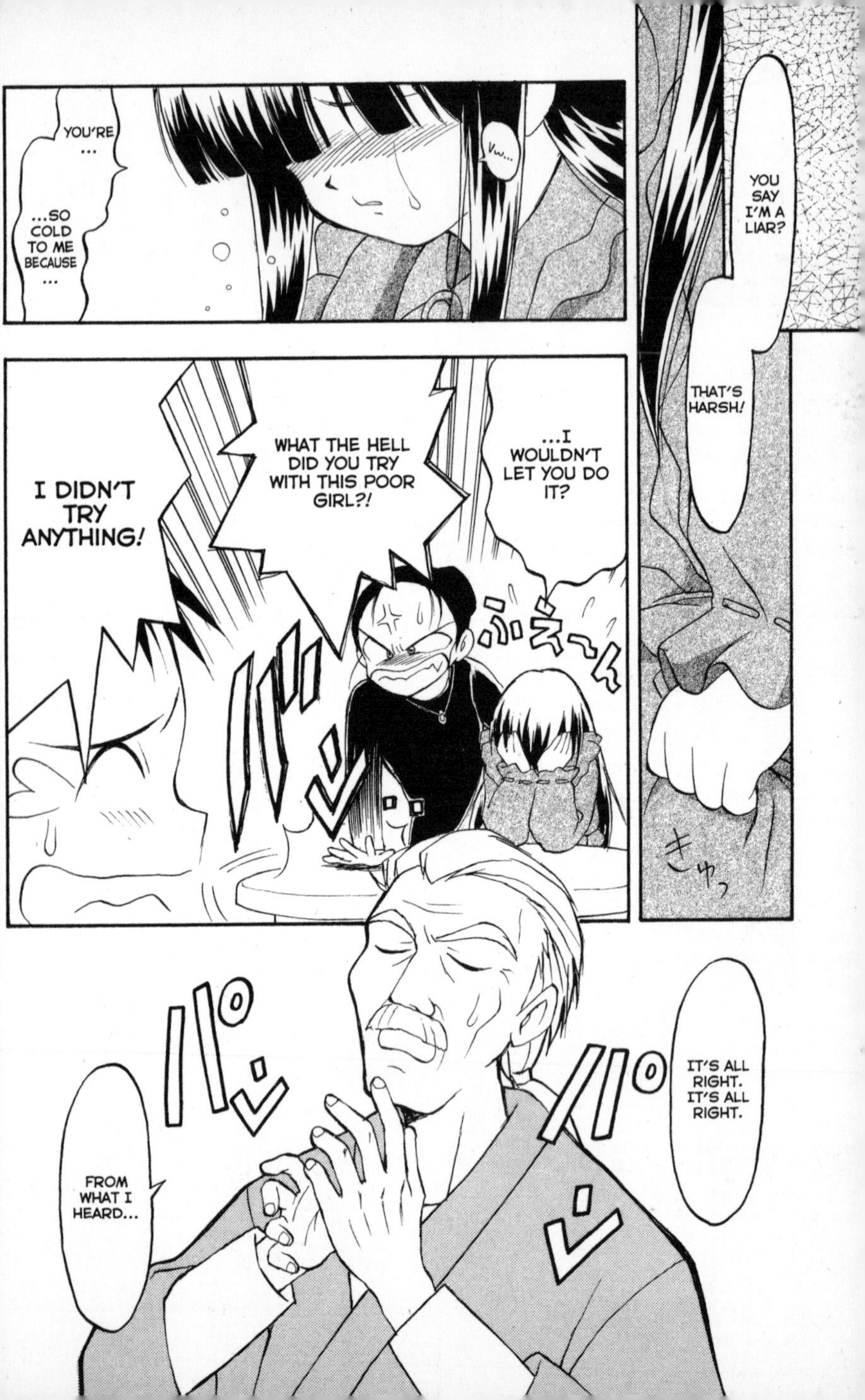
YOU SAY I'M A LIAR?
THAT'S HARSH!
きゅっ
Vw...
YOU'RE ...
...SO COLD TO ME BECAUSE ...
...I WOULDN'T LET YOU DO IT?
ふえ～ん
WHAT THE HELL DID YOU TRY WITH THIS POOR GIRL?!
I DIDN'T TRY ANYTHING!
バン
IT'S ALL RIGHT. IT'S ALL RIGHT.
パン
パン
FROM WHAT I HEARD...

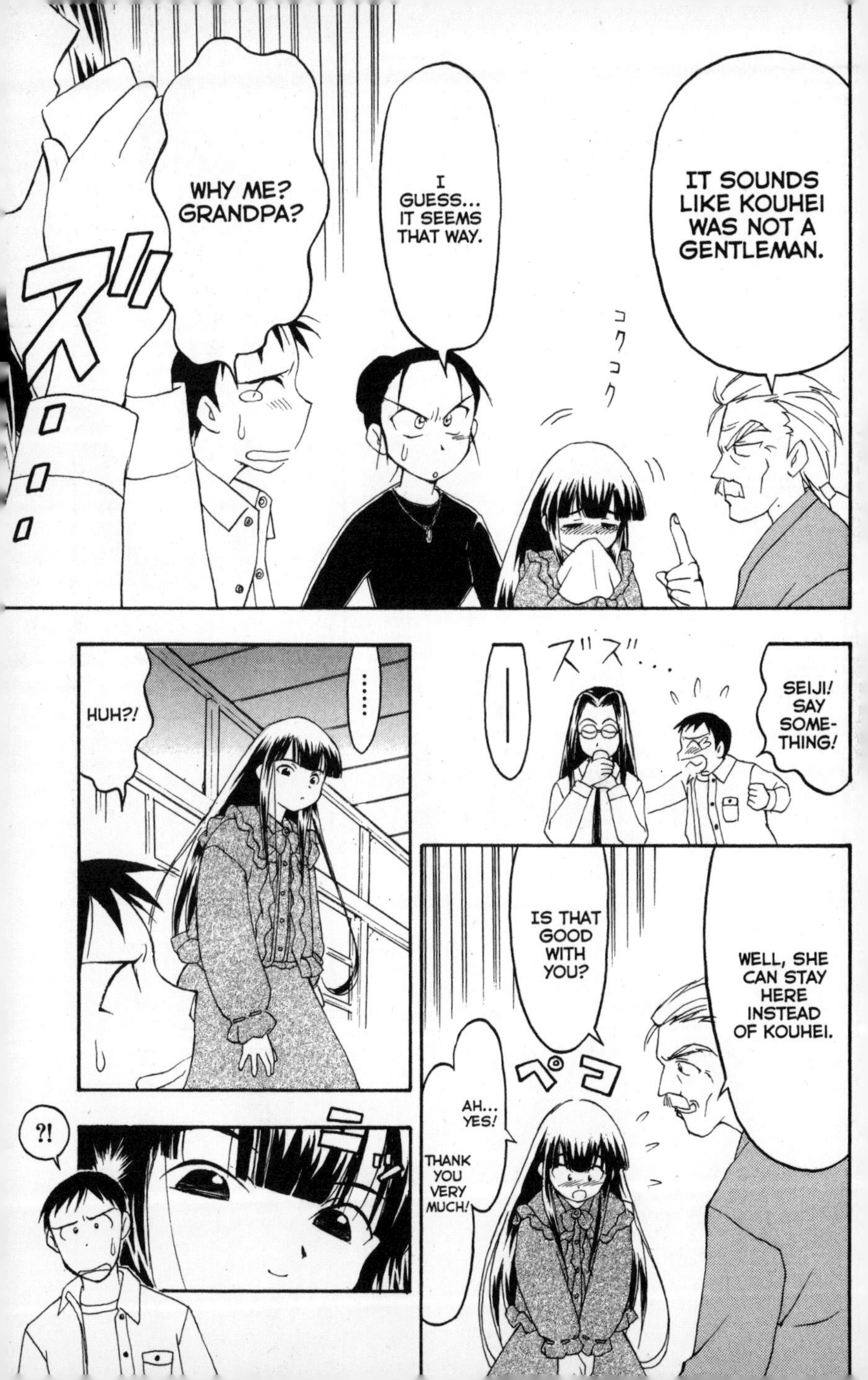
IT SOUNDS LIKE KOUHEI WAS NOT A GENTLEMAN.
コクコク
I GUESS... IT SEEMS THAT WAY.
WHY ME? GRANDPA?
SEIJI! SAY SOMETHING!
ズズ…
……
HUH?!
WELL, SHE CAN STAY HERE INSTEAD OF KOUHEI.
IS THAT GOOD WITH YOU?
ペコ
AH... YES!
THANK YOU VERY MUCH!
?!

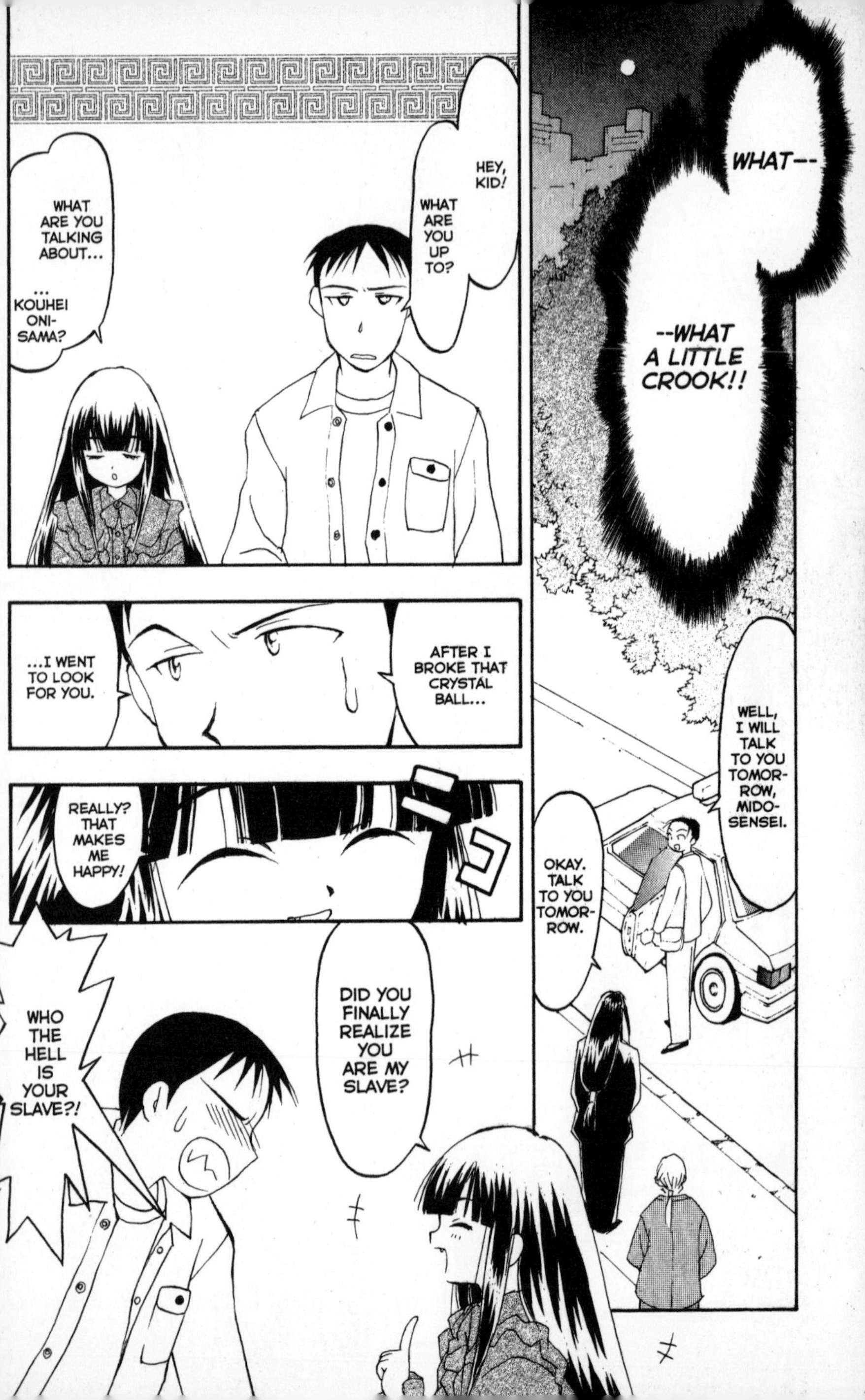
WHAT--
--WHAT A LITTLE CROOK!!
WELL, I WILL TALK TO YOU TOMORROW, MIDO-SENSEI.
OKAY. TALK TO YOU TOMORROW.
HEY, KID!
WHAT ARE YOU UP TO?
WHAT ARE YOU TALKING ABOUT...
... KOUHEI ONI-SAMA?
AFTER I BROKE THAT CRYSTAL BALL...
...I WENT TO LOOK FOR YOU.
REALLY? THAT MAKES ME HAPPY!
DID YOU FINALLY REALIZE YOU ARE MY SLAVE?
WHO THE HELL IS YOUR SLAVE?!

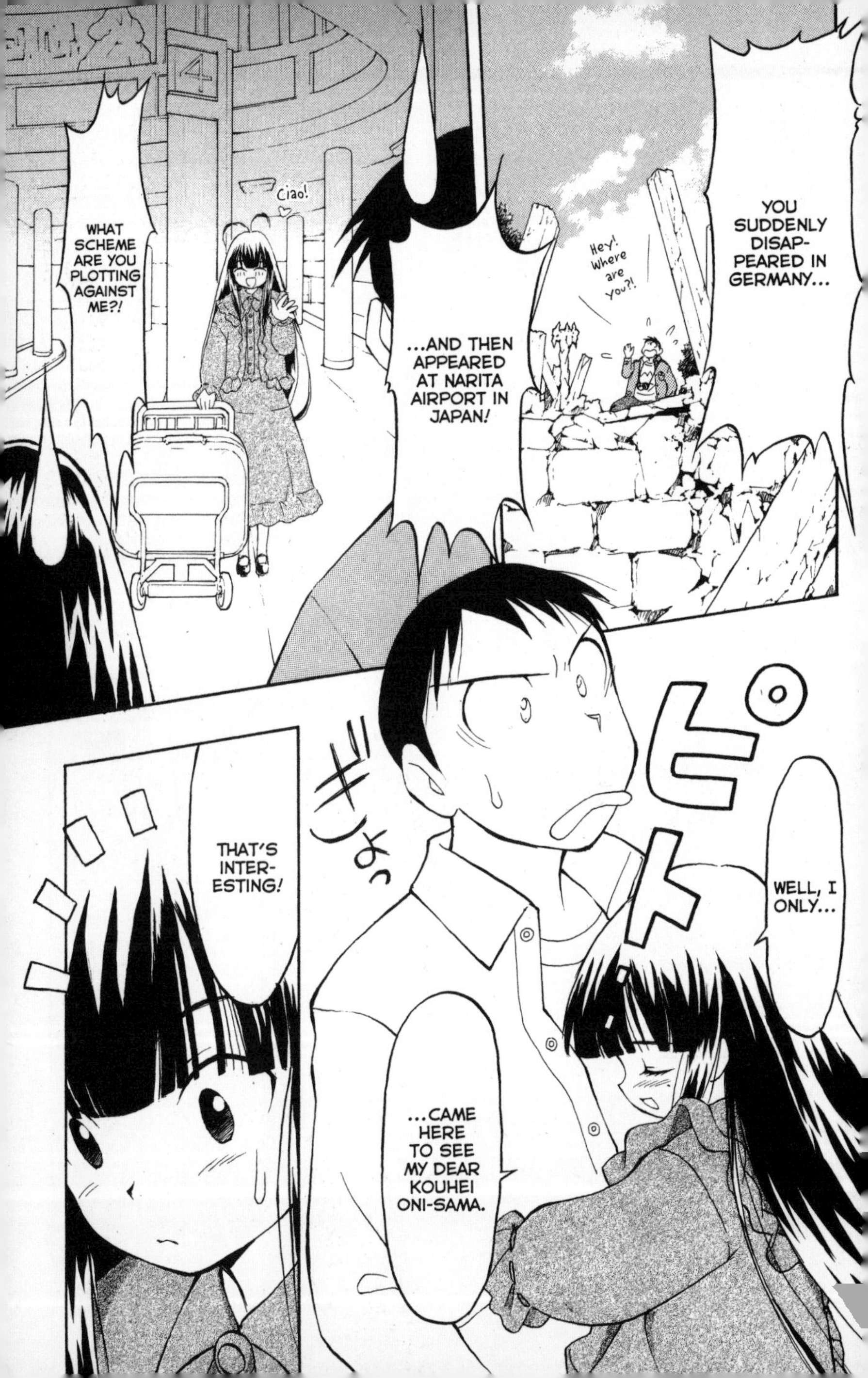
YOU SUDDENLY DISAP-PEARED IN GERMANY...
Hey! Where are You?!
...AND THEN APPEARED AT NARITA AIRPORT IN JAPAN!
Ciao!
WHAT SCHEME ARE YOU PLOTTING AGAINST ME?!
ピト
WELL, I ONLY...
...CAME HERE TO SEE MY DEAR KOUHEI ONI-SAMA.
ぎょっ
THAT'S INTER-ESTING!

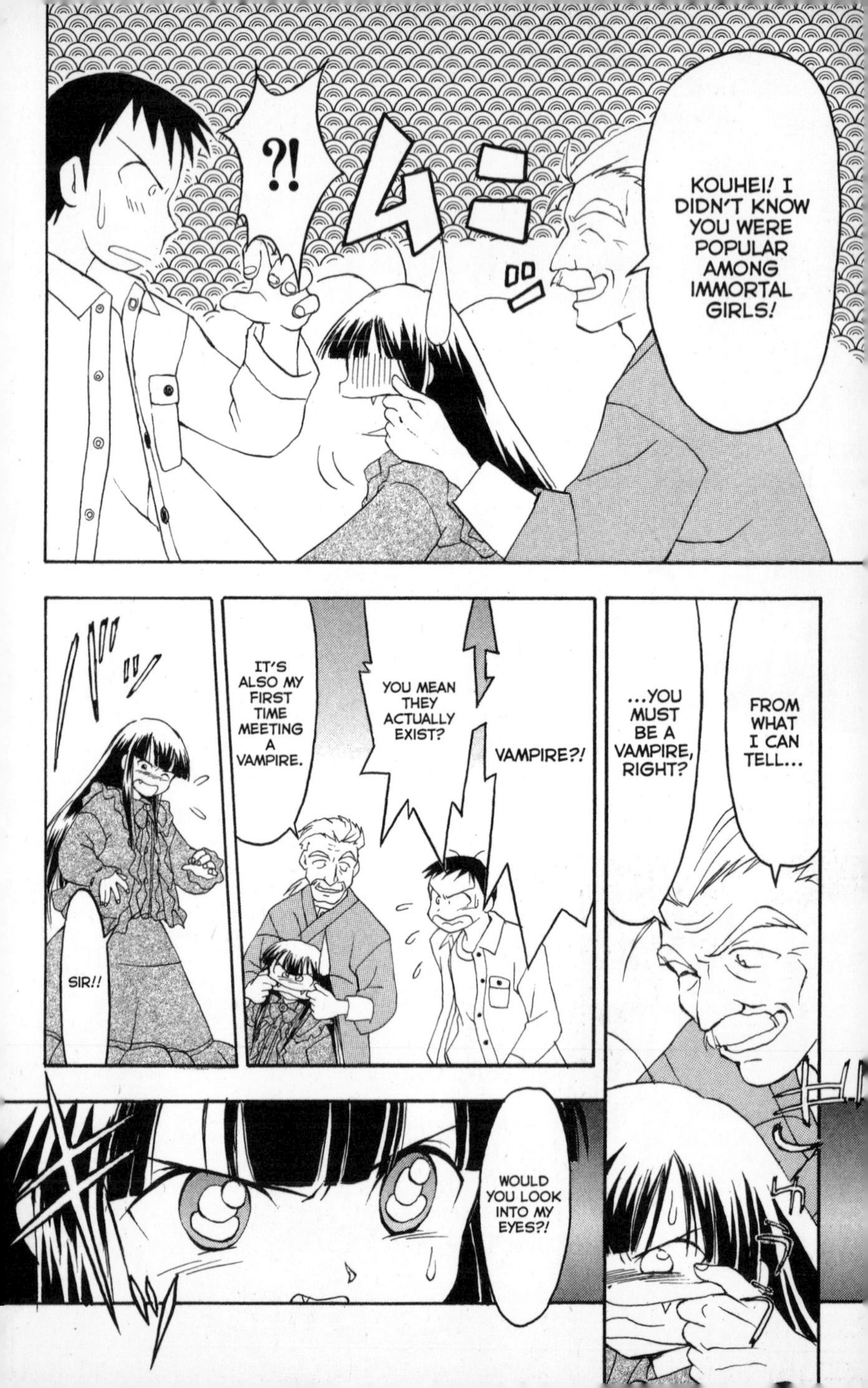
KOUHEI! I DIDN'T KNOW YOU WERE POPULAR AMONG IMMORTAL GIRLS!
?!
FROM WHAT I CAN TELL...
...YOU MUST BE A VAMPIRE, RIGHT?
VAMPIRE?!
YOU MEAN THEY ACTUALLY EXIST?
IT'S ALSO MY FIRST TIME MEETING A VAMPIRE.
SIR!!
WOULD YOU LOOK INTO MY EYES?!

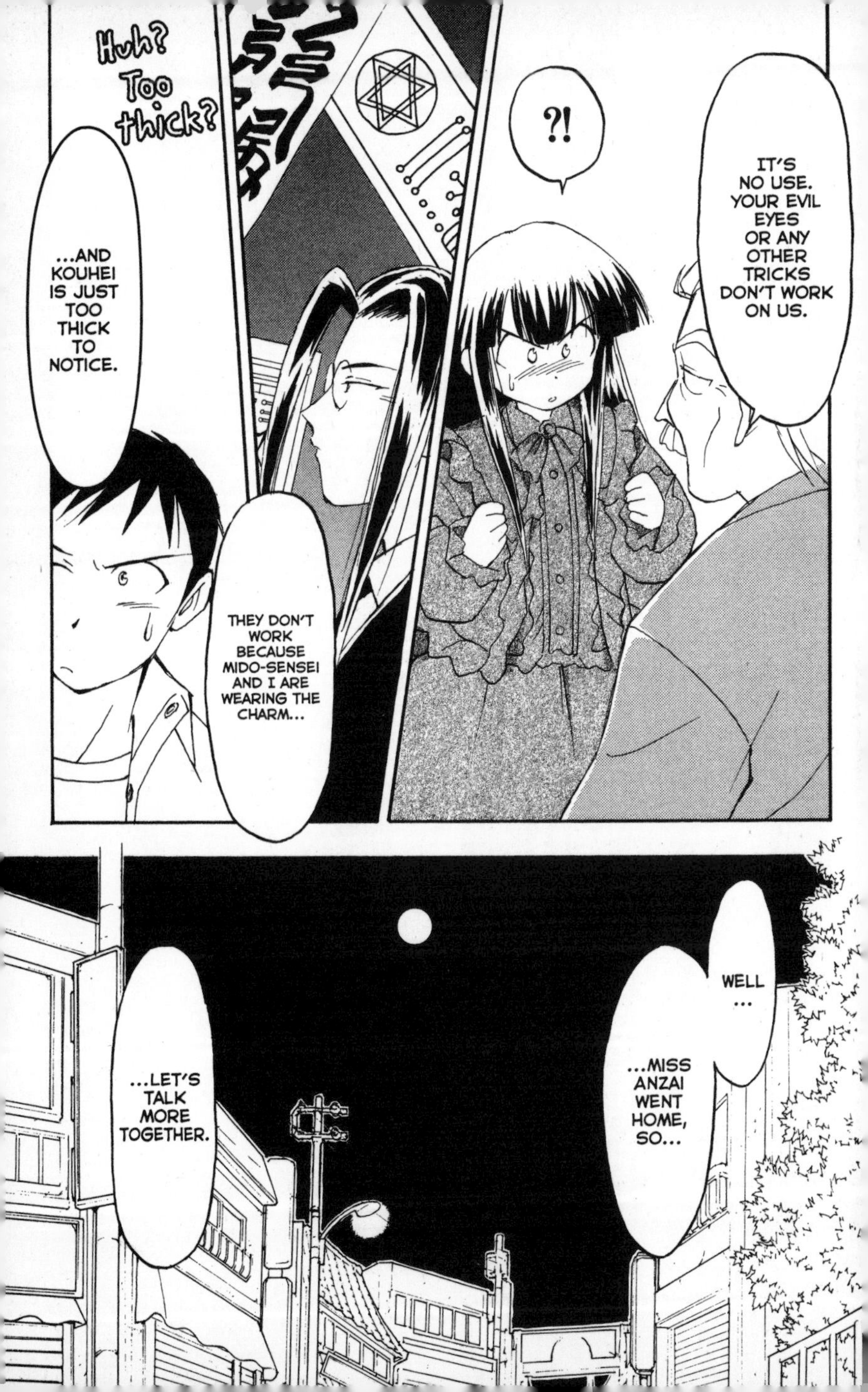
IT'S NO USE. YOUR EVIL EYES OR ANY OTHER TRICKS DON'T WORK ON US.
?!
THEY DON'T WORK BECAUSE MIDO-SENSEI AND I ARE WEARING THE CHARM...
...AND KOUHEI IS JUST TOO THICK TO NOTICE.
Huh? Too thick?
WELL...
...MISS ANZAI WENT HOME, SO...
...LET'S TALK MORE TOGETHER.

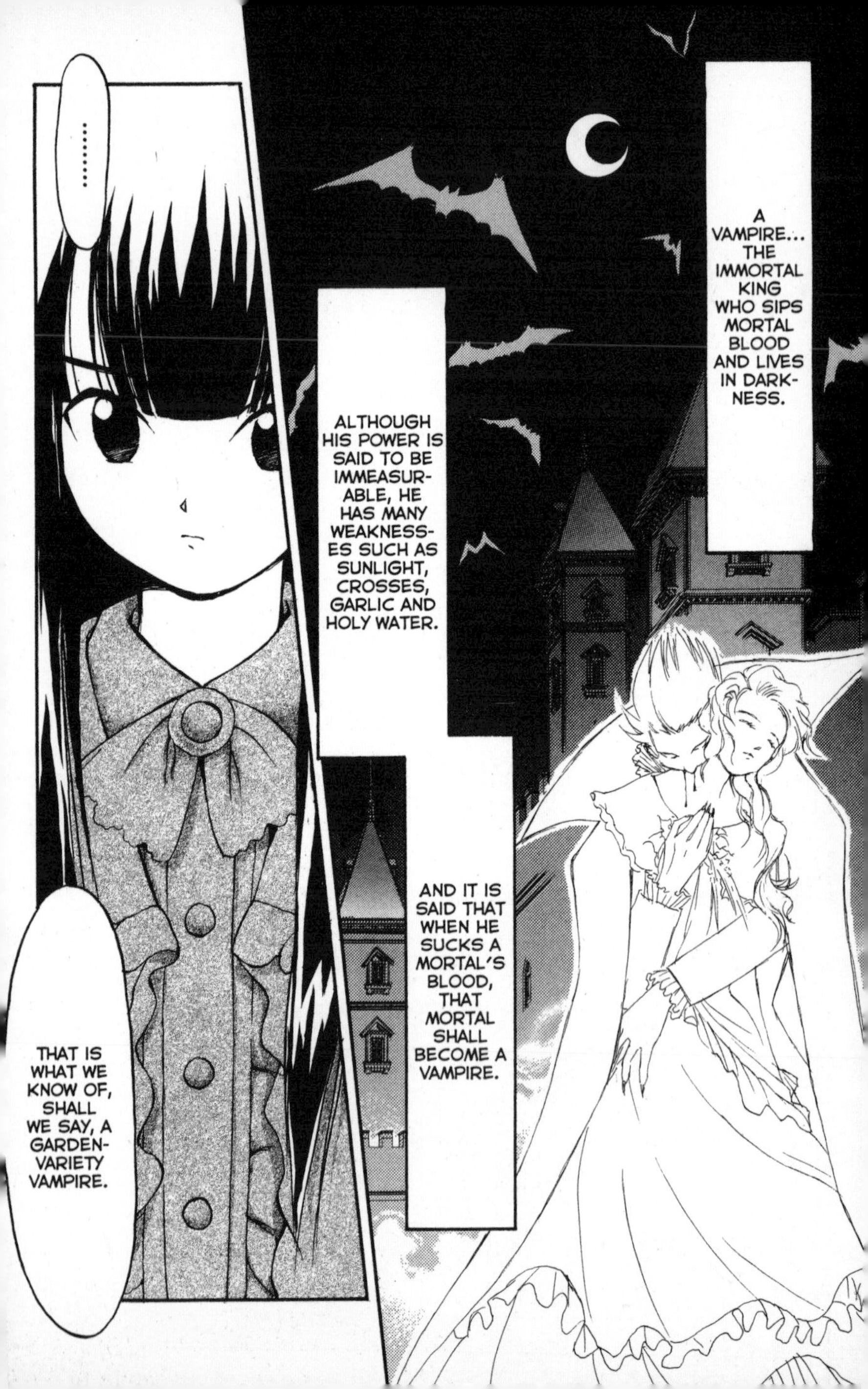
A VAMPIRE... THE IMMORTAL KING WHO SIPS MORTAL BLOOD AND LIVES IN DARKNESS.
ALTHOUGH HIS POWER IS SAID TO BE IMMEASURABLE, HE HAS MANY WEAKNESSES SUCH AS SUNLIGHT, CROSSES, GARLIC AND HOLY WATER.
AND IT IS SAID THAT WHEN HE SUCKS A MORTAL'S BLOOD, THAT MORTAL SHALL BECOME A VAMPIRE.
......
THAT IS WHAT WE KNOW OF, SHALL WE SAY, A GARDEN-VARIETY VAMPIRE.

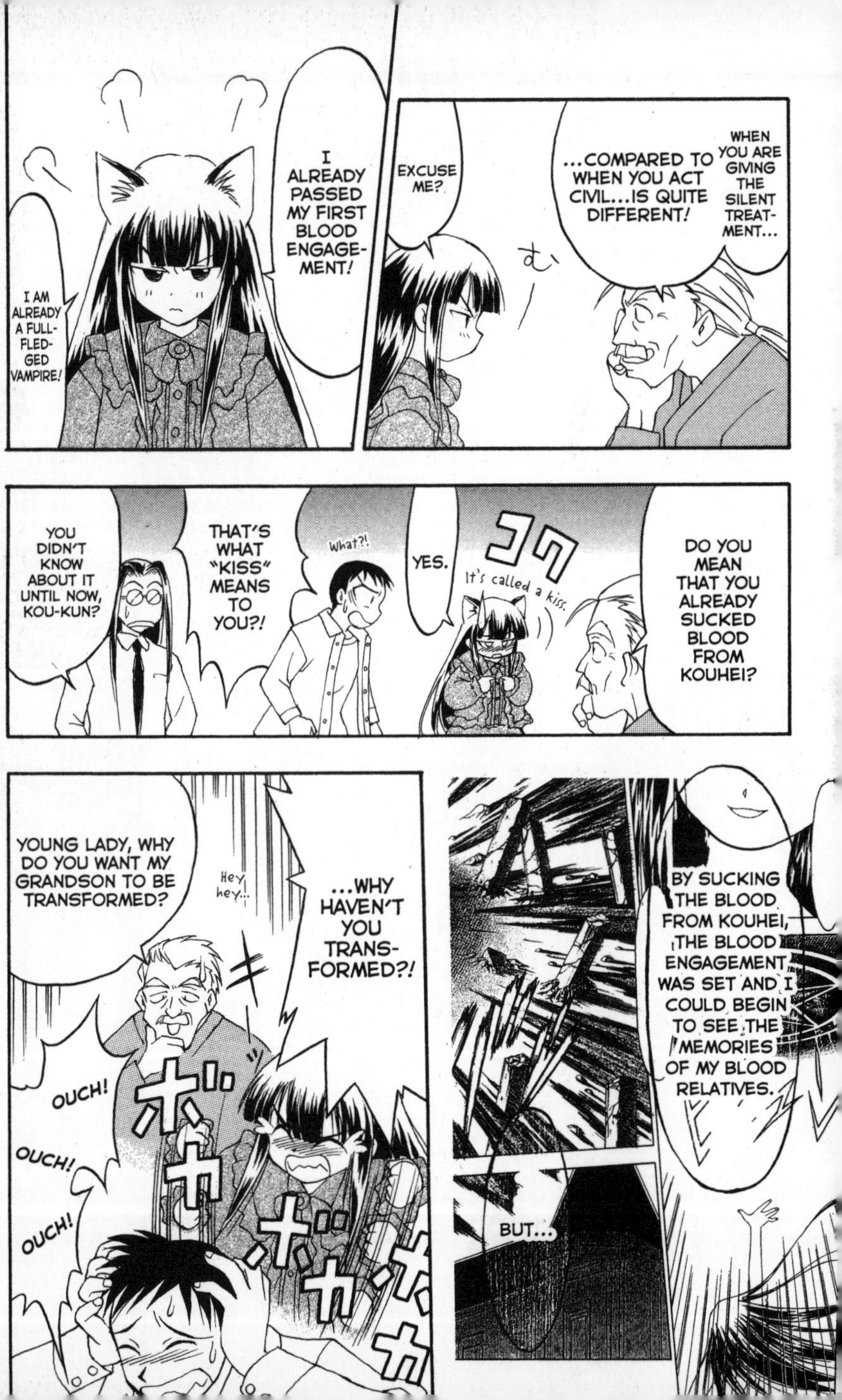
WHEN YOU ARE GIVING THE SILENT TREATMENT...
...COMPARED TO WHEN YOU ACT CIVIL...IS QUITE DIFFERENT!
EXCUSE ME?
む
I ALREADY PASSED MY FIRST BLOOD ENGAGEMENT!
I AM ALREADY A FULL-FLEDGED VAMPIRE!
DO YOU MEAN THAT YOU ALREADY SUCKED BLOOD FROM KOUHEI?
コク
It's called a kiss.
YES.
What?!
THAT'S WHAT "KISS" MEANS TO YOU?!
YOU DIDN'T KNOW ABOUT IT UNTIL NOW, KOU-KUN?
BY SUCKING THE BLOOD FROM KOUHEI, THE BLOOD ENGAGEMENT WAS SET AND I COULD BEGIN TO SEE THE MEMORIES OF MY BLOOD RELATIVES.
BUT...
...WHY HAVEN'T YOU TRANSFORMED?!
Hey hey..!
YOUNG LADY, WHY DO YOU WANT MY GRANDSON TO BE TRANSFORMED?
OUCH!
OUCH!
OUCH!

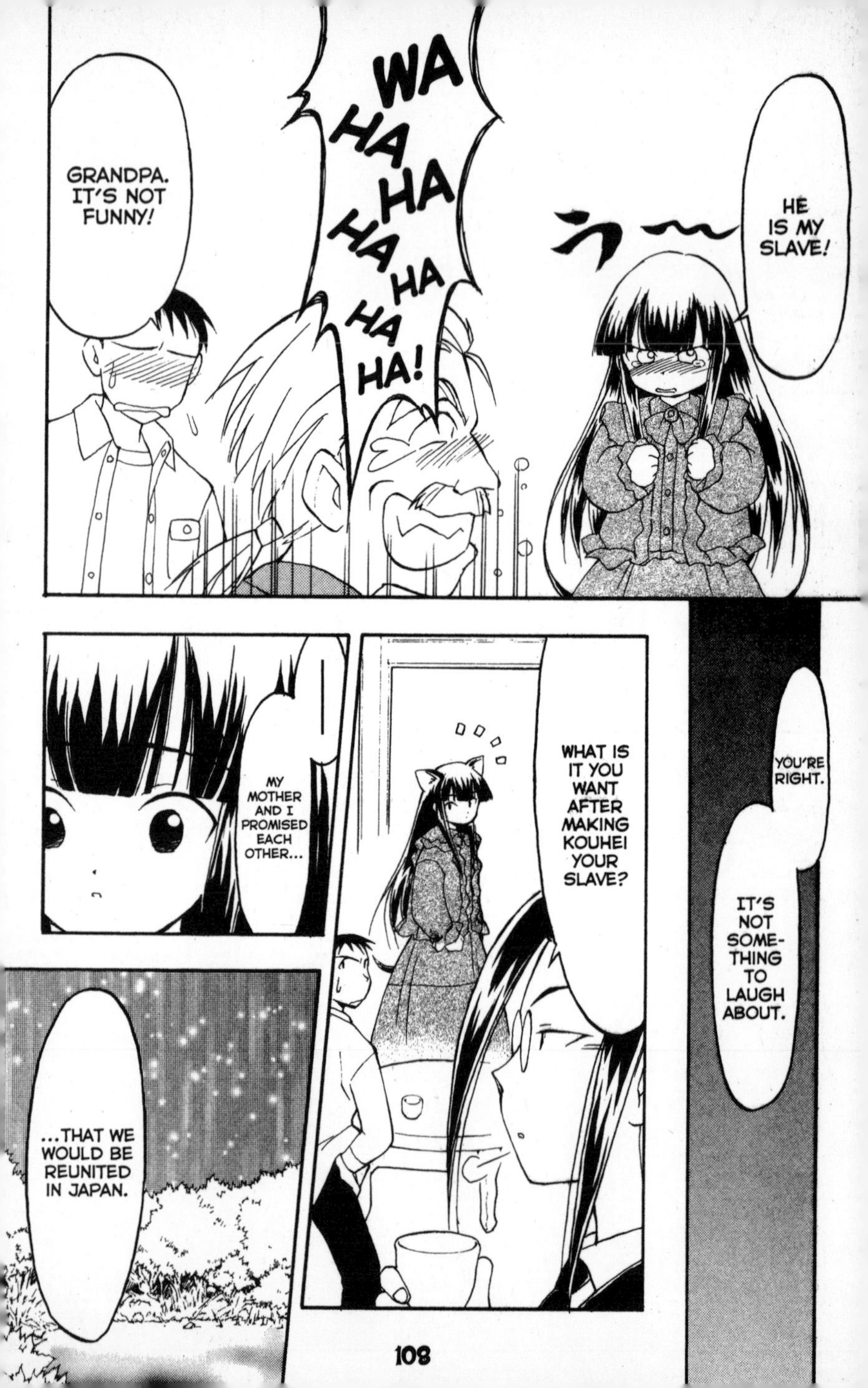
HE IS MY SLAVE!
う〜
WA HA HA HA HA HA HA HA!
GRANDPA. IT'S NOT FUNNY!
YOU'RE RIGHT.
IT'S NOT SOME-THING TO LAUGH ABOUT.
WHAT IS IT YOU WANT AFTER MAKING KOUHEI YOUR SLAVE?
MY MOTHER AND I PROMISED EACH OTHER...
...THAT WE WOULD BE REUNITED IN JAPAN.

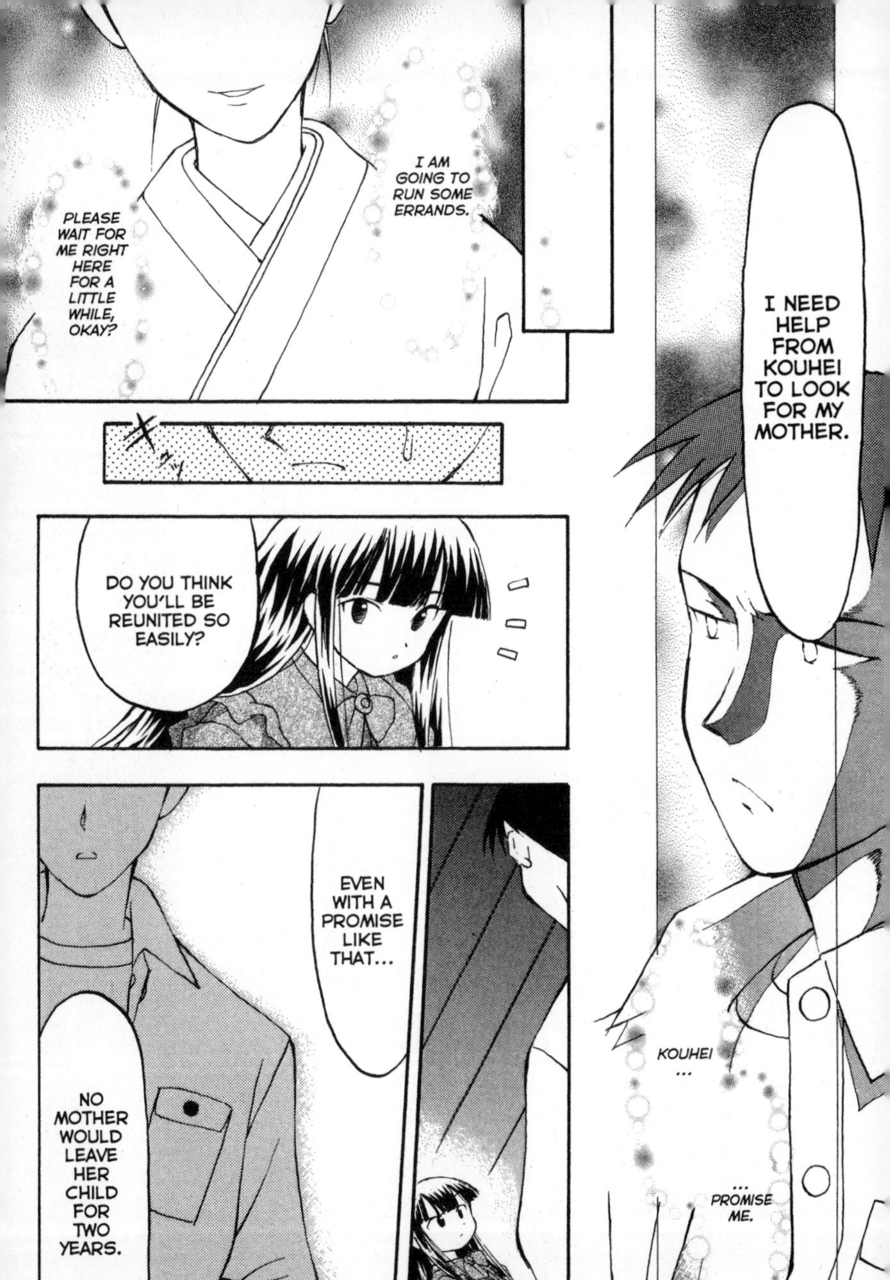
I NEED HELP FROM KOUHEI TO LOOK FOR MY MOTHER.
KOUHEI...
...PROMISE ME.
I AM GOING TO RUN SOME ERRANDS.
PLEASE WAIT FOR ME RIGHT HERE FOR A LITTLE WHILE, OKAY?
DO YOU THINK YOU'LL BE REUNITED SO EASILY?
EVEN WITH A PROMISE LIKE THAT...
NO MOTHER WOULD LEAVE HER CHILD FOR TWO YEARS.

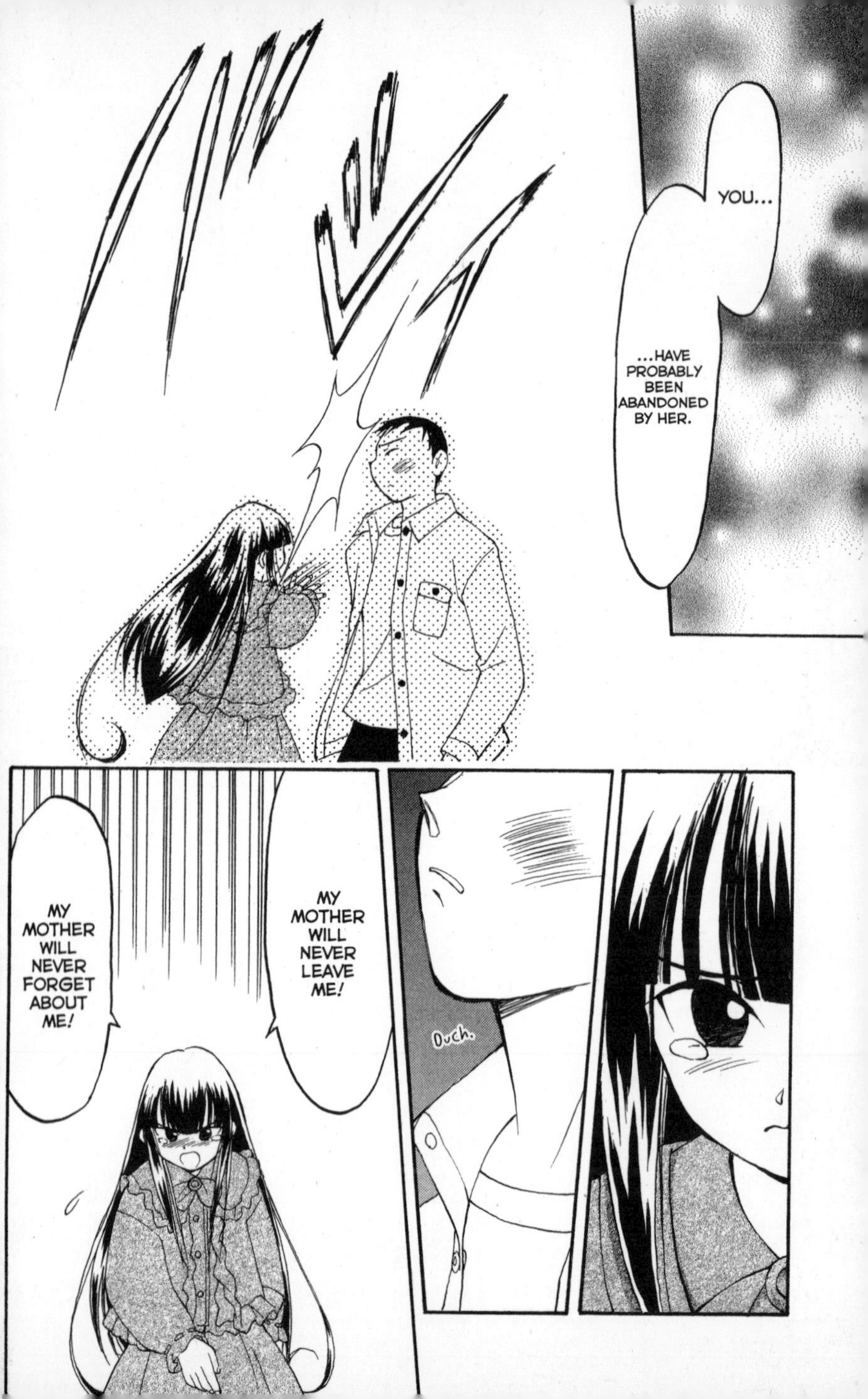
YOU...
...HAVE PROBABLY BEEN ABANDONED BY HER.
Ouch.
MY MOTHER WILL NEVER LEAVE ME!
MY MOTHER WILL NEVER FORGET ABOUT ME!

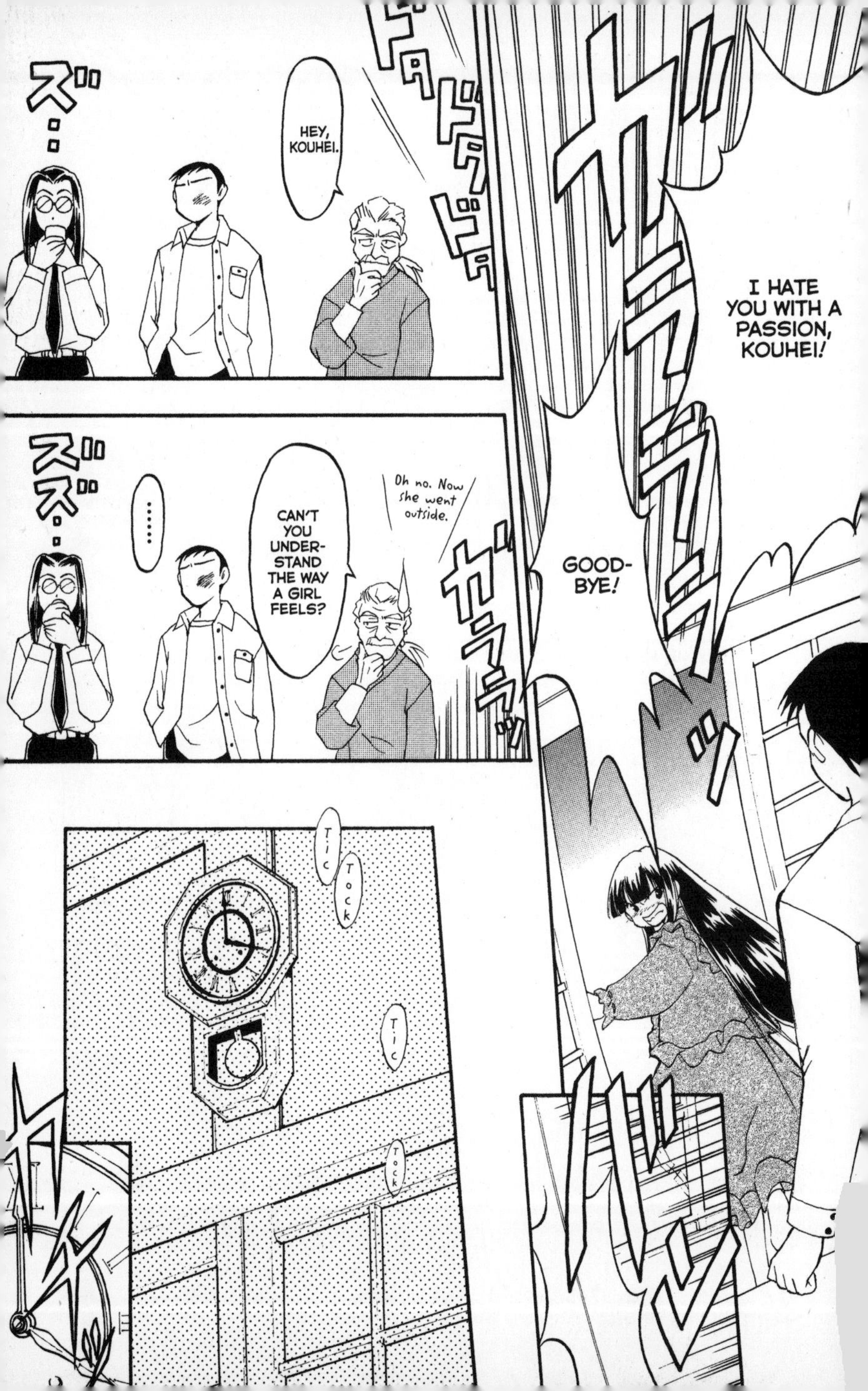
I HATE YOU WITH A PASSION, KOUHEI!
GOOD-BYE!
HEY, KOUHEI.
Oh no. Now she went outside.
CAN'T YOU UNDERSTAND THE WAY A GIRL FEELS?
......
Tic
Tock
Tic
Tock

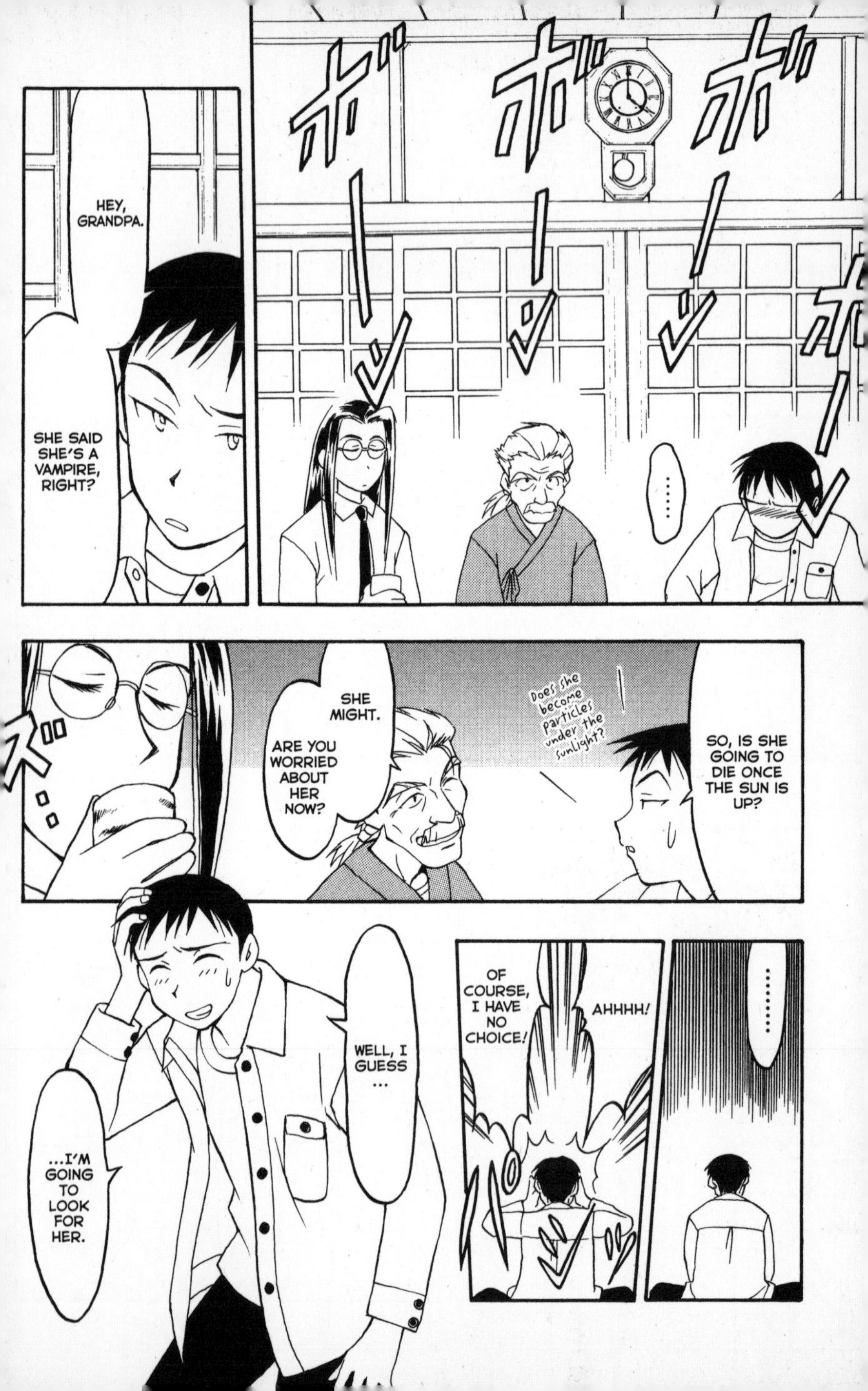
......
HEY, GRANDPA.
SHE SAID SHE'S A VAMPIRE, RIGHT?
SO, IS SHE GOING TO DIE ONCE THE SUN IS UP?
Does she become particles under the sunlight?
!
SHE MIGHT.
ARE YOU WORRIED ABOUT HER NOW?
......
AHHHH!
OF COURSE, I HAVE NO CHOICE!
WELL, I GUESS ...
...I'M GOING TO LOOK FOR HER.

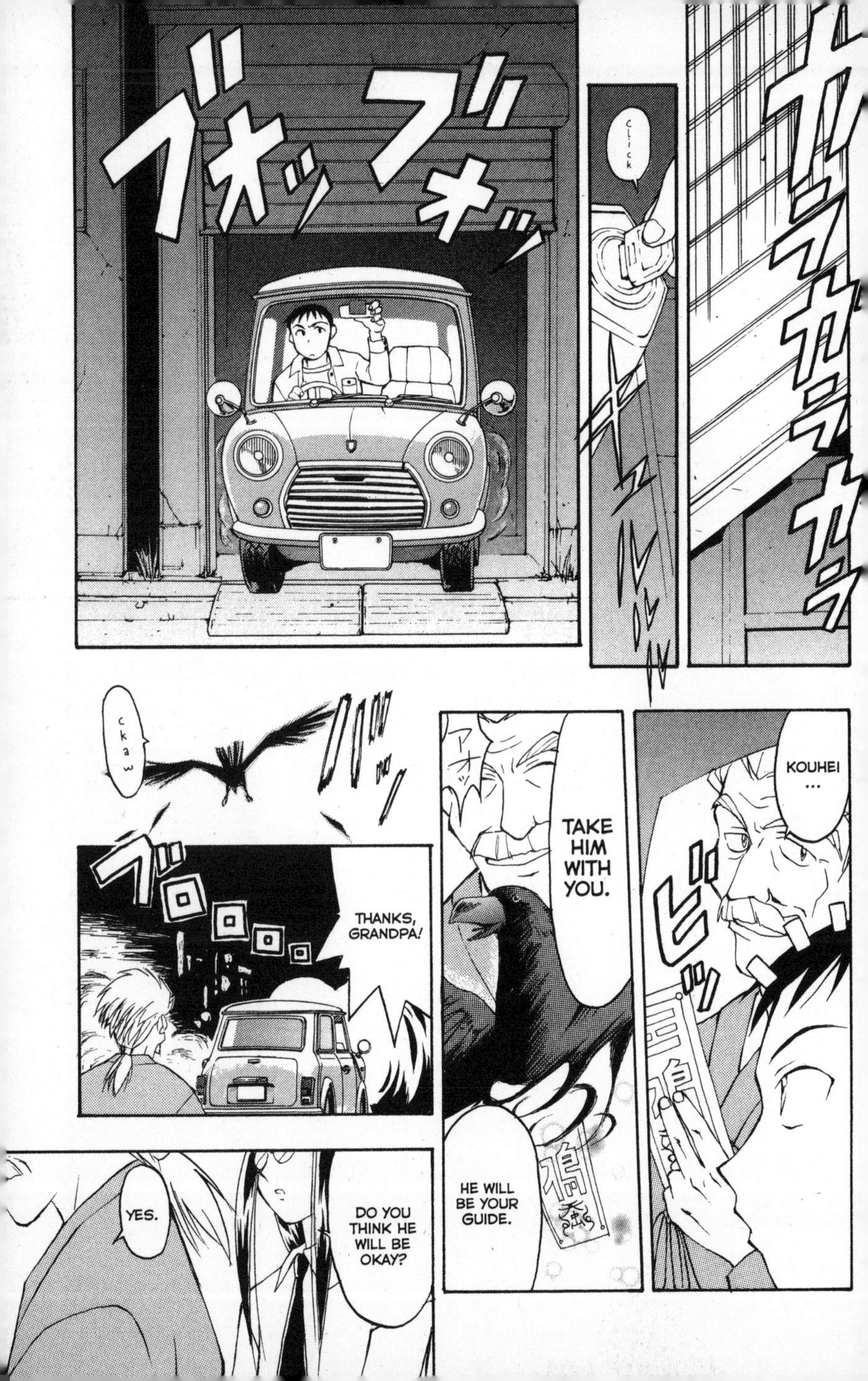
Click
KOUHEI ...
TAKE HIM WITH YOU.
HE WILL BE YOUR GUIDE.
Ckaw
THANKS, GRANDPA!
DO YOU THINK HE WILL BE OKAY?
YES.

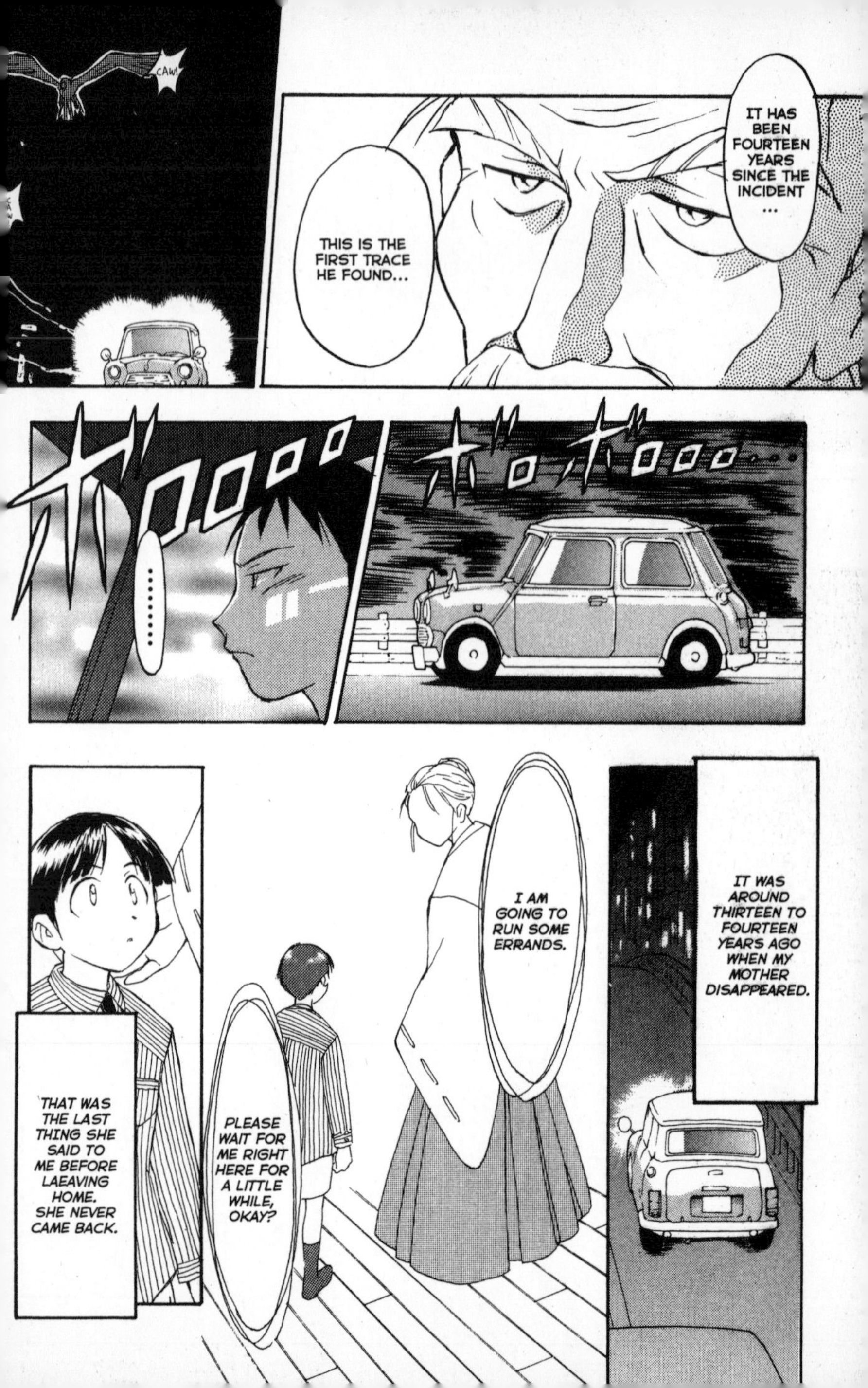
IT HAS BEEN FOURTEEN YEARS SINCE THE INCIDENT ...
THIS IS THE FIRST TRACE HE FOUND...
CAW!
CAW
....
IT WAS AROUND THIRTEEN TO FOURTEEN YEARS AGO WHEN MY MOTHER DISAPPEARED.
I AM GOING TO RUN SOME ERRANDS.
PLEASE WAIT FOR ME RIGHT HERE FOR A LITTLE WHILE, OKAY?
THAT WAS THE LAST THING SHE SAID TO ME BEFORE LAEAVING HOME. SHE NEVER CAME BACK.

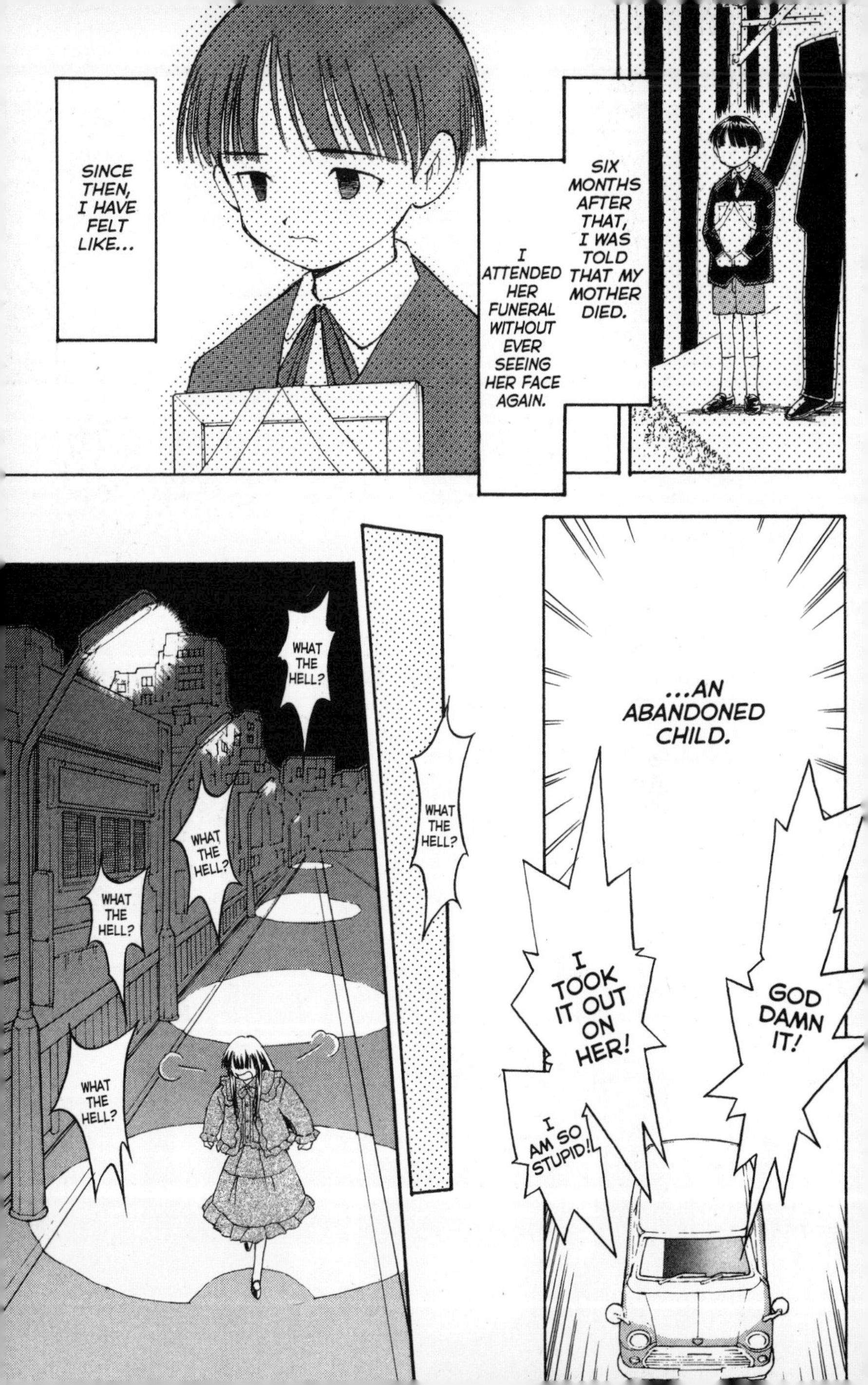
SIX MONTHS AFTER THAT, I WAS TOLD THAT MY MOTHER DIED.
I ATTENDED HER FUNERAL WITHOUT EVER SEEING HER FACE AGAIN.
SINCE THEN, I HAVE FELT LIKE...
...AN ABANDONED CHILD.
GOD DAMN IT!
I TOOK IT OUT ON HER!
I AM SO STUPID!
WHAT THE HELL?
WHAT THE HELL?
WHAT THE HELL?
WHAT THE HELL?
WHAT THE HELL?

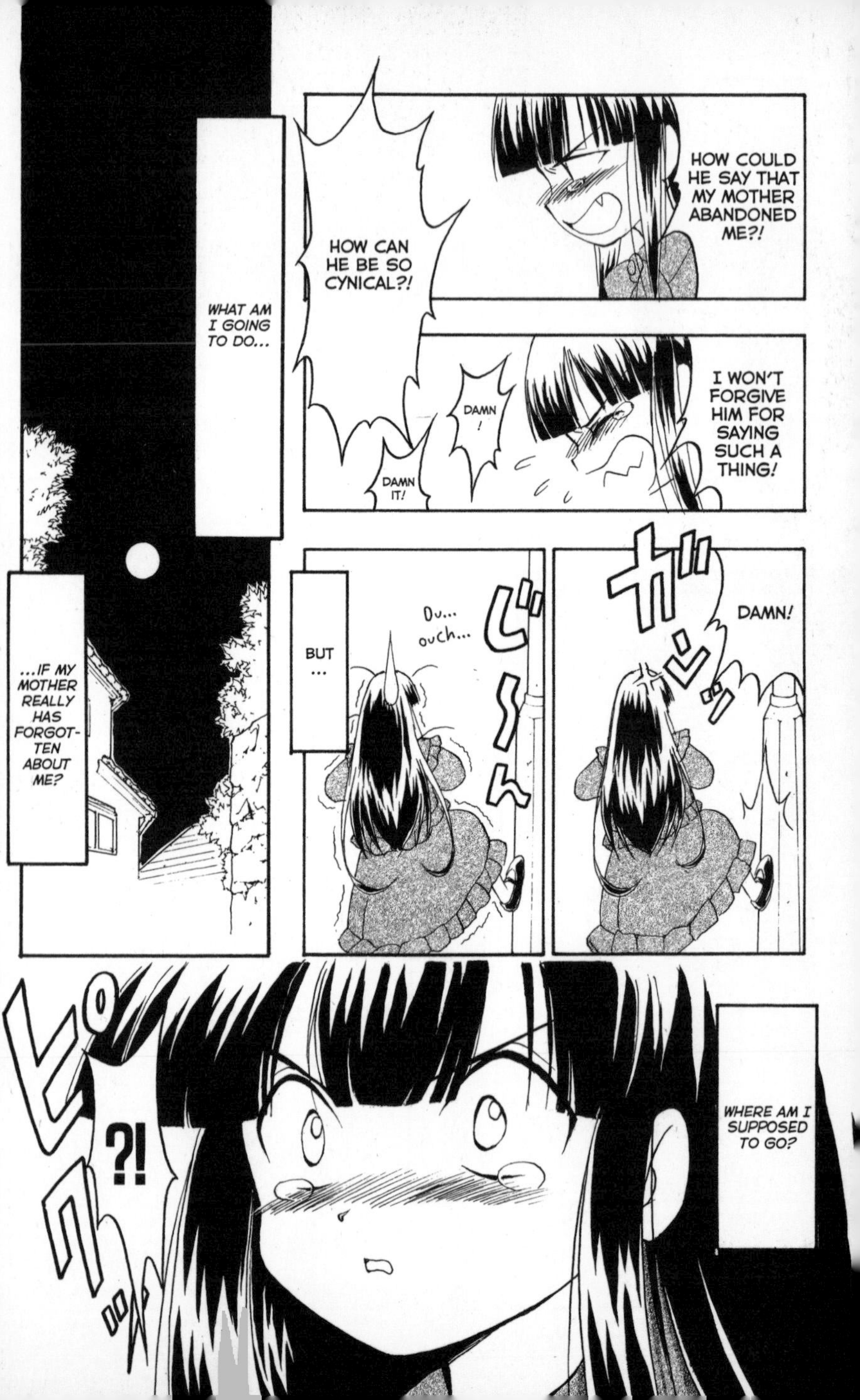
HOW COULD HE SAY THAT MY MOTHER ABANDONED ME?!
HOW CAN HE BE SO CYNICAL?!
I WON'T FORGIVE HIM FOR SAYING SUCH A THING!
DAMN!
DAMN IT!
DAMN!
ガン
BUT...
Ou... ouch...
じ〜ん
WHAT AM I GOING TO DO...
...IF MY MOTHER REALLY HAS FORGOT-TEN ABOUT ME?
WHERE AM I SUPPOSED TO GO?
?!
ピクッ

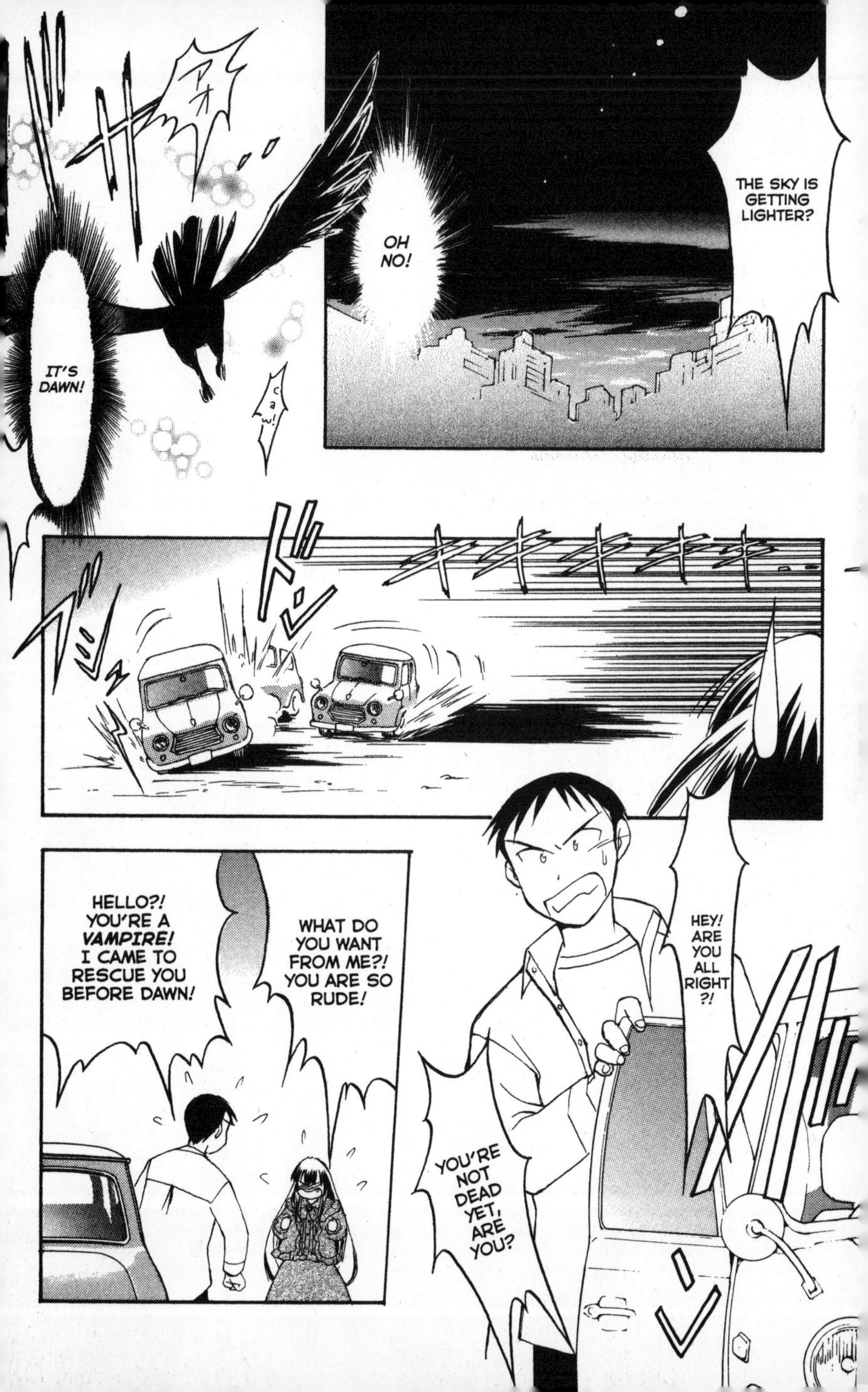
THE SKY IS GETTING LIGHTER?
OH NO!
IT'S DAWN!
caw!
HEY! ARE YOU ALL RIGHT?!
YOU'RE NOT DEAD YET, ARE YOU?
WHAT DO YOU WANT FROM ME?! YOU ARE SO RUDE!
HELLO?! YOU'RE A *VAMPIRE!* I CAME TO RESCUE YOU BEFORE DAWN!

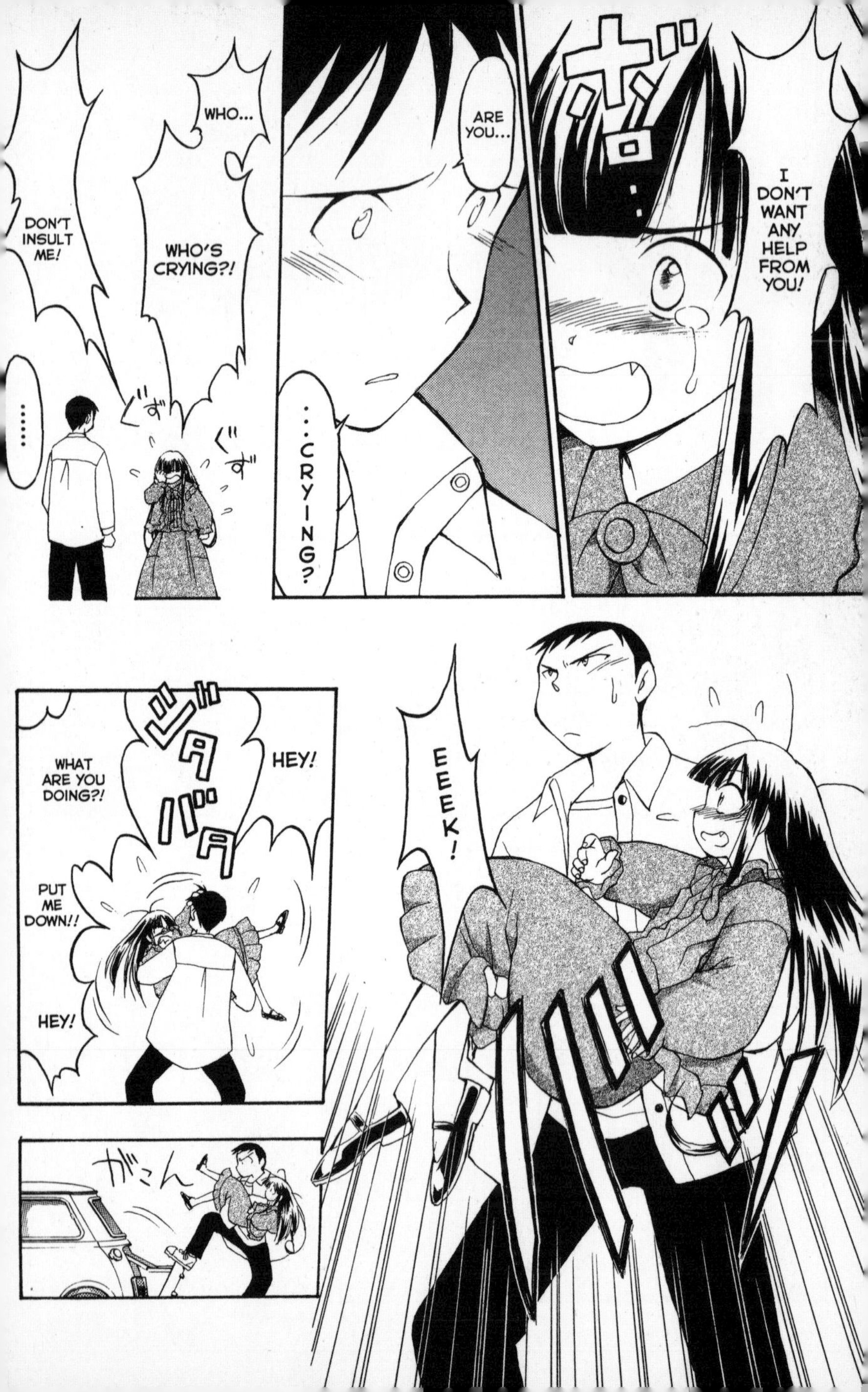
I DON'T WANT ANY HELP FROM YOU!
ARE YOU...
...CRYING?
WHO...
WHO'S CRYING?!
DON'T INSULT ME!
......
ぐず
ぐず
EEEK!
HEY!
WHAT ARE YOU DOING?!
ジタバタ
PUT ME DOWN!!
HEY!
がこん

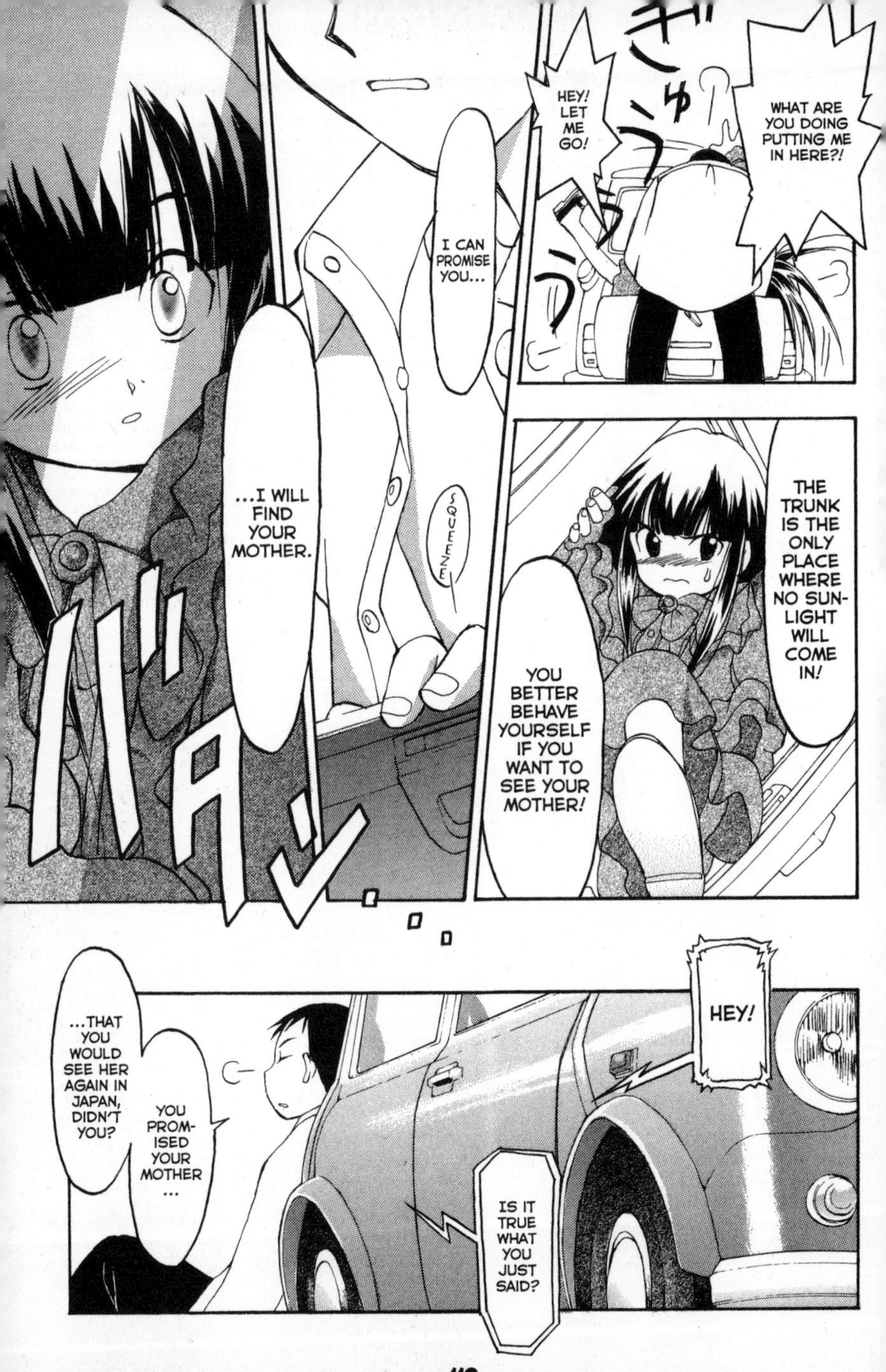
WHAT ARE YOU DOING PUTTING ME IN HERE?!
HEY! LET ME GO!
ぎゅうう
THE TRUNK IS THE ONLY PLACE WHERE NO SUN-LIGHT WILL COME IN!
YOU BETTER BEHAVE YOURSELF IF YOU WANT TO SEE YOUR MOTHER!
I CAN PROMISE YOU...
...I WILL FIND YOUR MOTHER.
SQUEEZE
バン
HEY!
IS IT TRUE WHAT YOU JUST SAID?
YOU PROM-ISED YOUR MOTHER ...
...THAT YOU WOULD SEE HER AGAIN IN JAPAN, DIDN'T YOU?

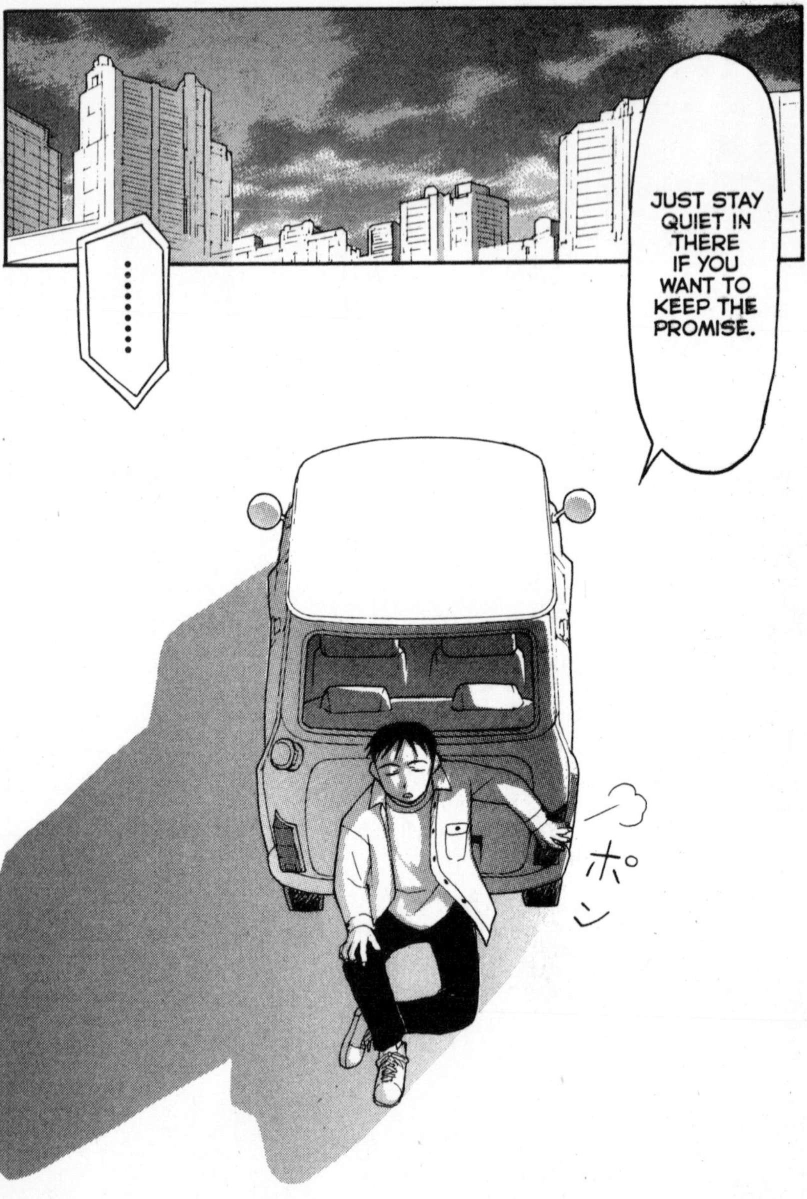
JUST STAY QUIET IN THERE IF YOU WANT TO KEEP THE PROMISE.
....
ポン

MOON 月詠 PHASE

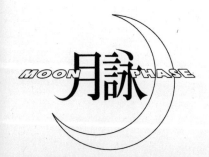

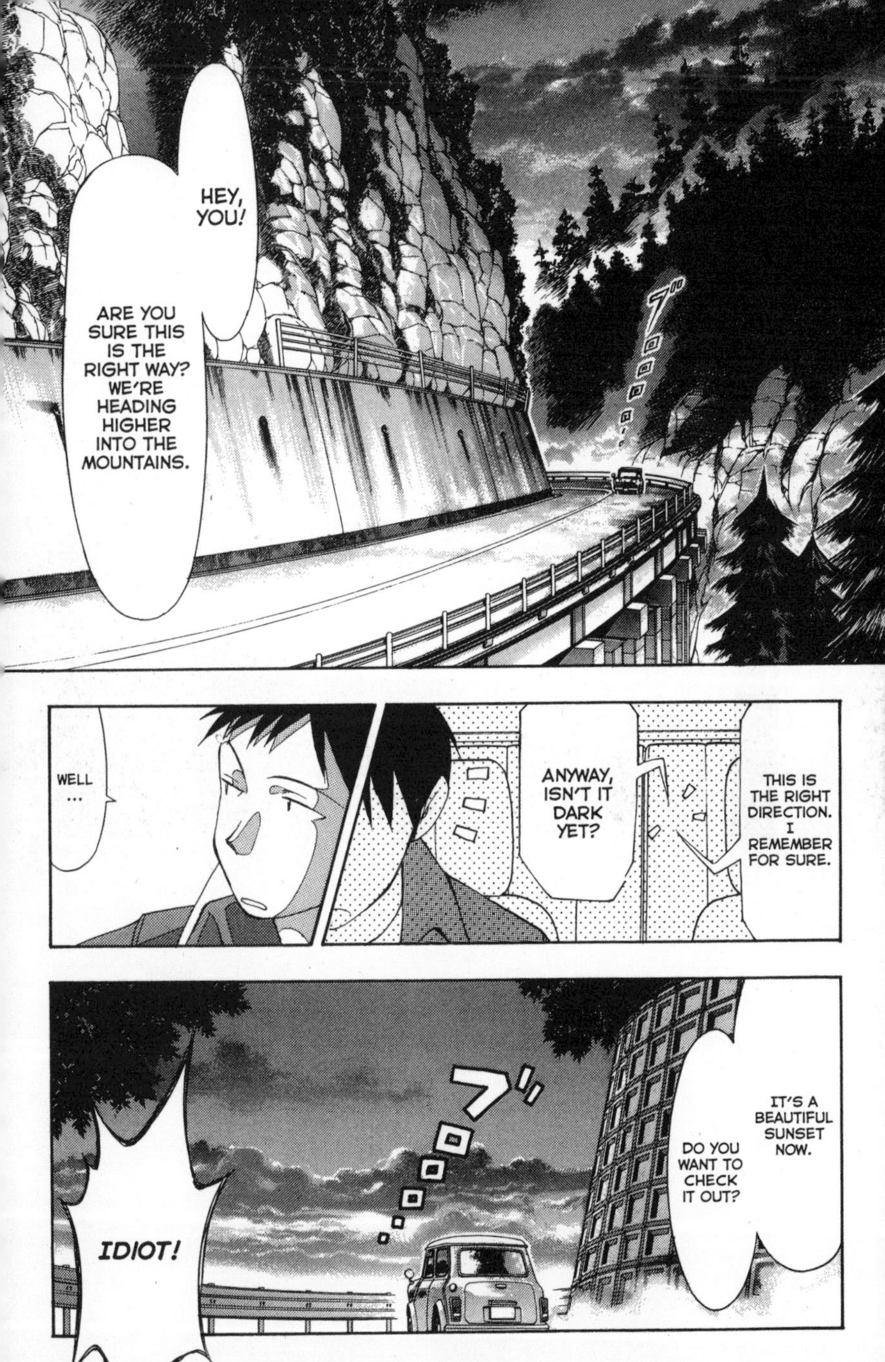
HEY, YOU!
ARE YOU SURE THIS IS THE RIGHT WAY? WE'RE HEADING HIGHER INTO THE MOUNTAINS.
ブロロロロ…
THIS IS THE RIGHT DIRECTION. I REMEMBER FOR SURE.
ANYWAY, ISN'T IT DARK YET?
WELL ...
IT'S A BEAUTIFUL SUNSET NOW.
DO YOU WANT TO CHECK IT OUT?
ブロロロロ
IDIOT!

Phase5 Meeting Again

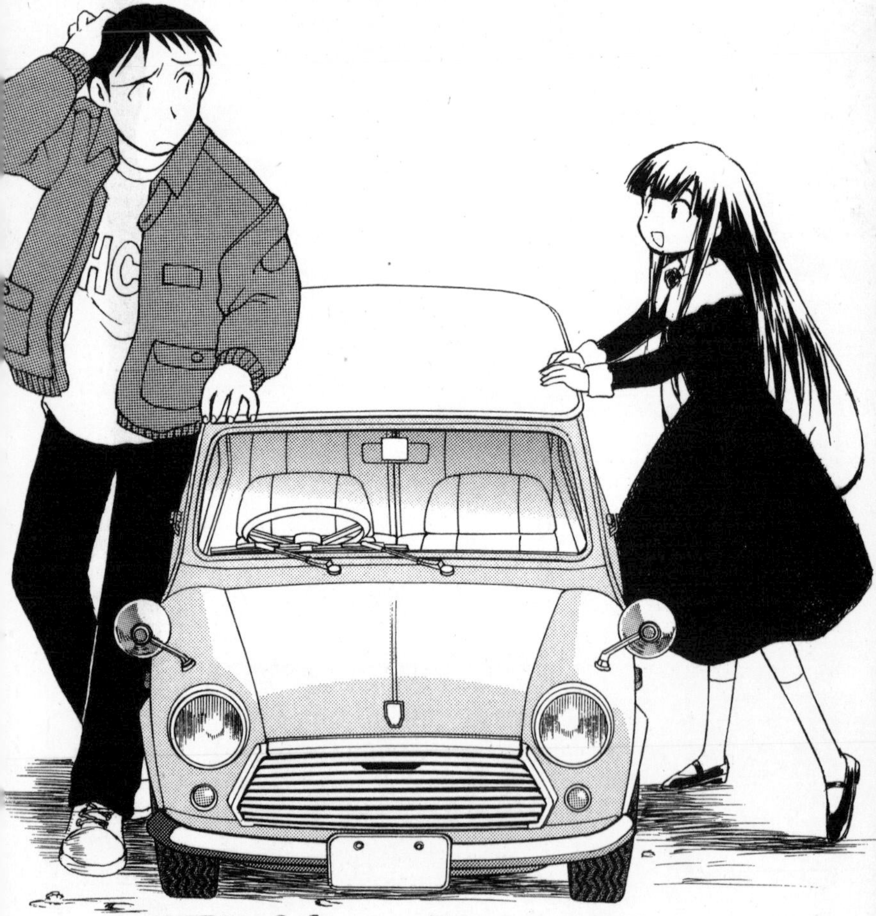

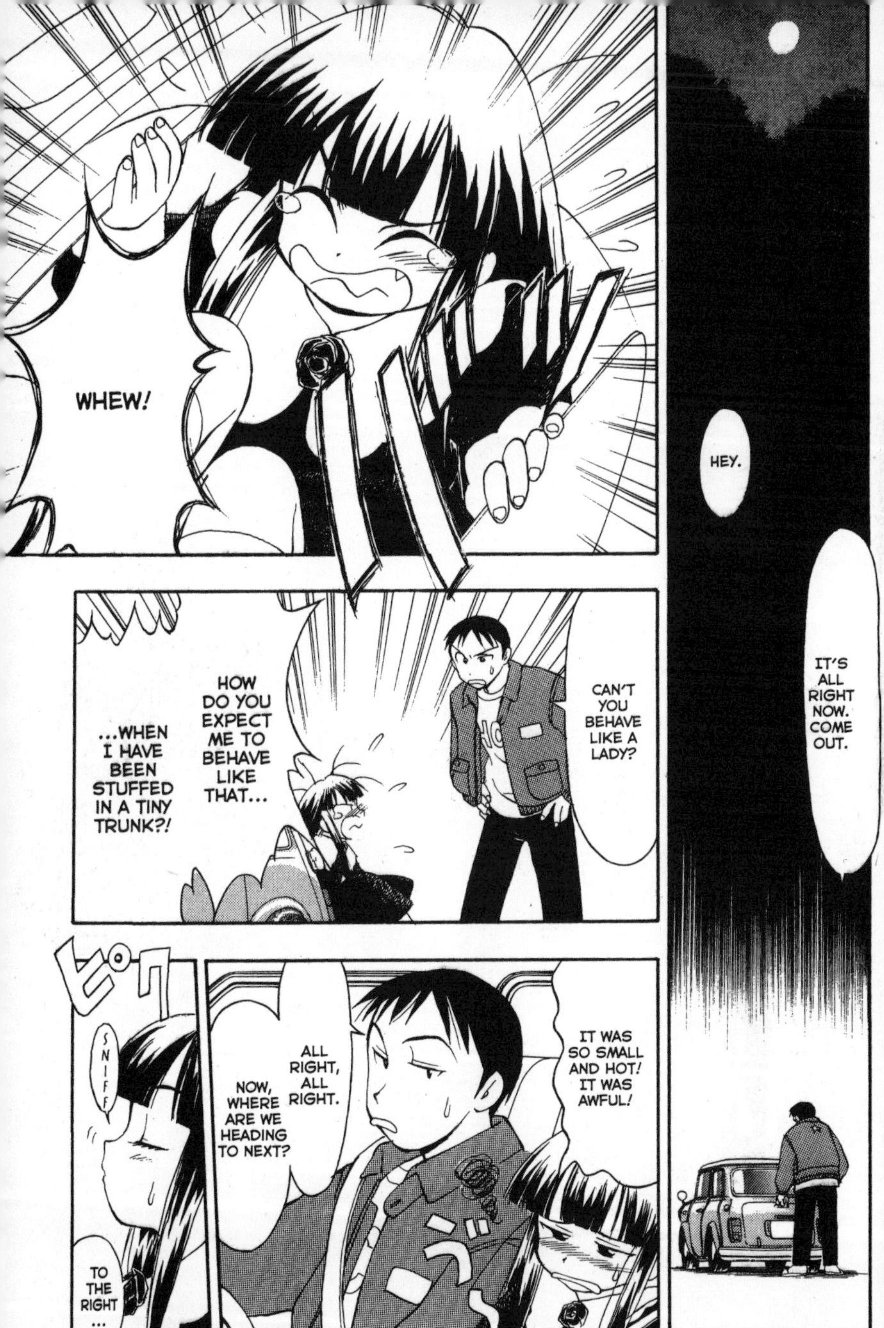
HEY.
IT'S ALL RIGHT NOW. COME OUT.
WHEW!
CAN'T YOU BEHAVE LIKE A LADY?
HOW DO YOU EXPECT ME TO BEHAVE LIKE THAT...
...WHEN I HAVE BEEN STUFFED IN A TINY TRUNK?!
IT WAS SO SMALL AND HOT! IT WAS AWFUL!
ALL RIGHT, ALL RIGHT.
NOW, WHERE ARE WE HEADING TO NEXT?
ピク
SNIFF
TO THE RIGHT...

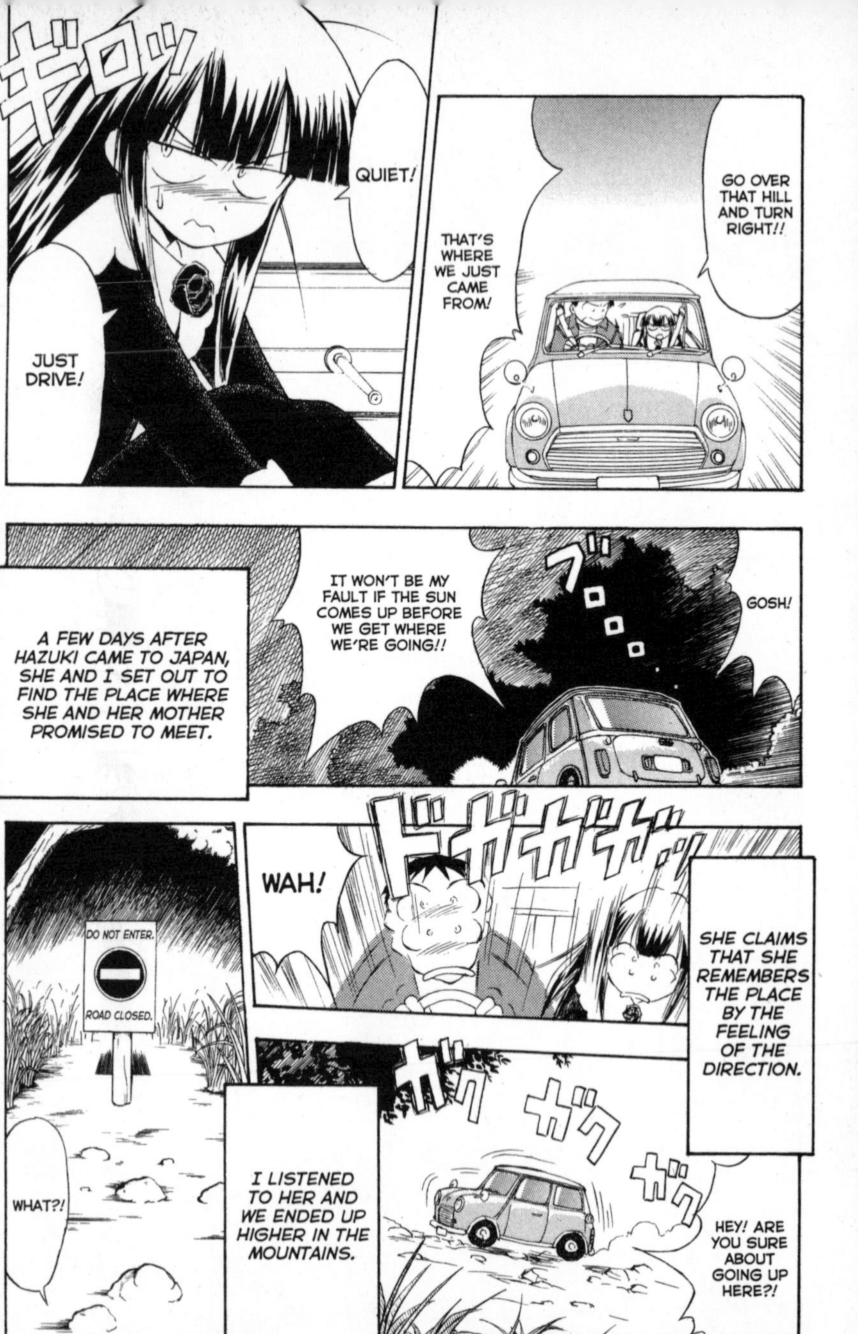
GO OVER THAT HILL AND TURN RIGHT!!
THAT'S WHERE WE JUST CAME FROM!
ギロッ
QUIET!
JUST DRIVE!
GOSH!
ブロロロ
IT WON'T BE MY FAULT IF THE SUN COMES UP BEFORE WE GET WHERE WE'RE GOING!!
A FEW DAYS AFTER HAZUKI CAME TO JAPAN, SHE AND I SET OUT TO FIND THE PLACE WHERE SHE AND HER MOTHER PROMISED TO MEET.
SHE CLAIMS THAT SHE REMEMBERS THE PLACE BY THE FEELING OF THE DIRECTION.
ドガガガッ
WAH!
HEY! ARE YOU SURE ABOUT GOING UP HERE?!
ガク
ガク
ガク
I LISTENED TO HER AND WE ENDED UP HIGHER IN THE MOUNTAINS.
DO NOT ENTER.
ROAD CLOSED.
WHAT?!

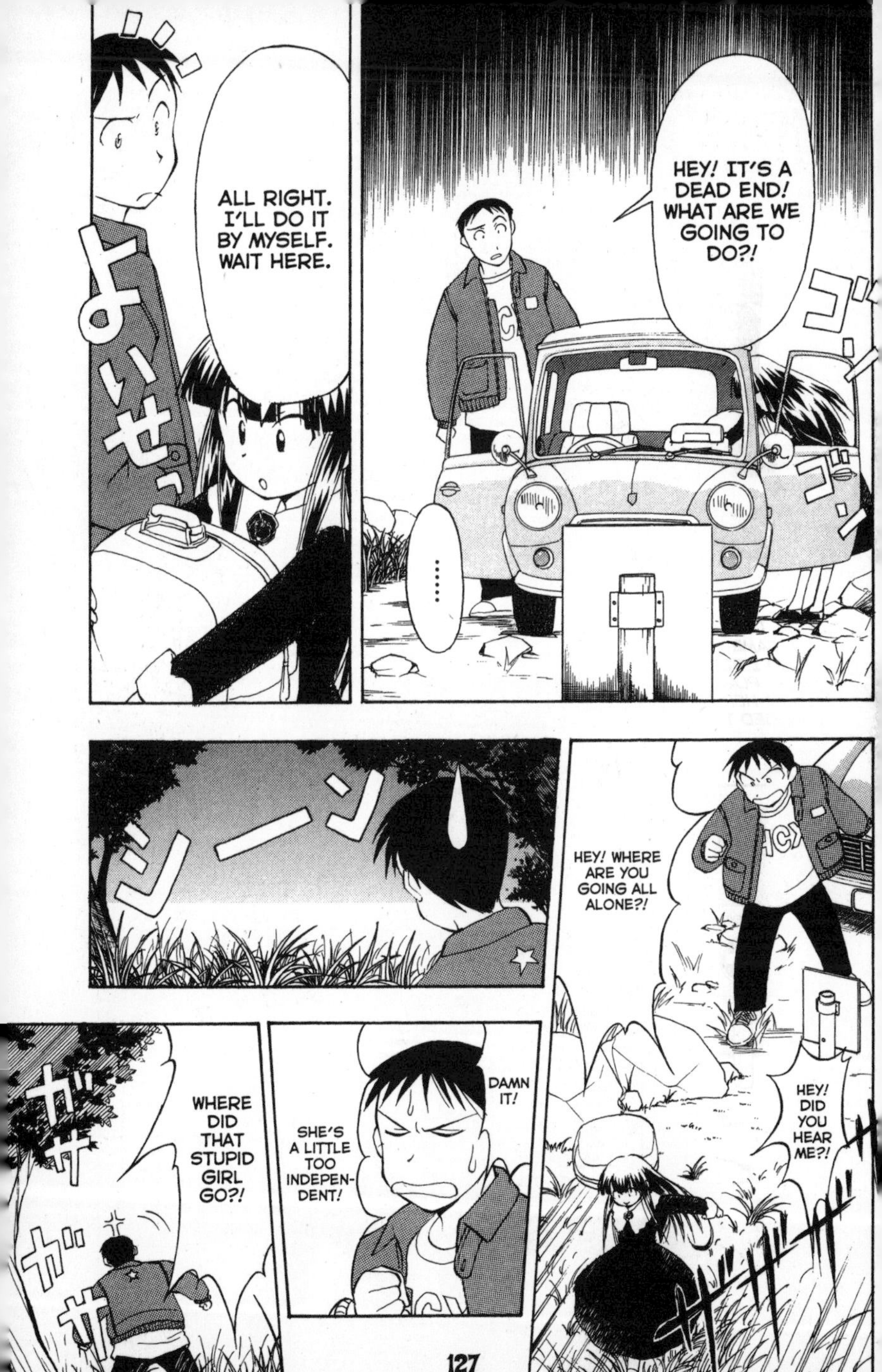
HEY! IT'S A DEAD END! WHAT ARE WE GOING TO DO?!
ゴ
ゴ
......
ALL RIGHT. I'LL DO IT BY MYSELF. WAIT HERE.
よいせっ
HEY! WHERE ARE YOU GOING ALL ALONE?!
HEY! DID YOU HEAR ME?!
シーン
DAMN IT!
SHE'S A LITTLE TOO INDEPENDENT!
WHERE DID THAT STUPID GIRL GO?!
ガサ
ガサ

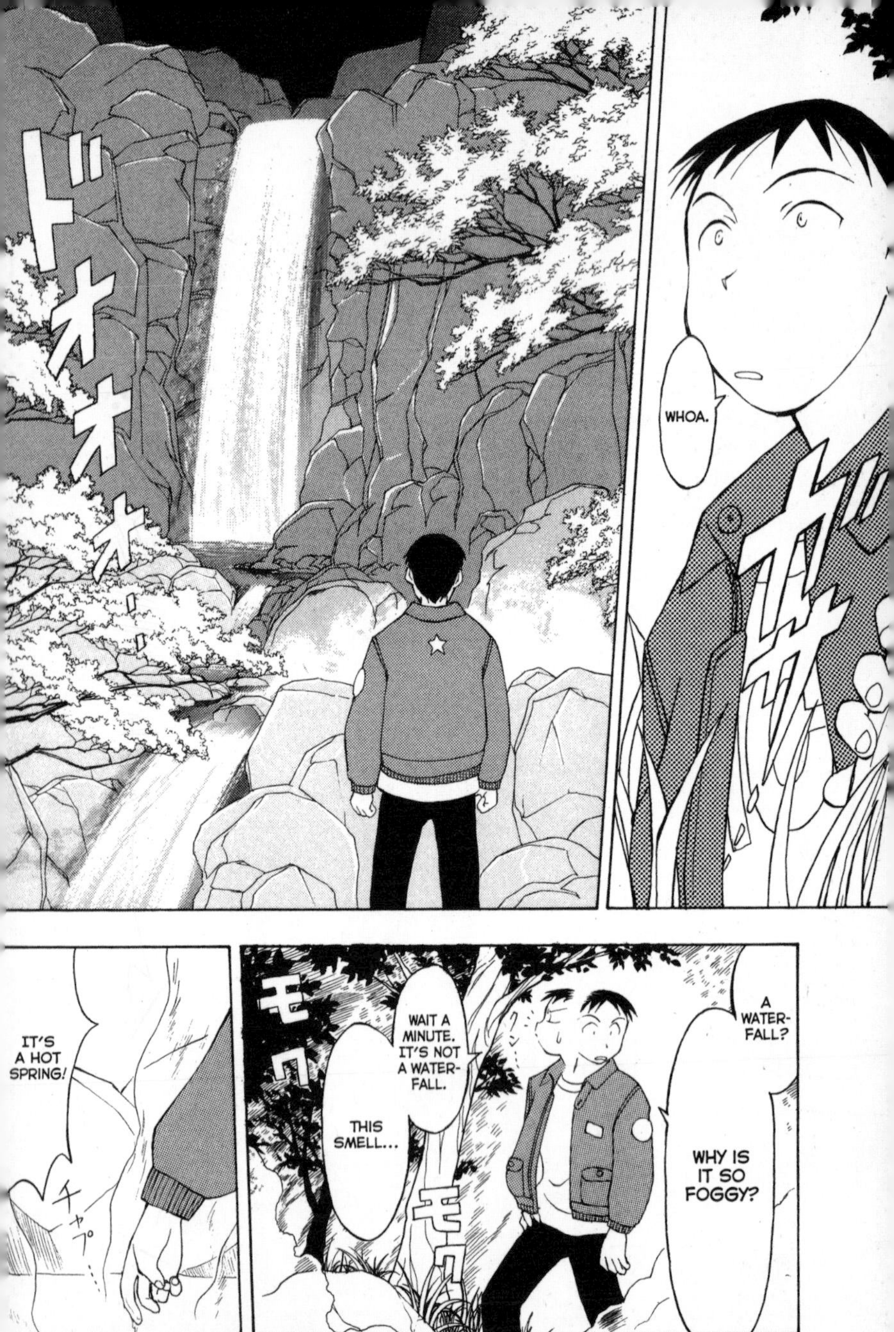
WHOA.
ガサ
ドォオオオ
A WATER-FALL?
WHY IS IT SO FOGGY?
WAIT A MINUTE. IT'S NOT A WATER-FALL.
THIS SMELL...
モク
モク
IT'S A HOT SPRING!
チャプ…

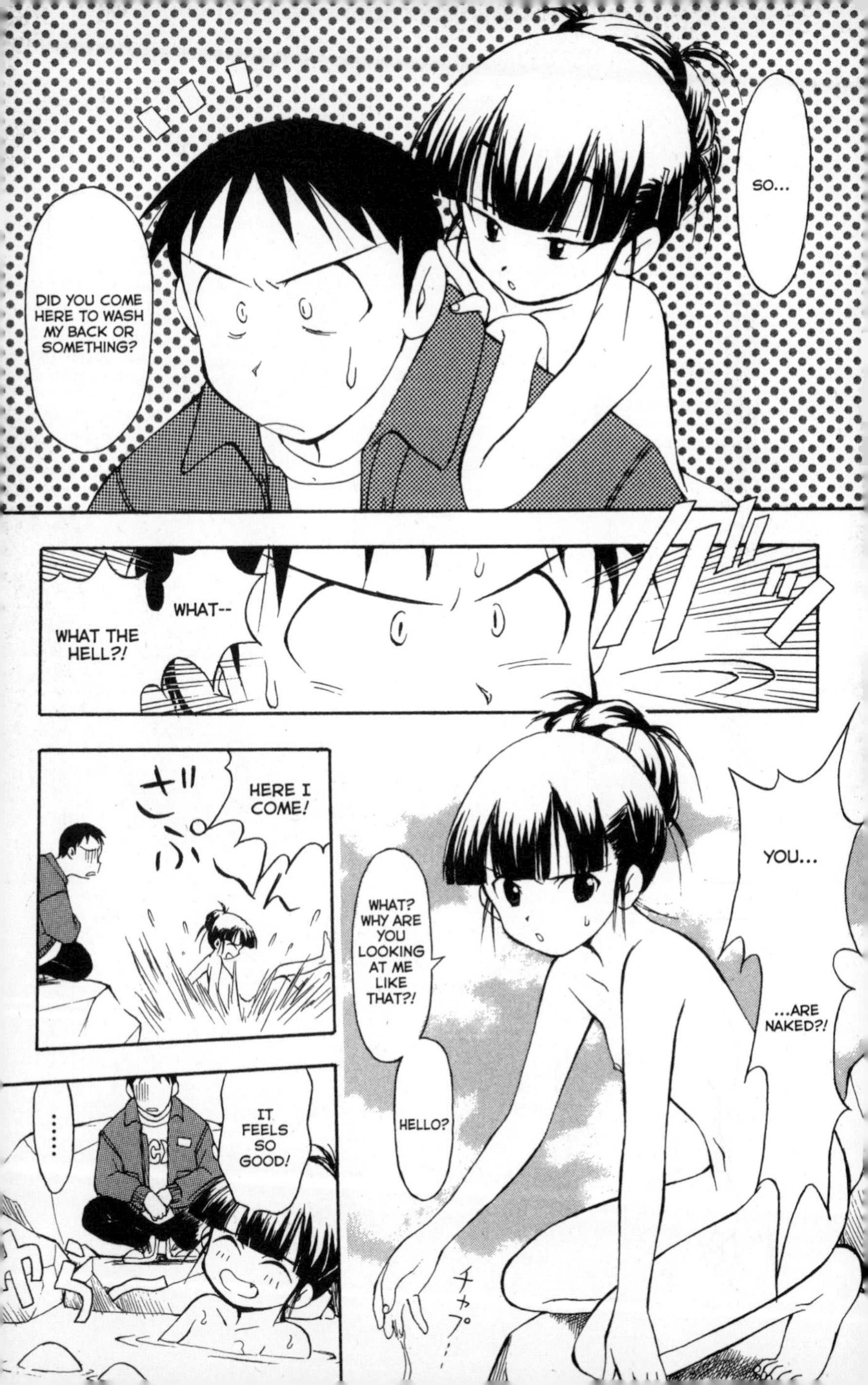
SO...
DID YOU COME HERE TO WASH MY BACK OR SOMETHING?
WHAT--
WHAT THE HELL?!
YOU...
...ARE NAKED?!
WHAT? WHY ARE YOU LOOKING AT ME LIKE THAT?!
HELLO?
チャプ...
HERE I COME!
IT FEELS SO GOOD!
......

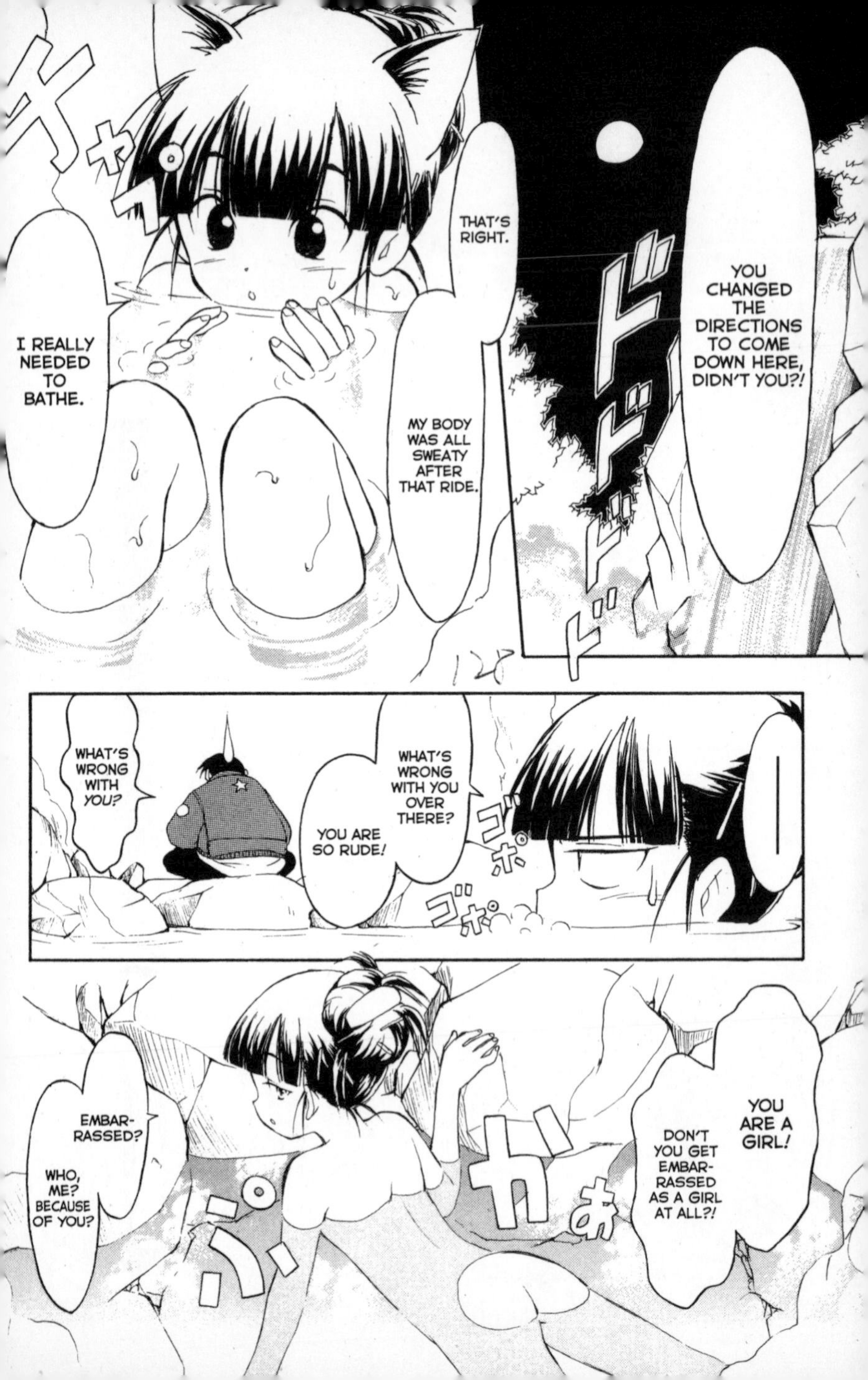
YOU CHANGED THE DIRECTIONS TO COME DOWN HERE, DIDN'T YOU?!
ドドドド
チャプ
THAT'S RIGHT.
MY BODY WAS ALL SWEATY AFTER THAT RIDE.
I REALLY NEEDED TO BATHE.
ゴポ ゴポ
WHAT'S WRONG WITH YOU OVER THERE?
YOU ARE SO RUDE!
WHAT'S WRONG WITH *YOU*?
YOU ARE A GIRL!
DON'T YOU GET EMBAR-RASSED AS A GIRL AT ALL?!
かあ
EMBAR-RASSED?
WHO, ME? BECAUSE OF YOU?
ぷい

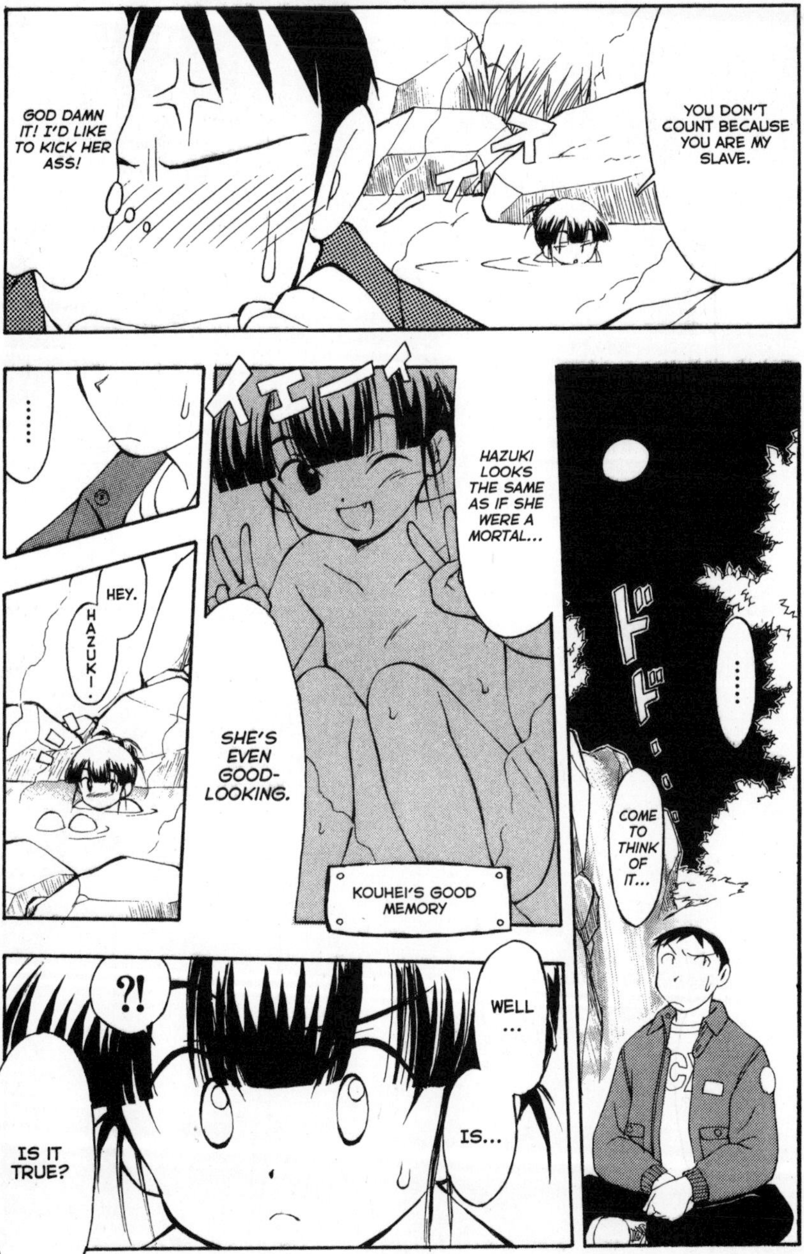
YOU DON'T COUNT BECAUSE YOU ARE MY SLAVE.
GOD DAMN IT! I'D LIKE TO KICK HER ASS!
......
COME TO THINK OF IT...
HAZUKI LOOKS THE SAME AS IF SHE WERE A MORTAL...
イエーイ
SHE'S EVEN GOOD-LOOKING.
KOUHEI'S GOOD MEMORY
......
HEY.
HAZUKI.
WELL ...
IS...
?!
IS IT TRUE?

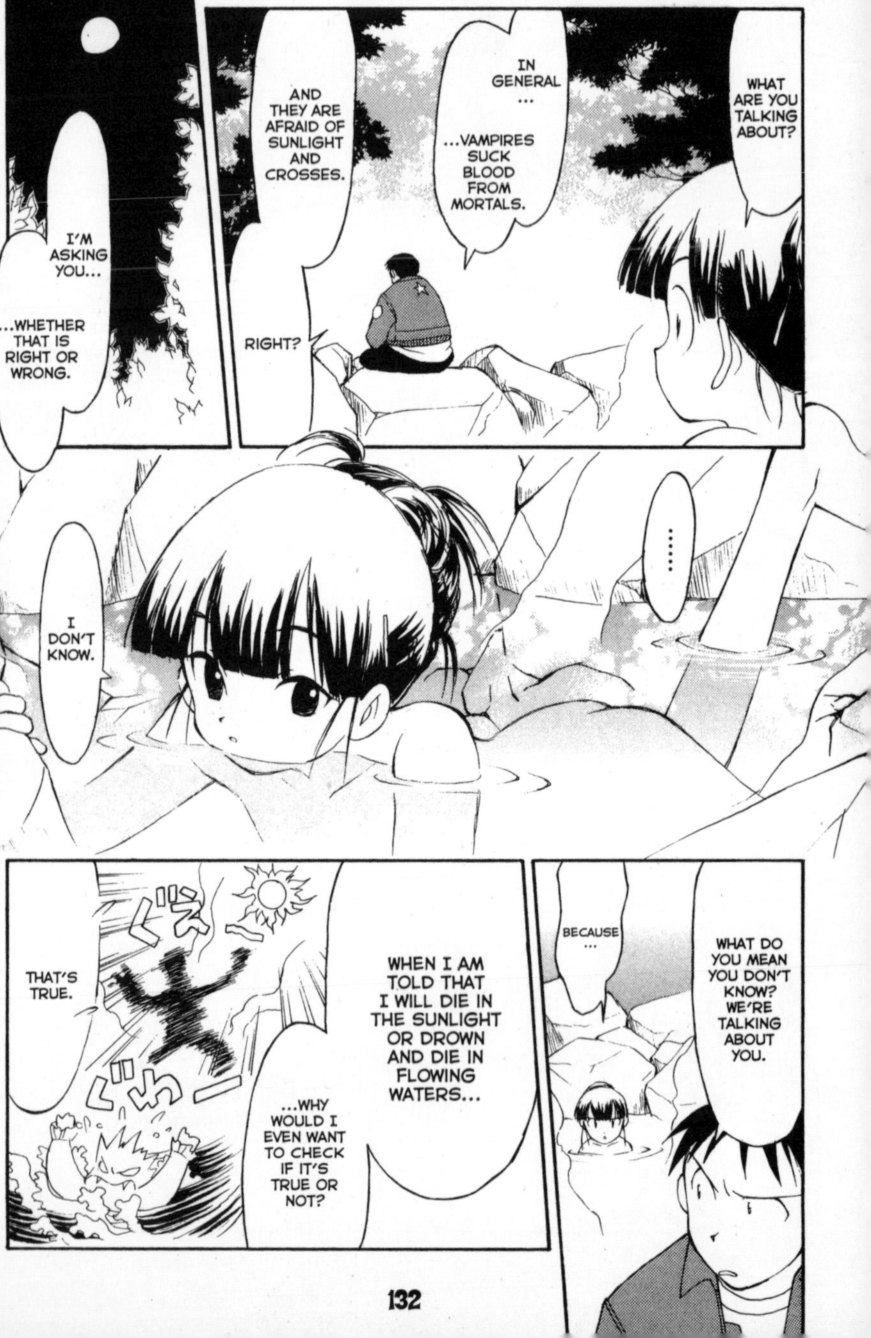
WHAT ARE YOU TALKING ABOUT?
IN GENERAL ...
...VAMPIRES SUCK BLOOD FROM MORTALS.
AND THEY ARE AFRAID OF SUNLIGHT AND CROSSES.
RIGHT?
I'M ASKING YOU...
...WHETHER THAT IS RIGHT OR WRONG.
......
I DON'T KNOW.
WHAT DO YOU MEAN YOU DON'T KNOW? WE'RE TALKING ABOUT YOU.
BECAUSE ...
WHEN I AM TOLD THAT I WILL DIE IN THE SUNLIGHT OR DROWN AND DIE IN FLOWING WATERS...
...WHY WOULD I EVEN WANT TO CHECK IF IT'S TRUE OR NOT?
THAT'S TRUE.
ぐえ～
ぐわー

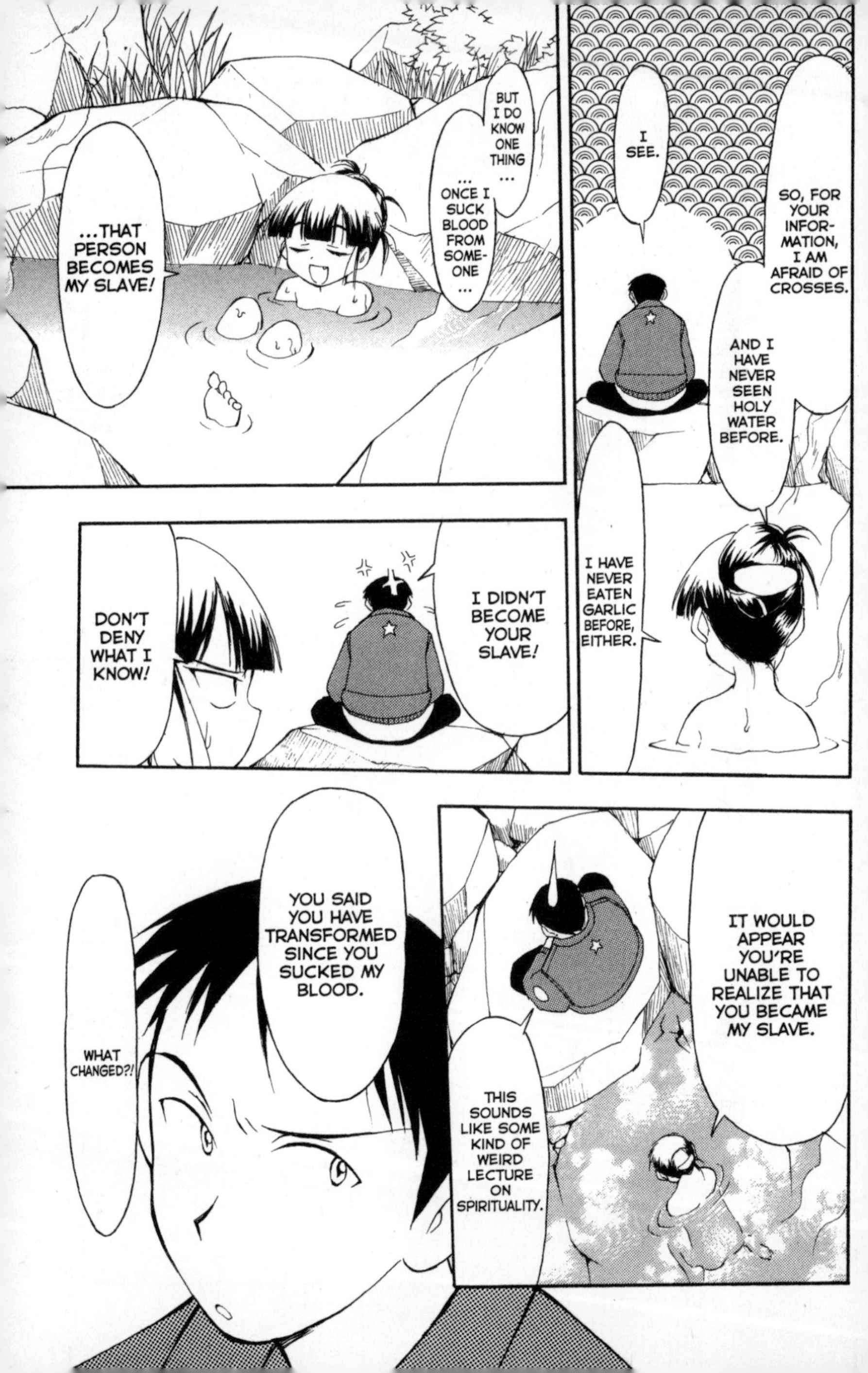
I SEE.
SO, FOR YOUR INFORMATION, I AM AFRAID OF CROSSES.
AND I HAVE NEVER SEEN HOLY WATER BEFORE.
I HAVE NEVER EATEN GARLIC BEFORE, EITHER.
BUT I DO KNOW ONE THING ...
... ONCE I SUCK BLOOD FROM SOMEONE ...
...THAT PERSON BECOMES MY SLAVE!
I DIDN'T BECOME YOUR SLAVE!
DON'T DENY WHAT I KNOW!
IT WOULD APPEAR YOU'RE UNABLE TO REALIZE THAT YOU BECAME MY SLAVE.
THIS SOUNDS LIKE SOME KIND OF WEIRD LECTURE ON SPIRITUALITY.
YOU SAID YOU HAVE TRANSFORMED SINCE YOU SUCKED MY BLOOD.
WHAT CHANGED?!

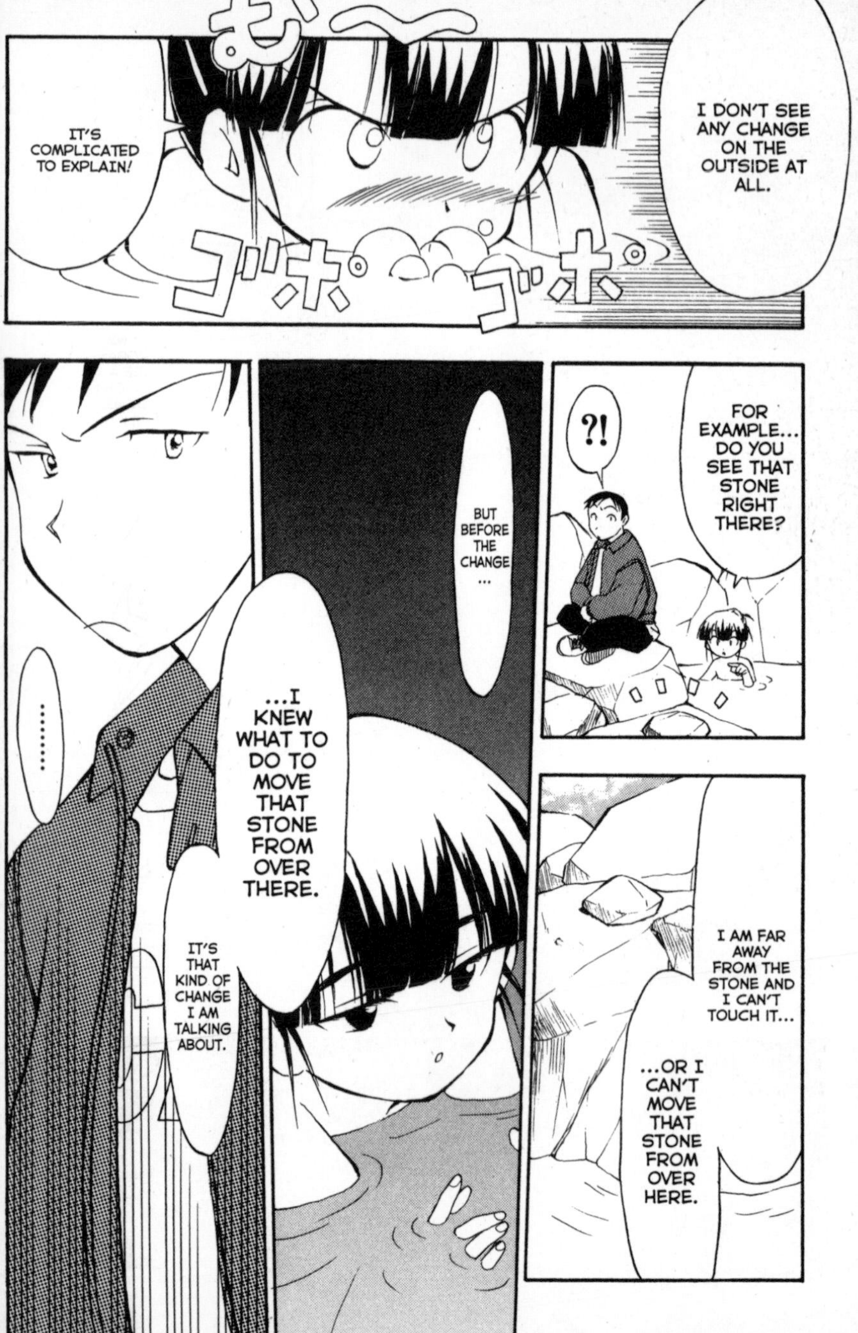
I DON'T SEE ANY CHANGE ON THE OUTSIDE AT ALL.
むー
IT'S COMPLICATED TO EXPLAIN!
ゴポ゜ゴポ゜
FOR EXAMPLE... DO YOU SEE THAT STONE RIGHT THERE?
?!
I AM FAR AWAY FROM THE STONE AND I CAN'T TOUCH IT...
...OR I CAN'T MOVE THAT STONE FROM OVER HERE.
BUT BEFORE THE CHANGE...
...I KNEW WHAT TO DO TO MOVE THAT STONE FROM OVER THERE.
IT'S THAT KIND OF CHANGE I AM TALKING ABOUT.
....

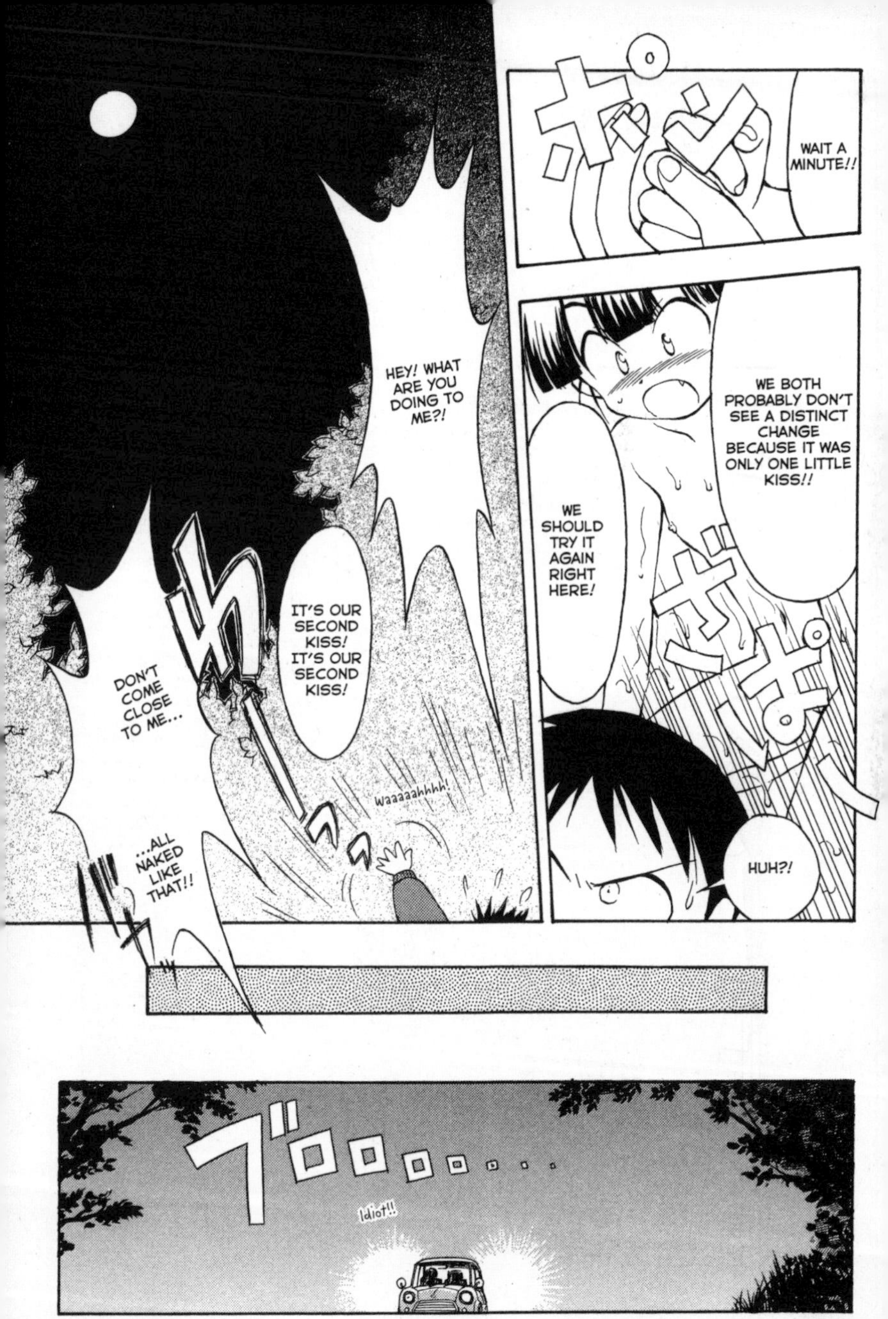
WAIT A MINUTE!!
WE BOTH PROBABLY DON'T SEE A DISTINCT CHANGE BECAUSE IT WAS ONLY ONE LITTLE KISS!!
WE SHOULD TRY IT AGAIN RIGHT HERE!
HUH?!
HEY! WHAT ARE YOU DOING TO ME?!
IT'S OUR SECOND KISS! IT'S OUR SECOND KISS!
DON'T COME CLOSE TO ME...
...ALL NAKED LIKE THAT!!
Waaaaahhhh!
Idiot!!

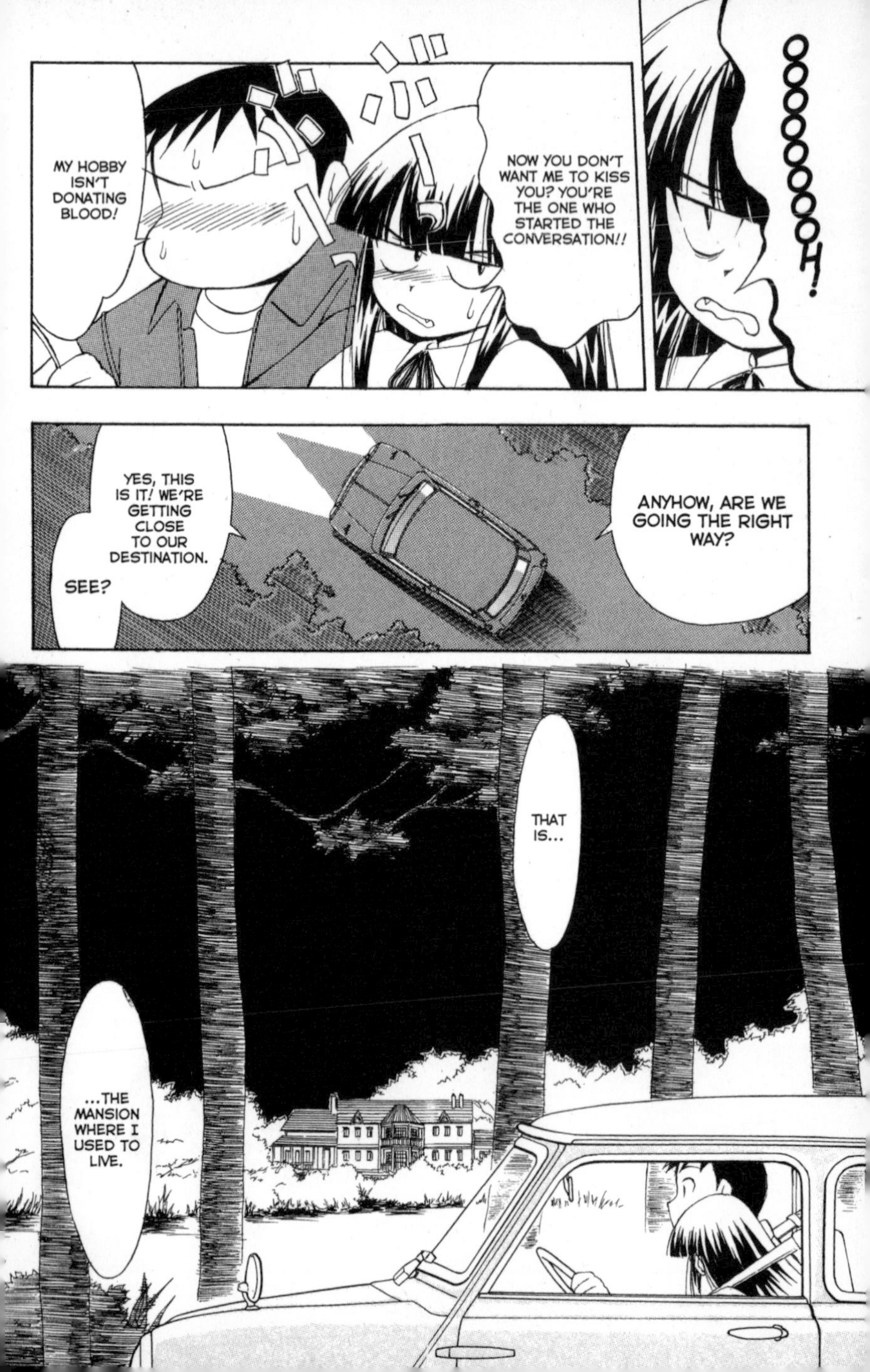
OOOOOOOOH!
NOW YOU DON'T WANT ME TO KISS YOU? YOU'RE THE ONE WHO STARTED THE CONVERSATION!!
MY HOBBY ISN'T DONATING BLOOD!
ANYHOW, ARE WE GOING THE RIGHT WAY?
YES, THIS IS IT! WE'RE GETTING CLOSE TO OUR DESTINATION.
SEE?
THAT IS...
...THE MANSION WHERE I USED TO LIVE.

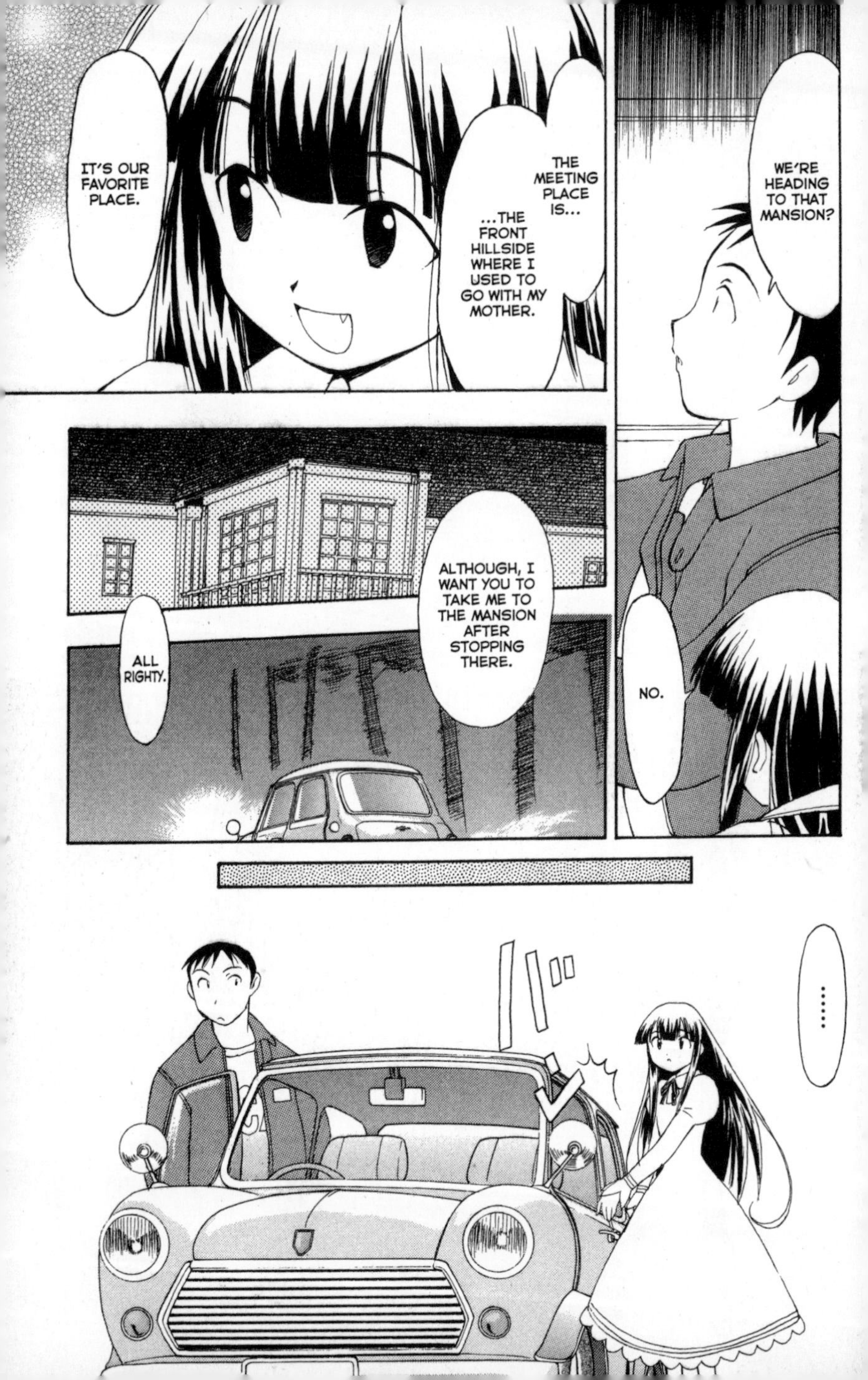
WE'RE HEADING TO THAT MANSION?
NO.
THE MEETING PLACE IS...
...THE FRONT HILLSIDE WHERE I USED TO GO WITH MY MOTHER.
IT'S OUR FAVORITE PLACE.
ALTHOUGH, I WANT YOU TO TAKE ME TO THE MANSION AFTER STOPPING THERE.
ALL RIGHTY.
......

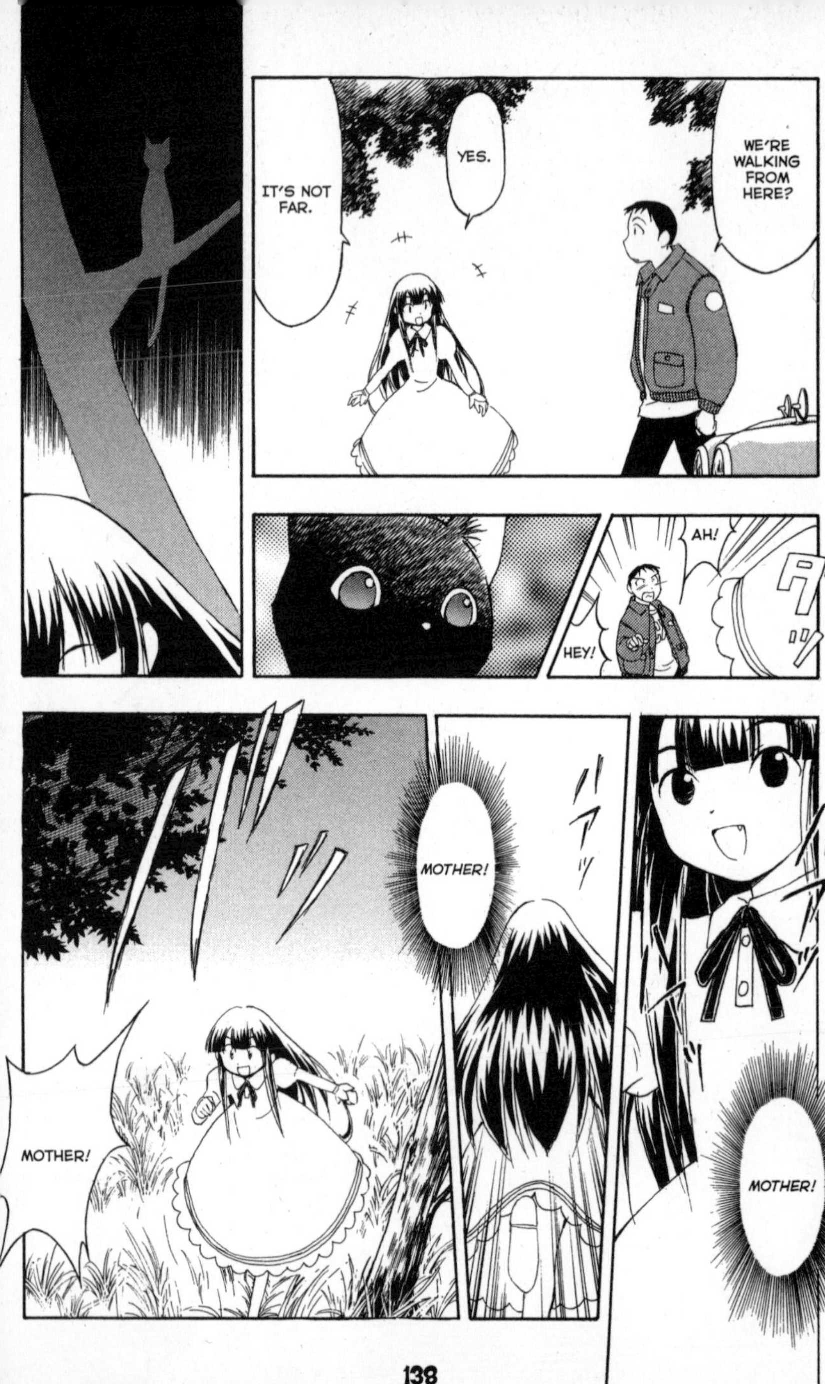
WE'RE WALKING FROM HERE?
YES.
IT'S NOT FAR.
AH!
HEY!
ダッ
MOTHER!
ハアッ
MOTHER!
MOTHER!

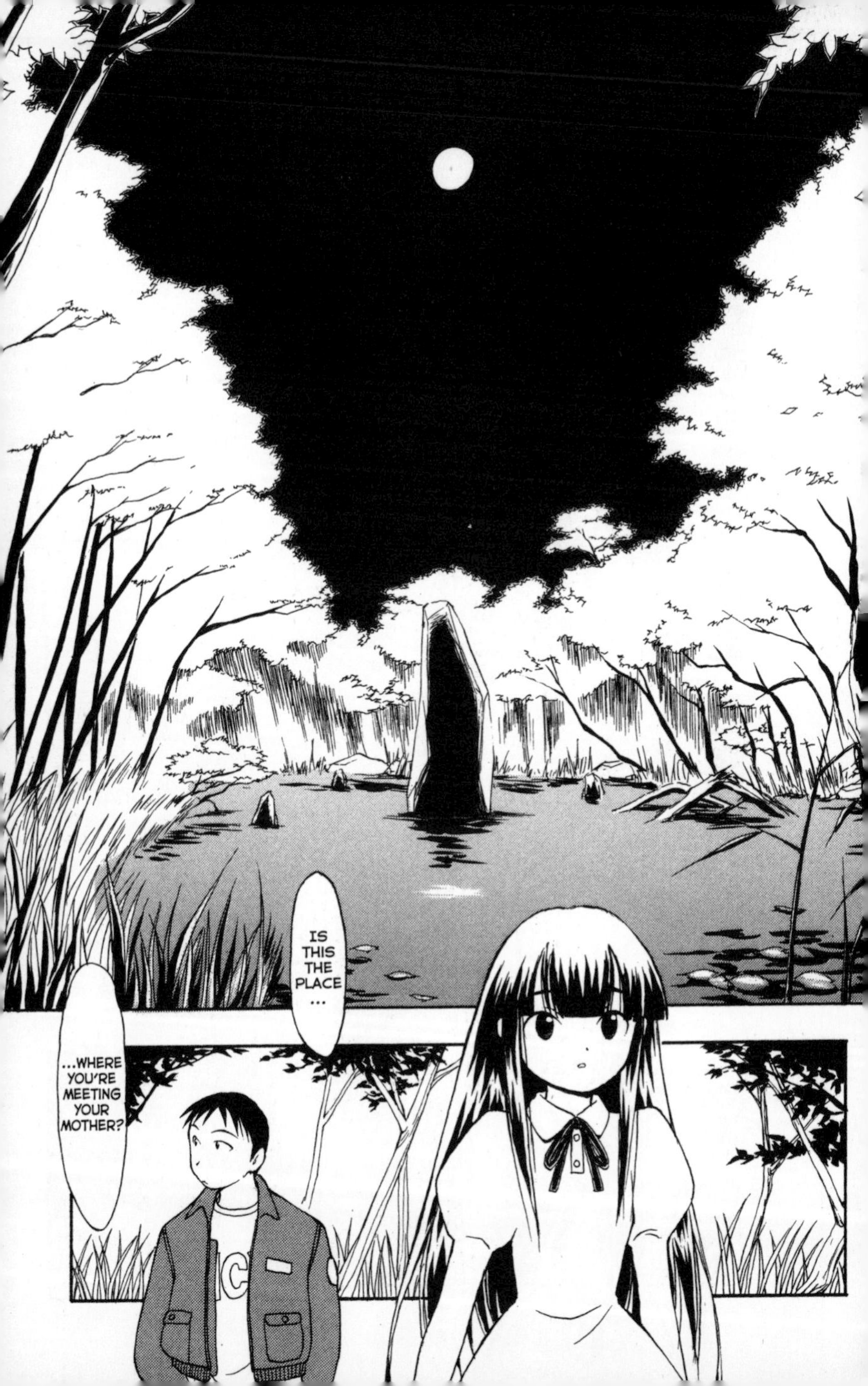
IS THIS THE PLACE...
...WHERE YOU'RE MEETING YOUR MOTHER?

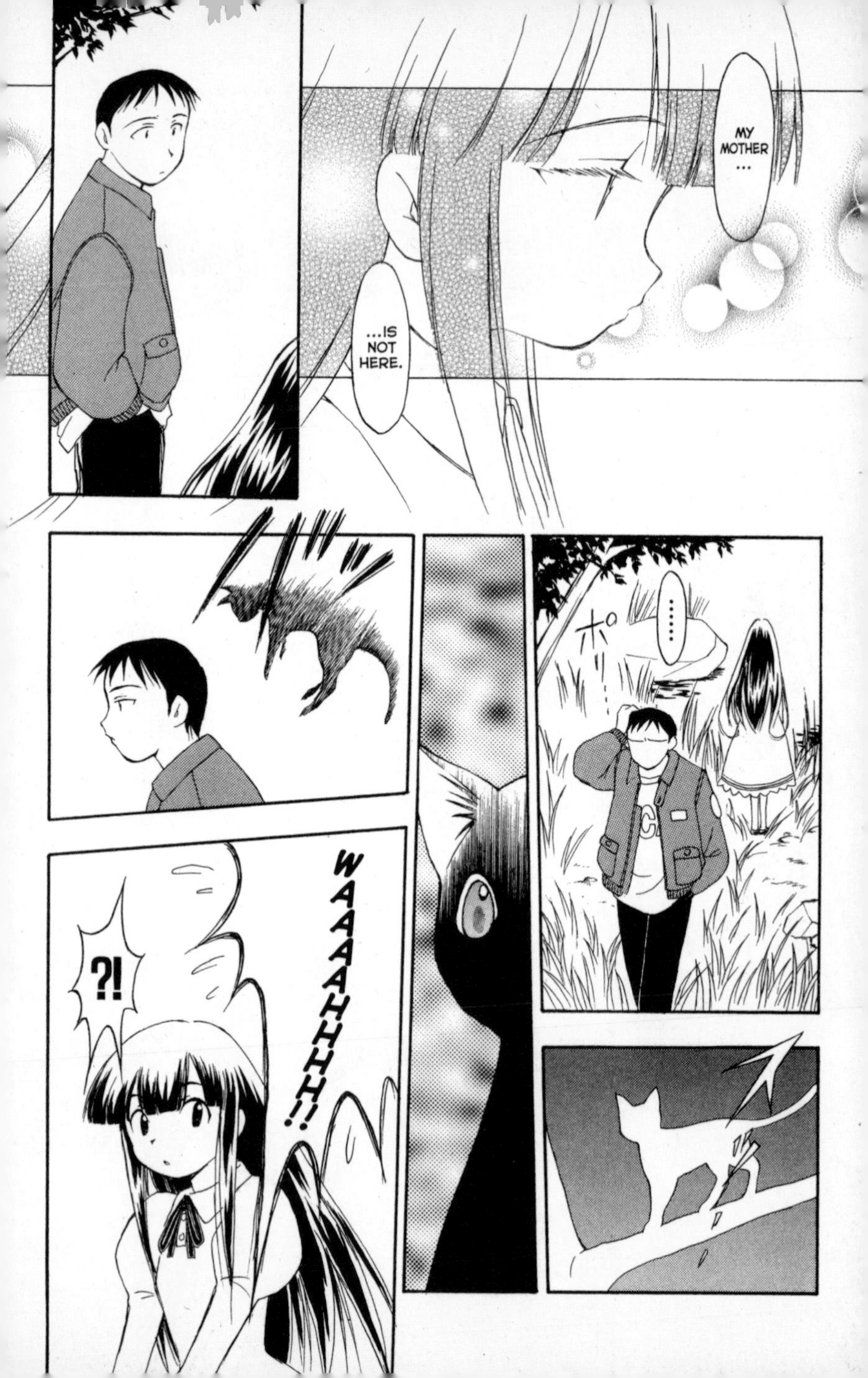
MY MOTHER ...
...IS NOT HERE.
......
ポ
WAAAAHHHH!!
?!

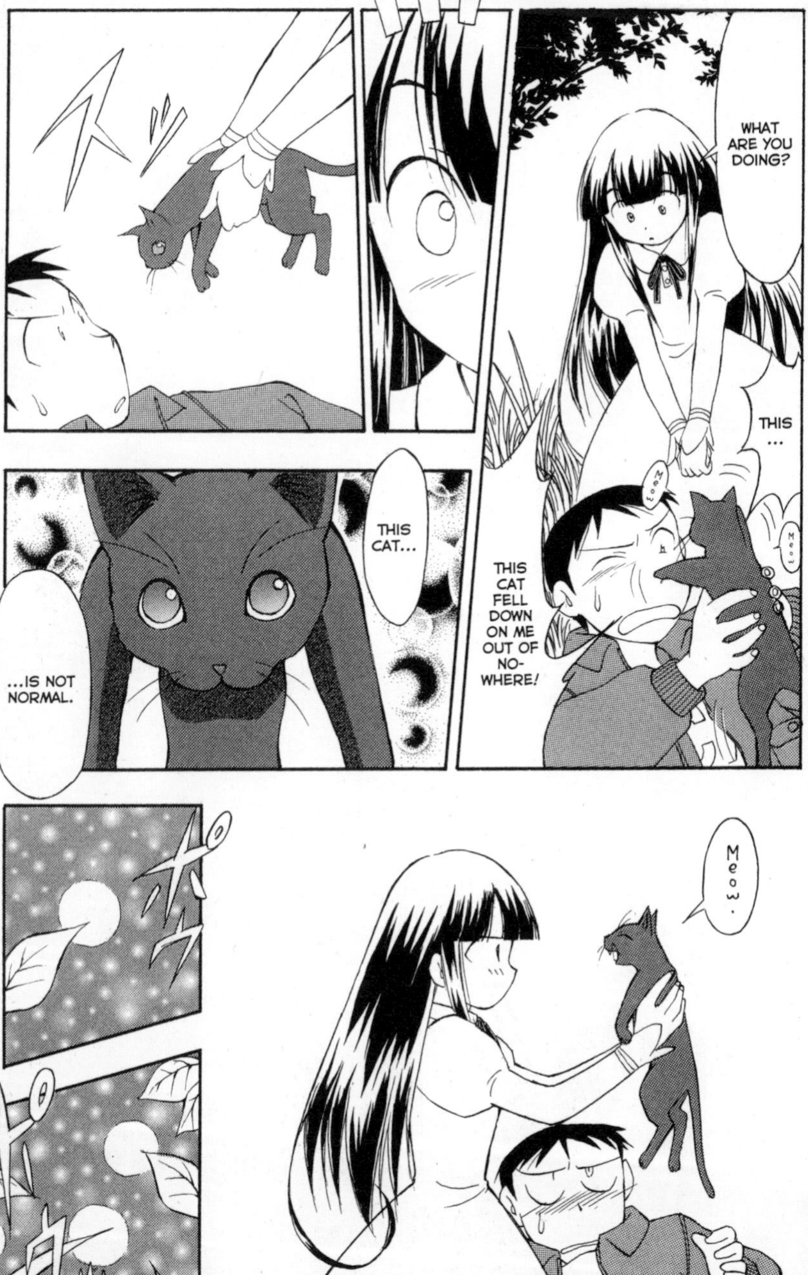
WHAT ARE YOU DOING?
THIS ...
Meow
Meow
THIS CAT FELL DOWN ON ME OUT OF NO-WHERE!
THIS CAT...
...IS NOT NORMAL.
Meow.

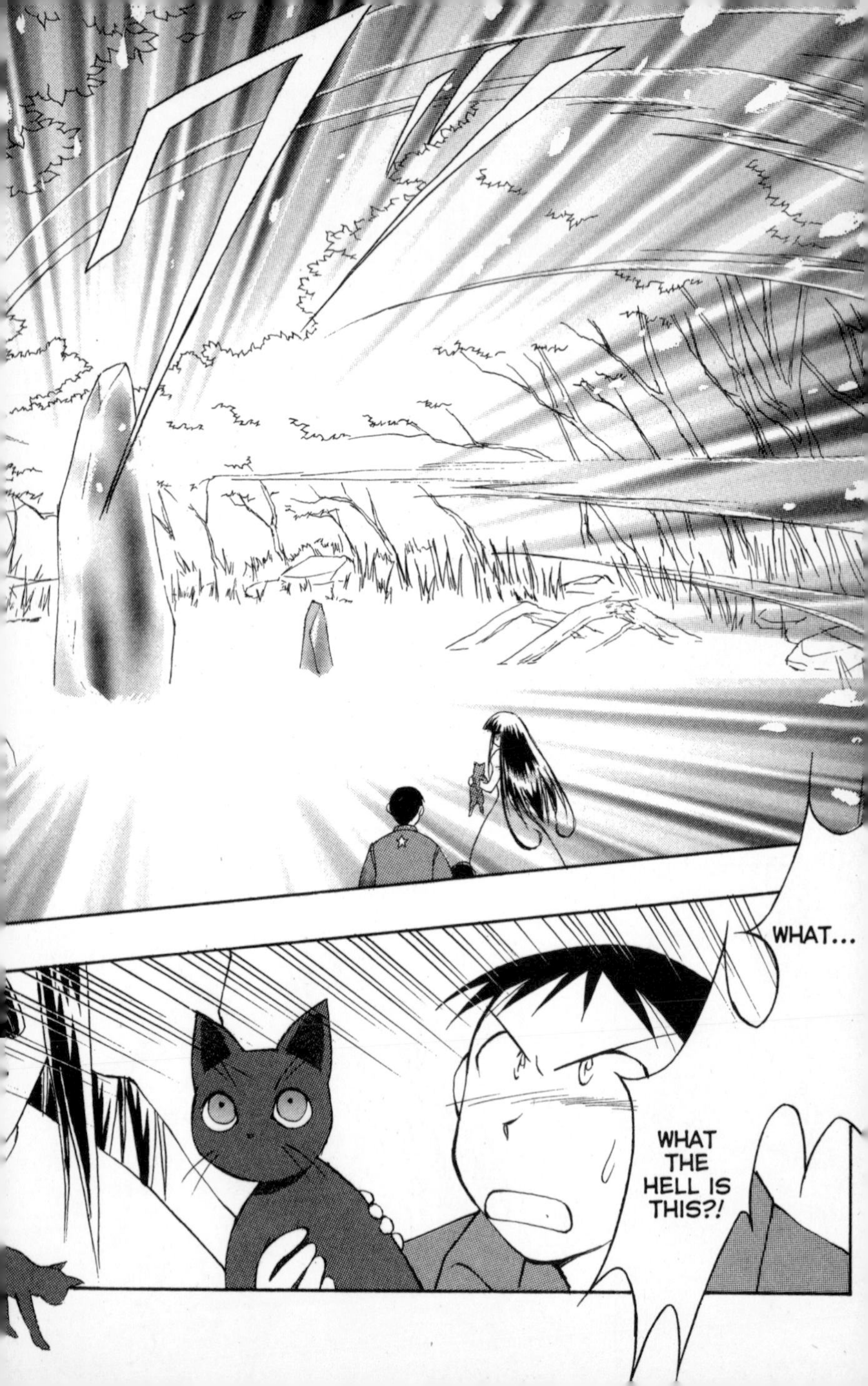
WHAT...
WHAT THE HELL IS THIS?!

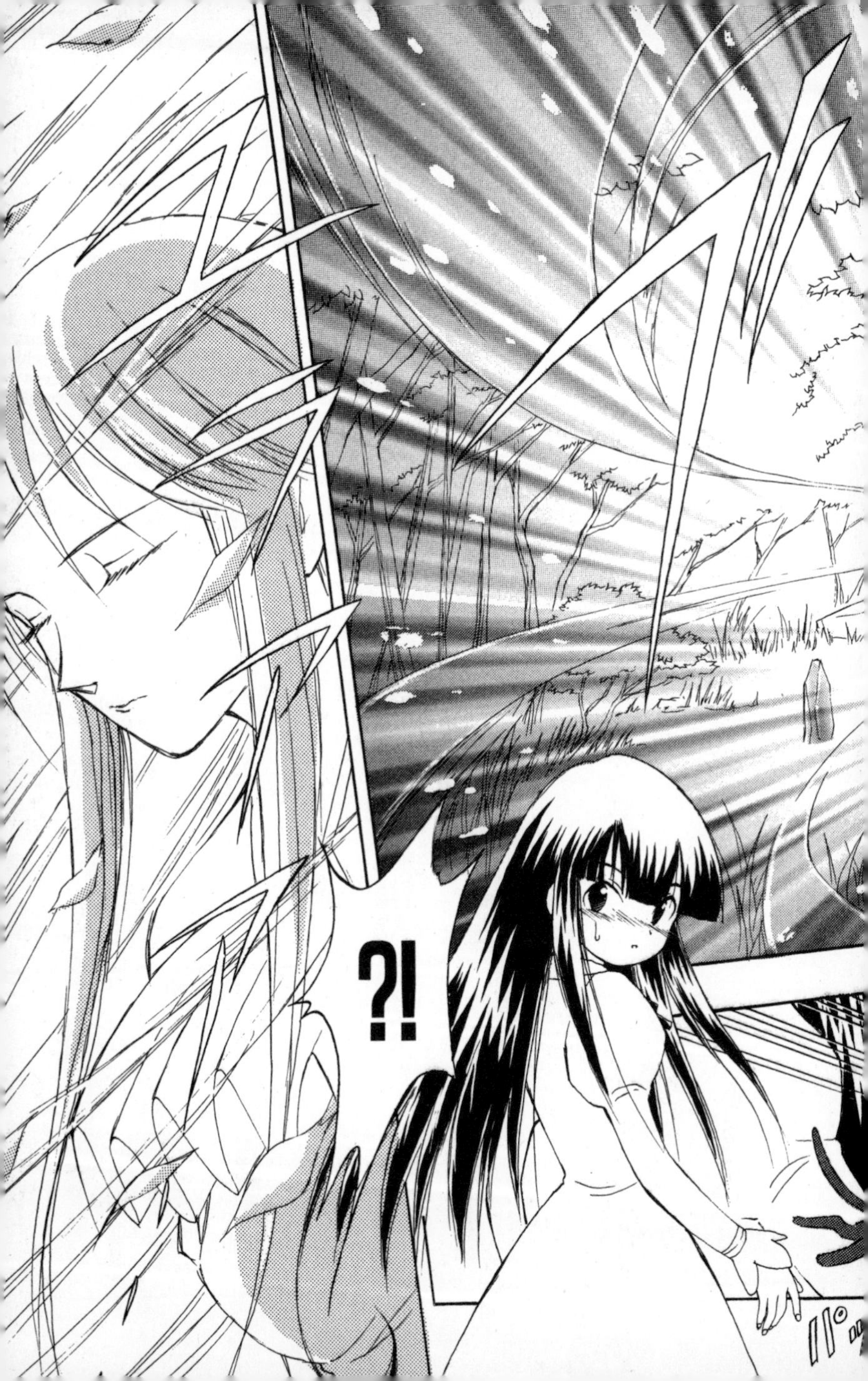
?!

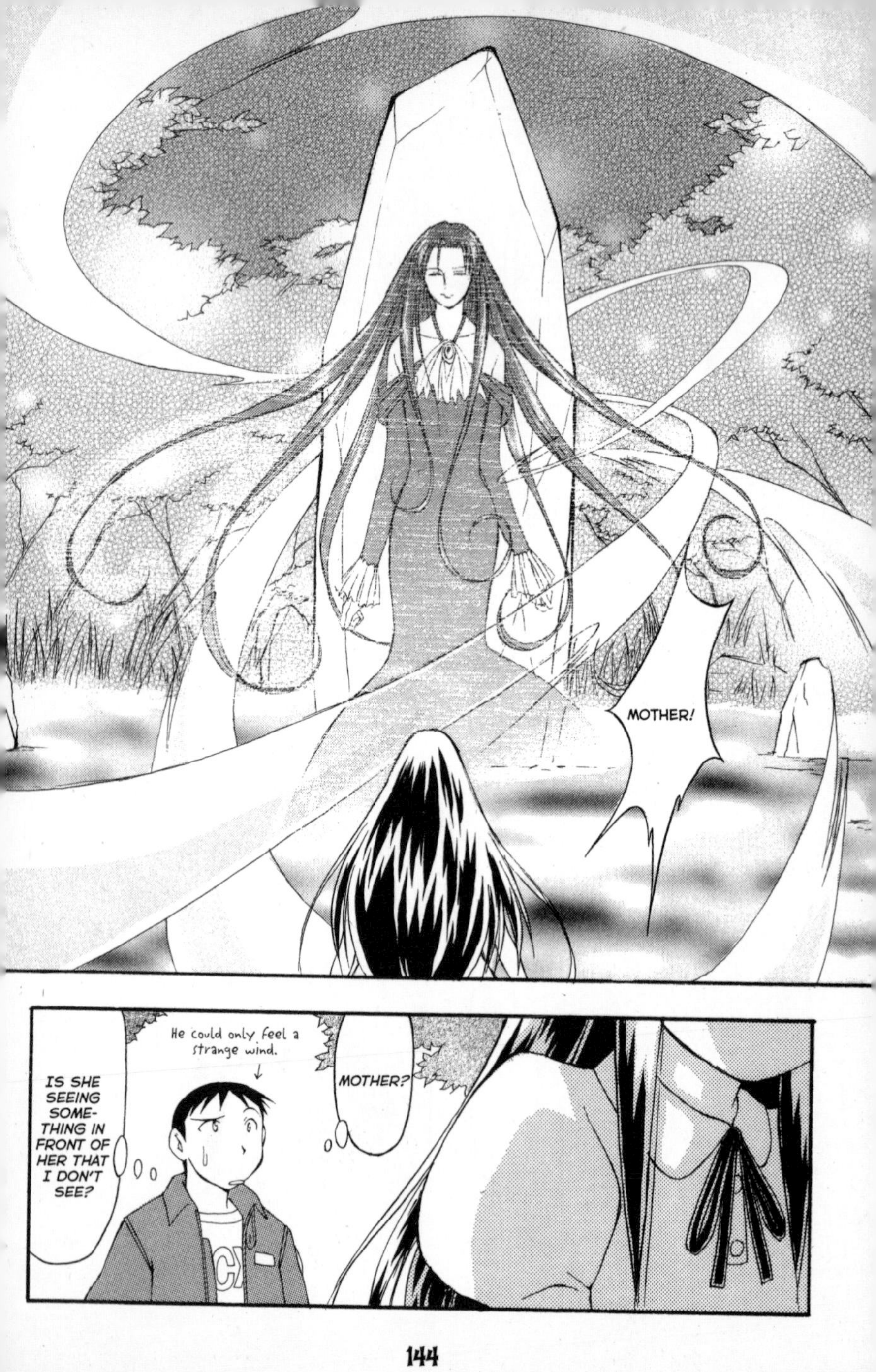
MOTHER!
MOTHER?
He could only feel a strange wind.
IS SHE SEEING SOME-THING IN FRONT OF HER THAT I DON'T SEE?

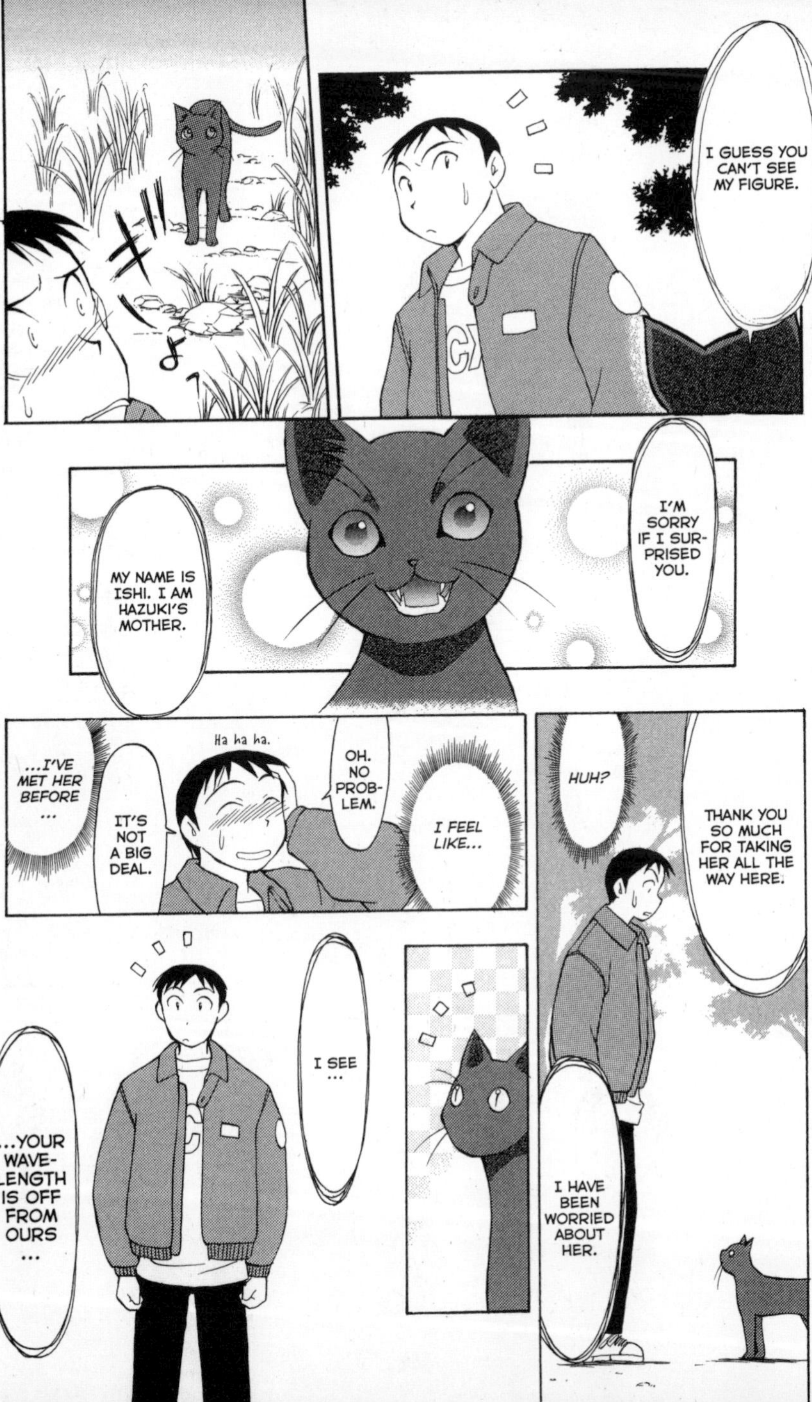
I GUESS YOU CAN'T SEE MY FIGURE.
I'M SORRY IF I SURPRISED YOU.
MY NAME IS ISHI. I AM HAZUKI'S MOTHER.
HUH?
THANK YOU SO MUCH FOR TAKING HER ALL THE WAY HERE.
I HAVE BEEN WORRIED ABOUT HER.
I FEEL LIKE...
OH. NO PROBLEM.
Ha ha ha.
IT'S NOT A BIG DEAL.
...I'VE MET HER BEFORE...
I SEE...
...YOUR WAVELENGTH IS OFF FROM OURS...

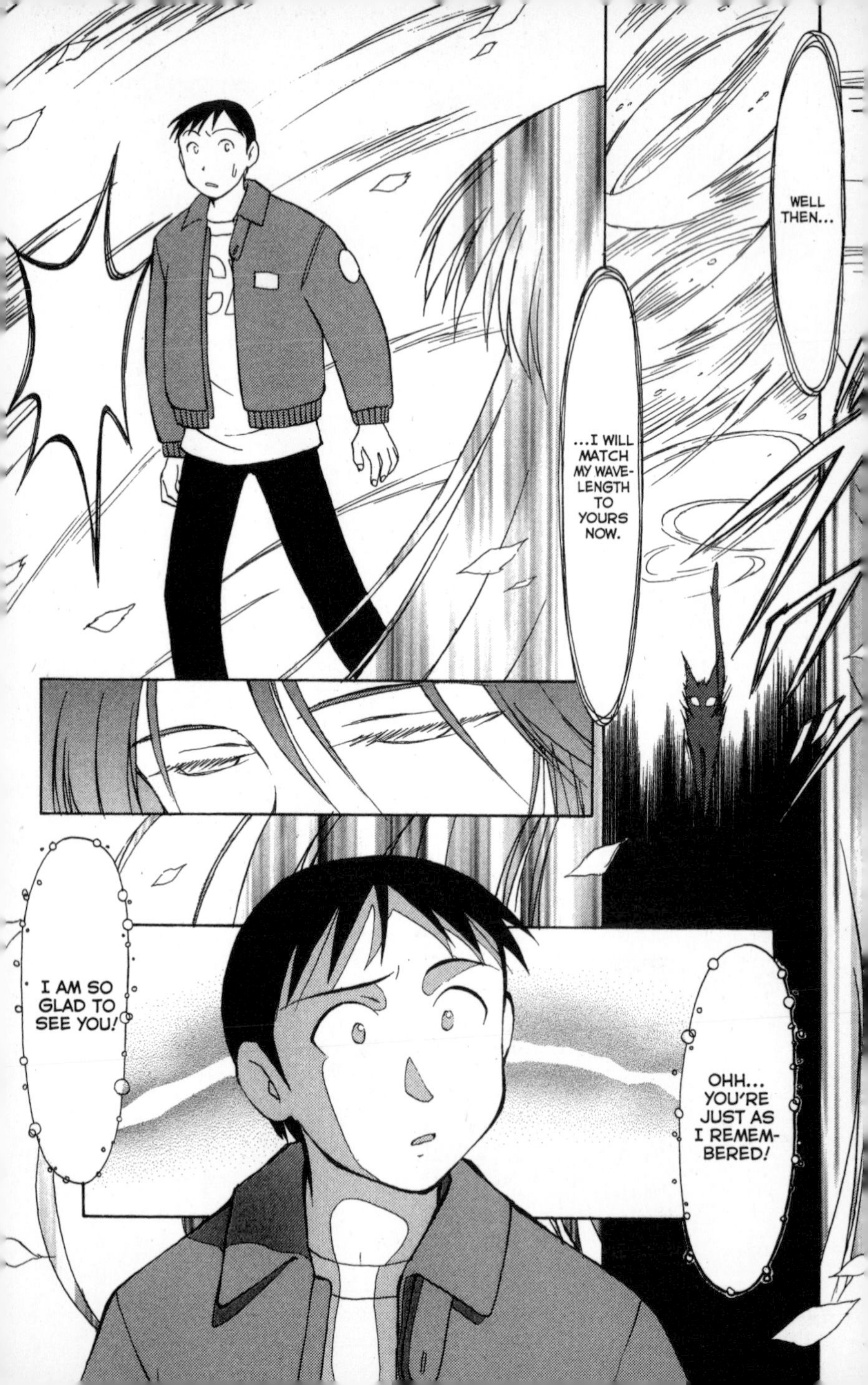
WELL THEN...
...I WILL MATCH MY WAVE-LENGTH TO YOURS NOW.
OHH... YOU'RE JUST AS I REMEM-BERED!
I AM SO GLAD TO SEE YOU!

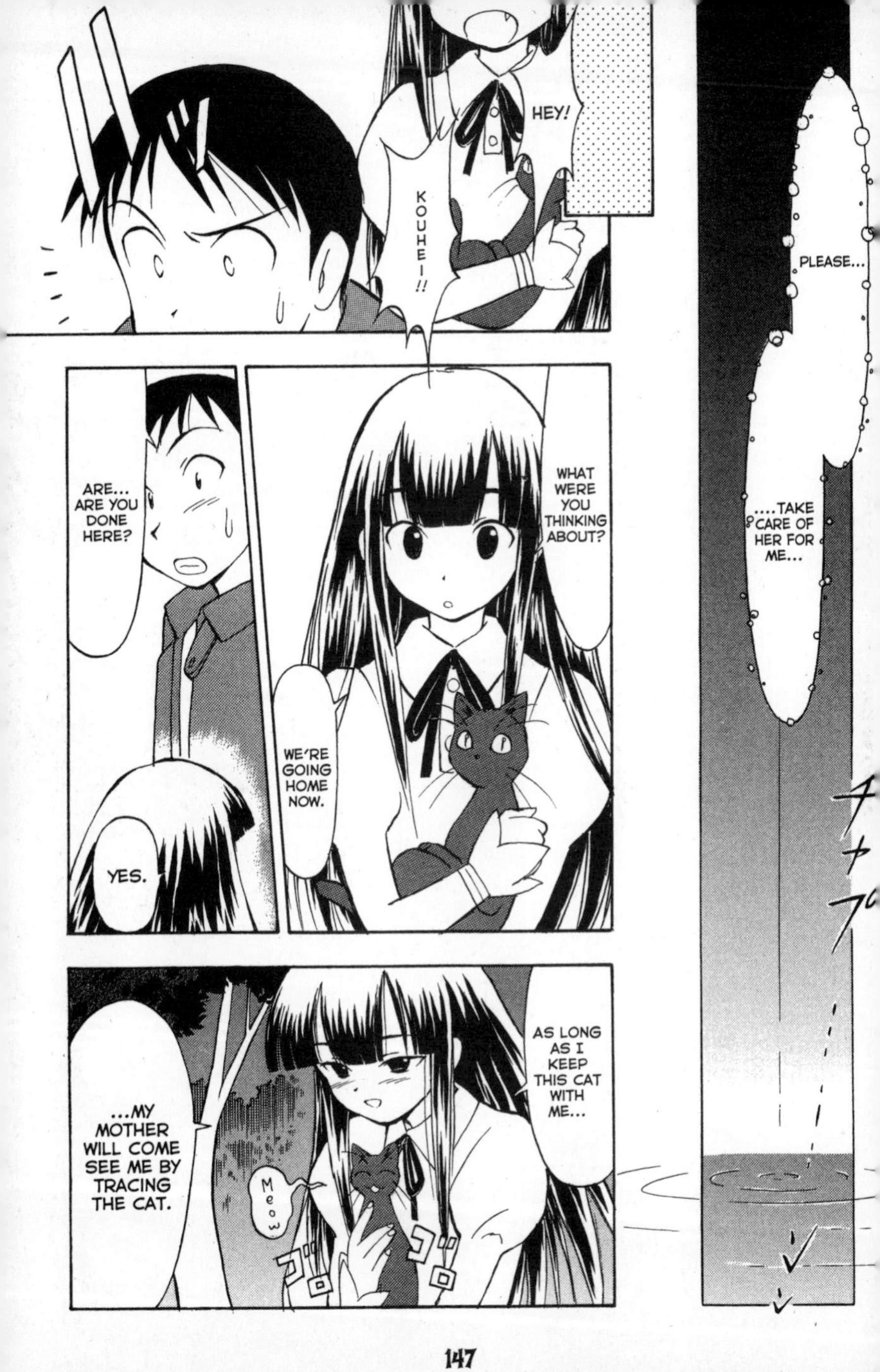
PLEASE...
....TAKE CARE OF HER FOR ME...
HEY!
KOUHEI!!
WHAT WERE YOU THINKING ABOUT?
WE'RE GOING HOME NOW.
ARE... ARE YOU DONE HERE?
YES.
AS LONG AS I KEEP THIS CAT WITH ME...
...MY MOTHER WILL COME SEE ME BY TRACING THE CAT.
Meow

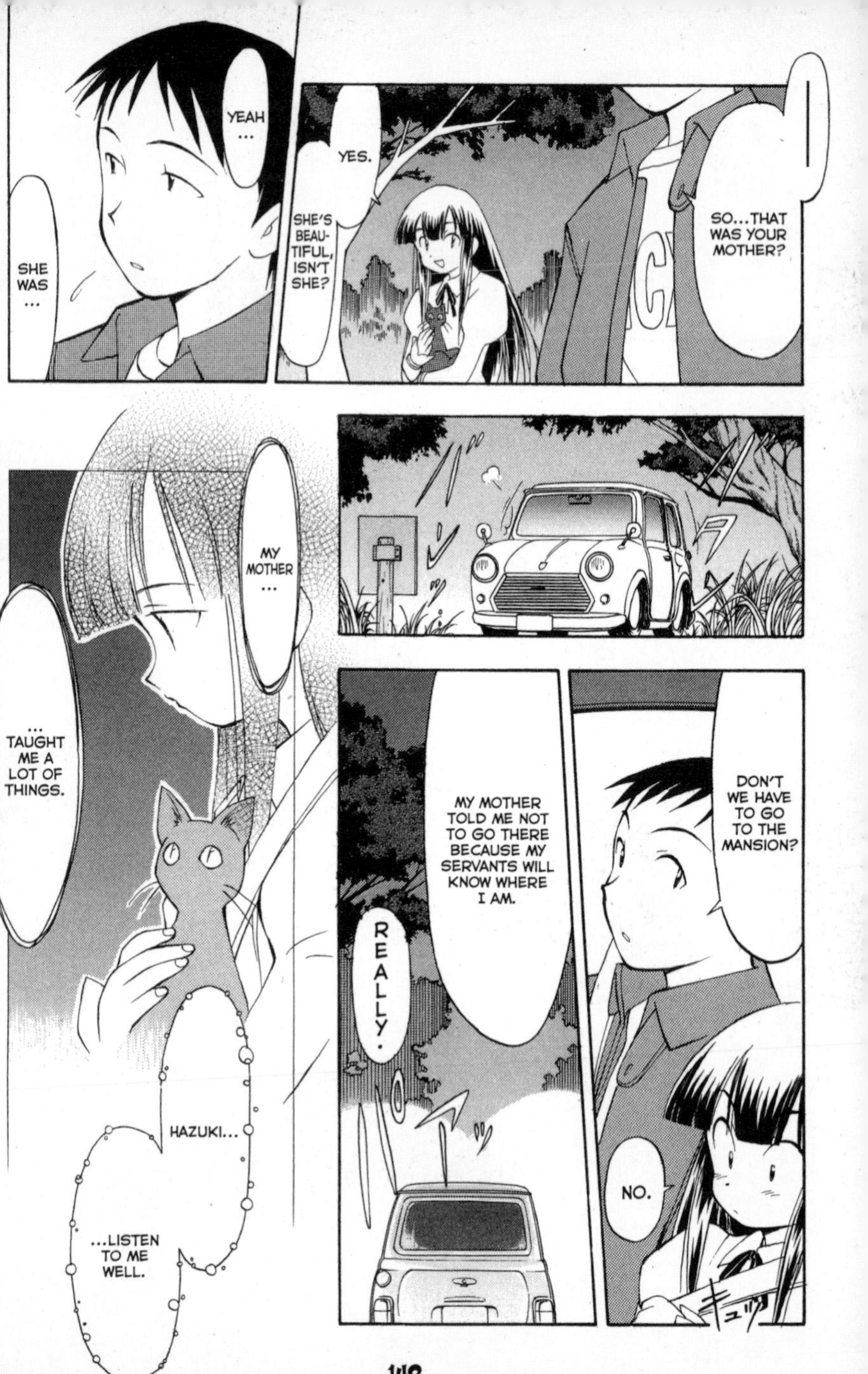
SO...THAT WAS YOUR MOTHER?
YES.
SHE'S BEAU-TIFUL, ISN'T SHE?
YEAH...
SHE WAS...
DON'T WE HAVE TO GO TO THE MANSION?
NO.
MY MOTHER TOLD ME NOT TO GO THERE BECAUSE MY SERVANTS WILL KNOW WHERE I AM.
REALLY.
MY MOTHER...
...TAUGHT ME A LOT OF THINGS.
HAZUKI...
...LISTEN TO ME WELL.

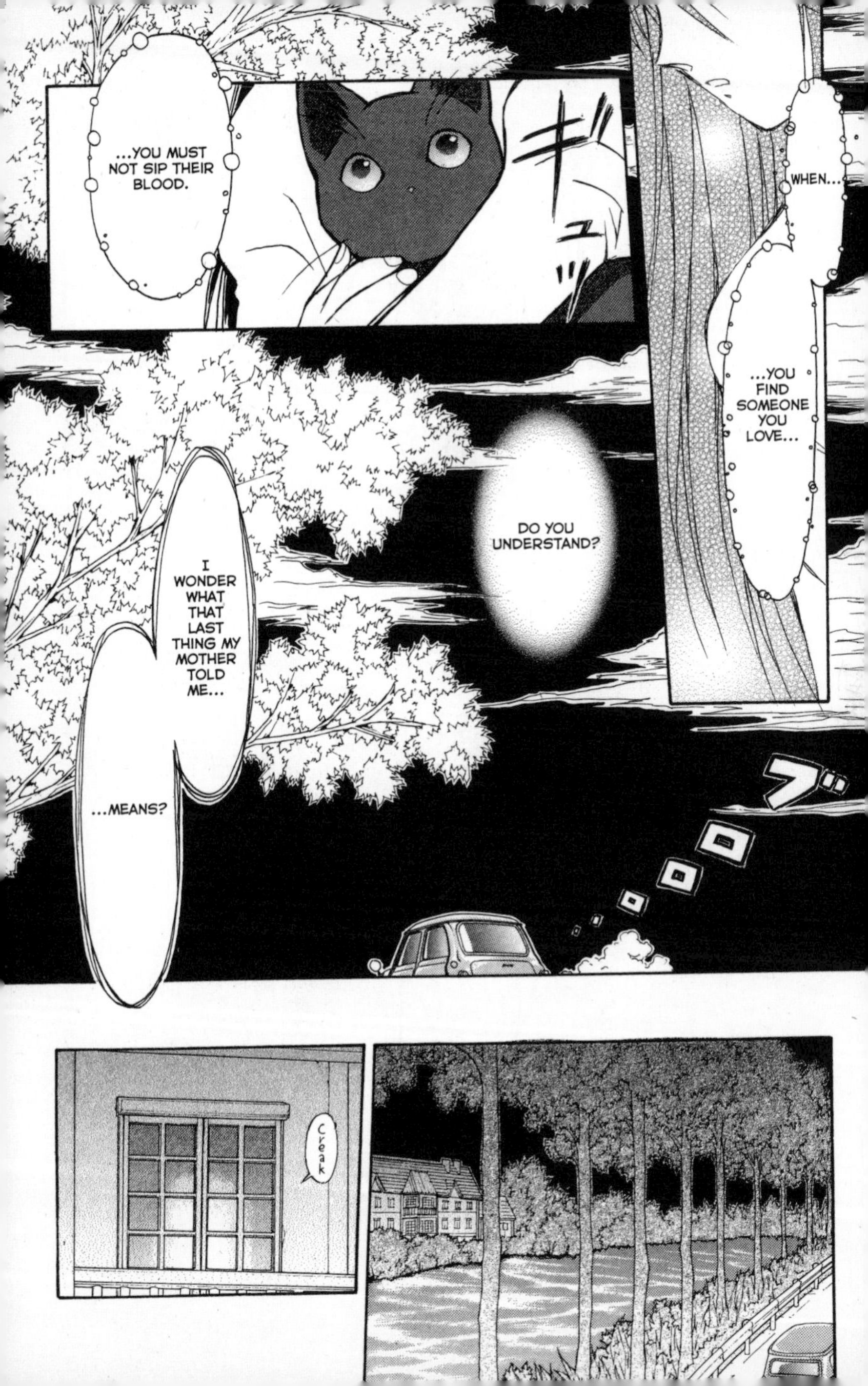
WHEN...
...YOU FIND SOMEONE YOU LOVE...
...YOU MUST NOT SIP THEIR BLOOD.
DO YOU UNDERSTAND?
I WONDER WHAT THAT LAST THING MY MOTHER TOLD ME...
...MEANS?
Creak

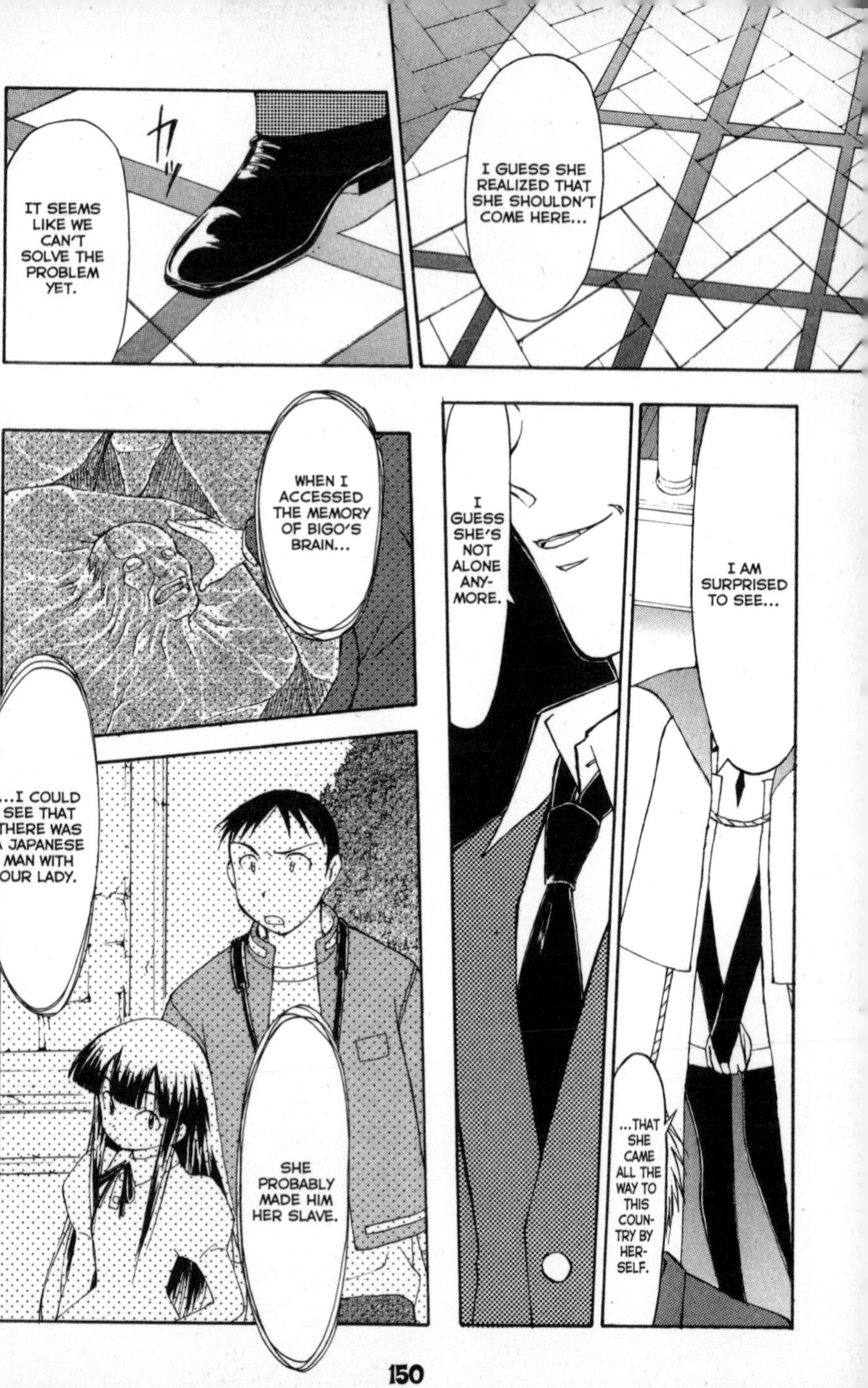
I GUESS SHE REALIZED THAT SHE SHOULDN'T COME HERE...
ガッ
IT SEEMS LIKE WE CAN'T SOLVE THE PROBLEM YET.
I AM SURPRISED TO SEE...
...THAT SHE CAME ALL THE WAY TO THIS COUNTRY BY HER-SELF.
I GUESS SHE'S NOT ALONE ANY-MORE.
WHEN I ACCESSED THE MEMORY OF BIGO'S BRAIN...
...I COULD SEE THAT THERE WAS A JAPANESE MAN WITH OUR LADY.
SHE PROBABLY MADE HIM HER SLAVE.

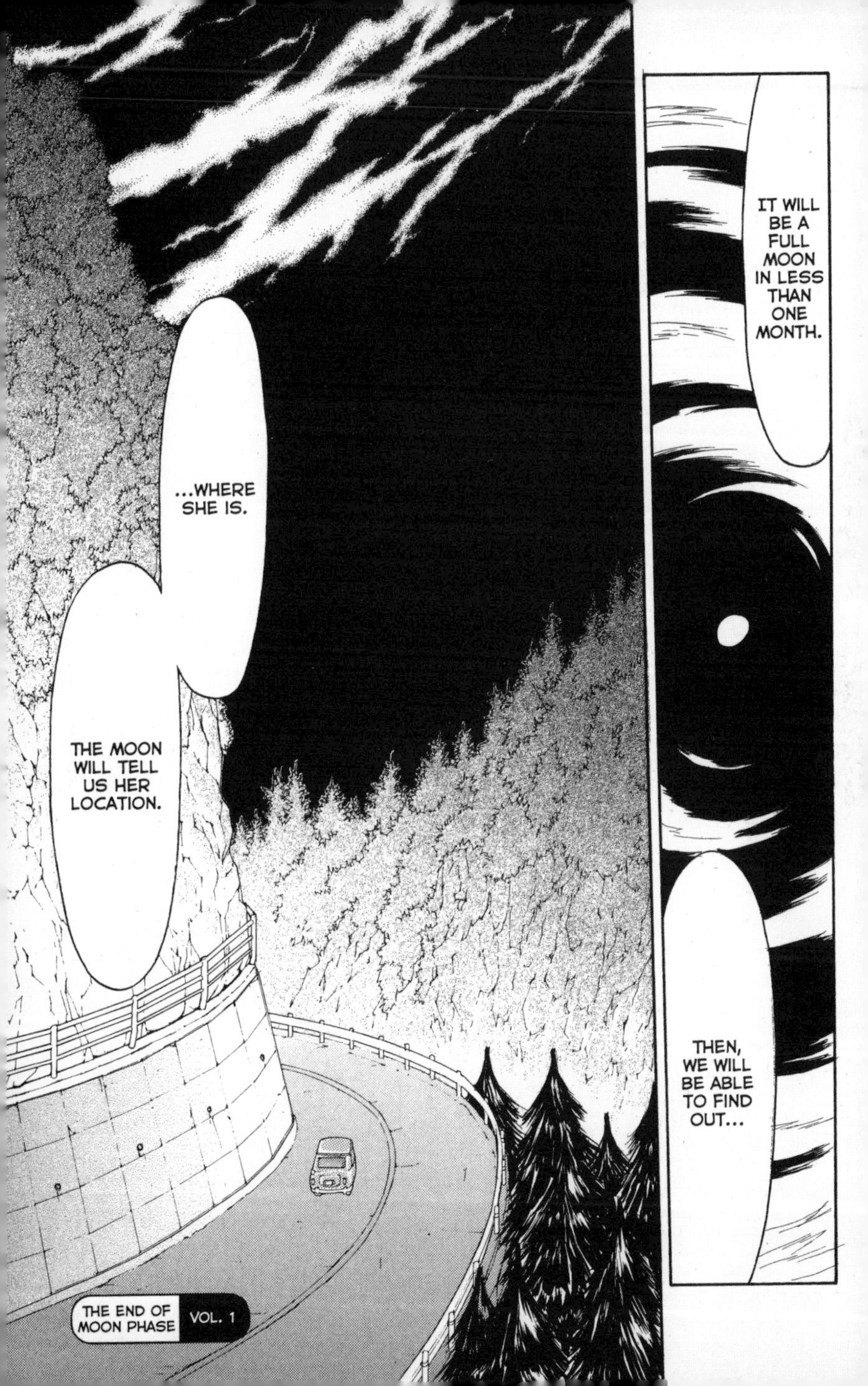
IT WILL BE A FULL MOON IN LESS THAN ONE MONTH.
THEN, WE WILL BE ABLE TO FIND OUT...
...WHERE SHE IS.
THE MOON WILL TELL US HER LOCATION.
THE END OF MOON PHASE VOL. 1

MOON PHASE
~ 4-PANEL THEATER ~

YOUR NAME IS...

エヘヘ Eh heh heh.
WE WILL ALWAYS BE TOGETHER FROM NOW ON.
LET'S BE FRIENDS, HAIJI!
?!
Meow!
SO YOU KNOW HER NAME NOW?
Is her name the same as the girl from Alps?
BUT WHY DID YOU NAME HER HAIJI?
BECAUSE SHE'S GRAY.
The abbreviation of this name is Haiji!
GIVEN NAME: HAIJIROU
HAIJIROU

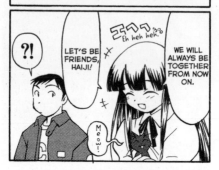

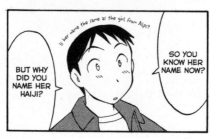

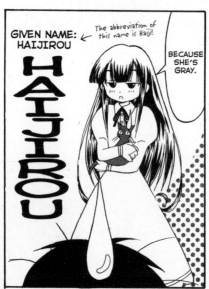

[Addition]

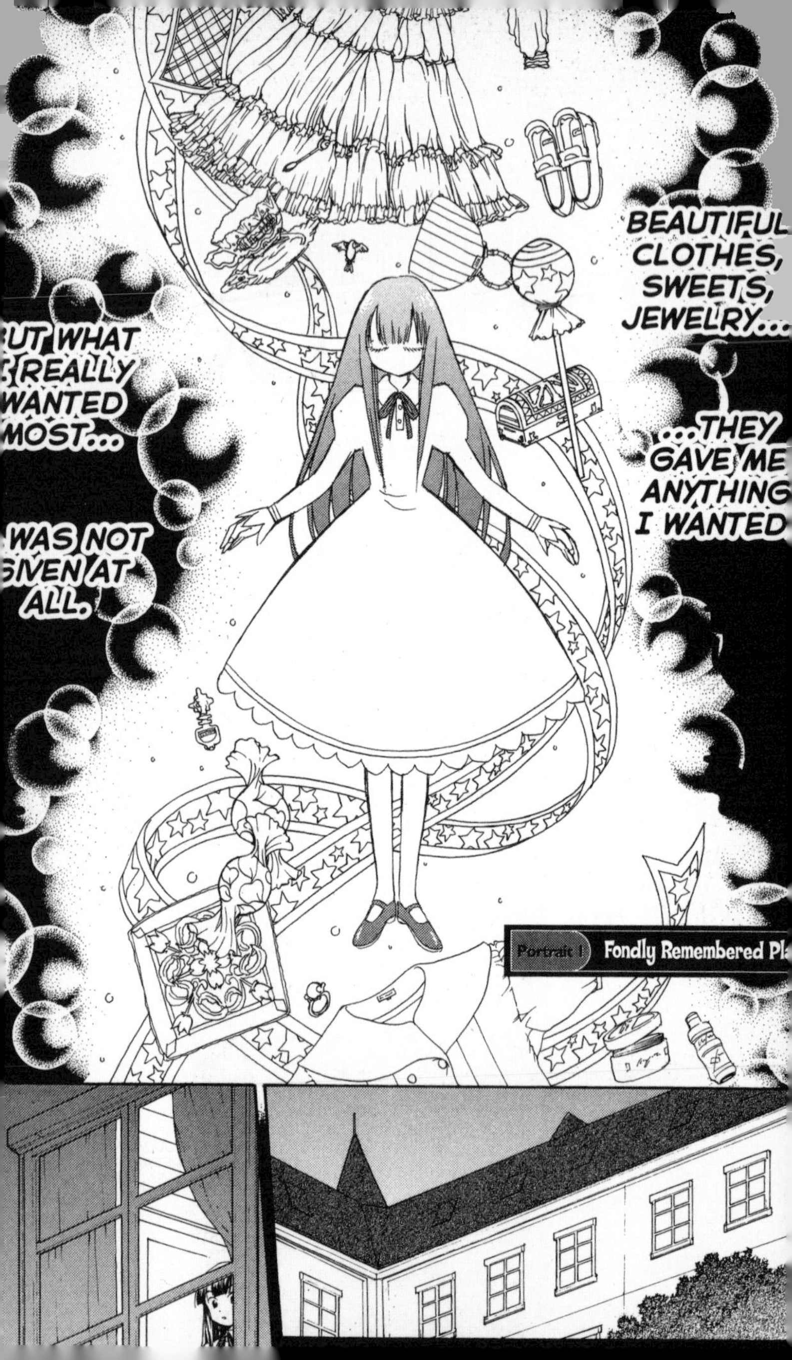
BEAUTIFUL CLOTHES, SWEETS, JEWELRY...
...THEY GAVE ME ANYTHING I WANTED
UT WHAT REALLY WANTED MOST...
WAS NOT IVEN AT ALL.
Portrait 1 Fondly Remembered Pla

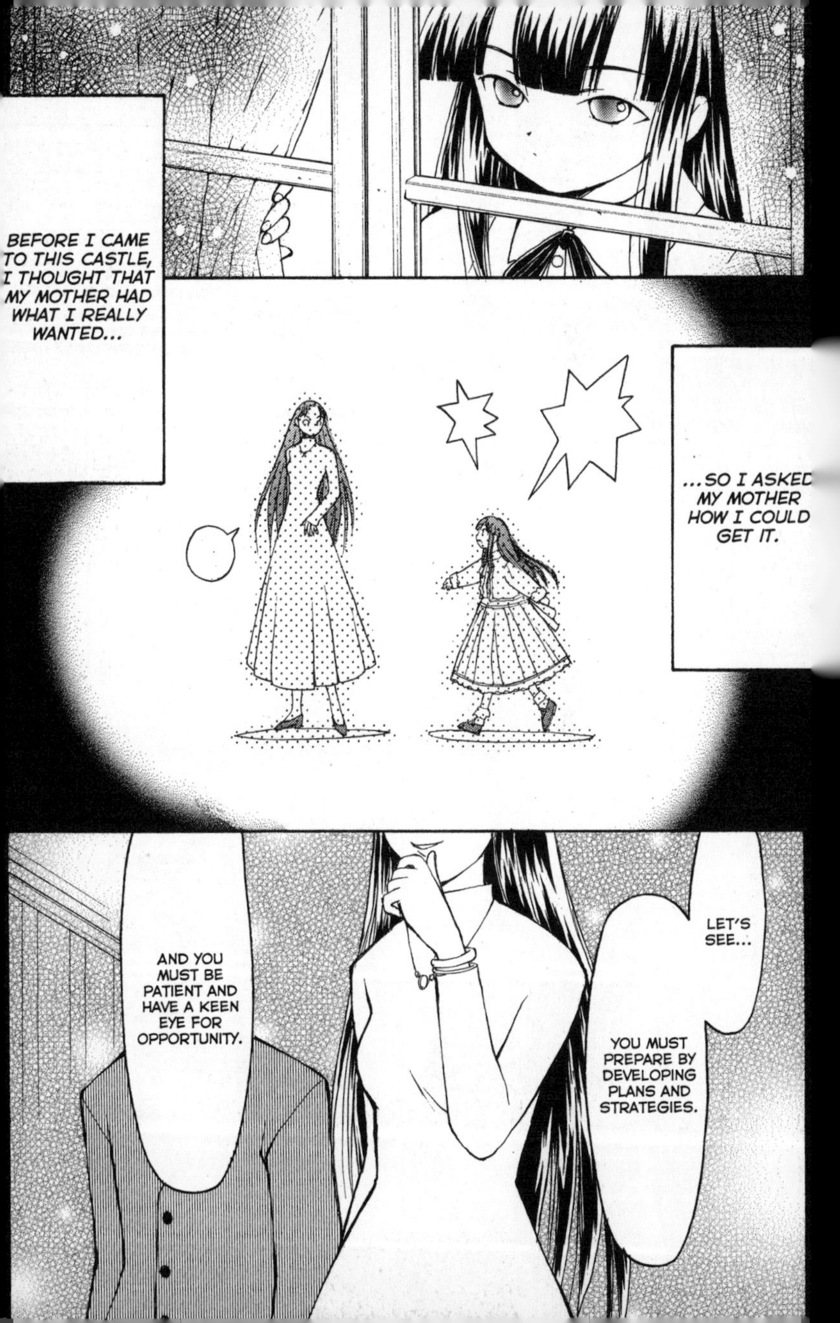
BEFORE I CAME TO THIS CASTLE, I THOUGHT THAT MY MOTHER HAD WHAT I REALLY WANTED...
...SO I ASKED MY MOTHER HOW I COULD GET IT.
LET'S SEE...
YOU MUST PREPARE BY DEVELOPING PLANS AND STRATEGIES.
AND YOU MUST BE PATIENT AND HAVE A KEEN EYE FOR OPPORTUNITY.

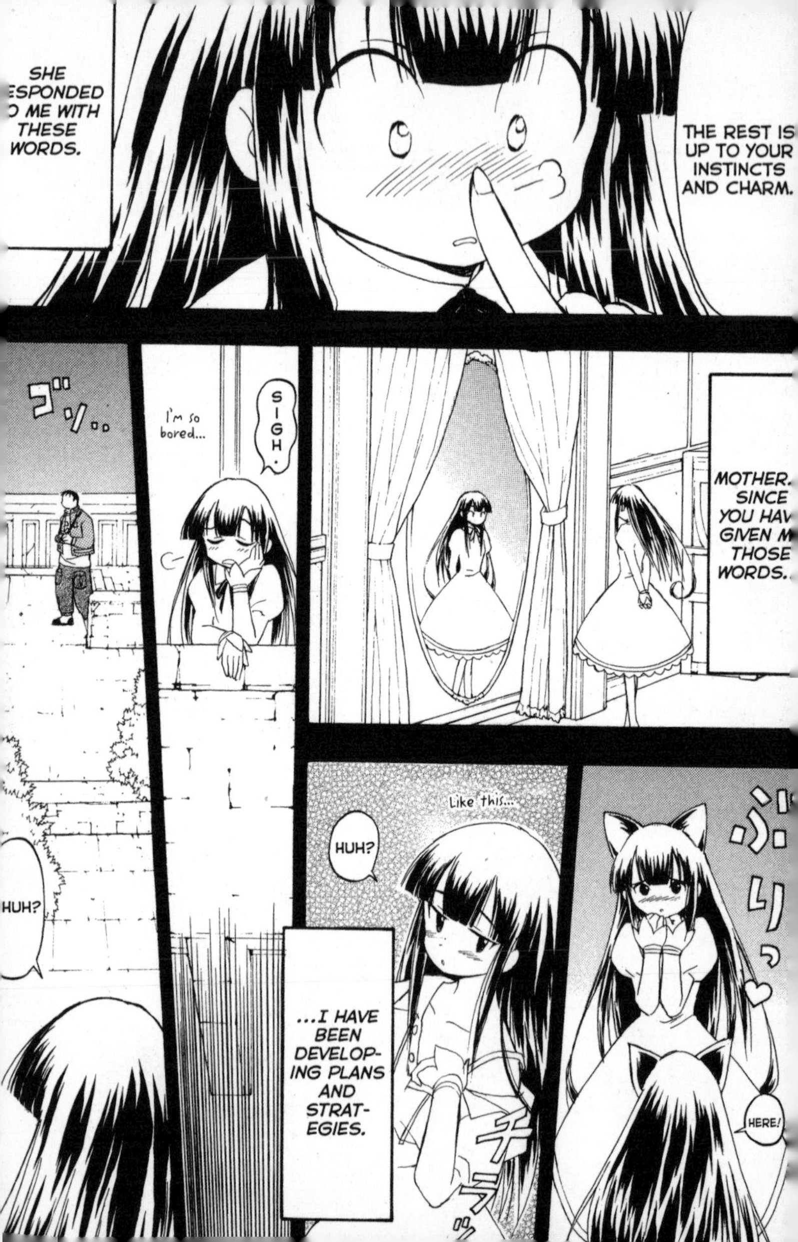
THE REST IS UP TO YOUR INSTINCTS AND CHARM.
SHE RESPONDED TO ME WITH THESE WORDS.
MOTHER.. SINCE YOU HAV GIVEN M THOSE WORDS..
SIGH.
I'm so bored...
ぶりっ
HERE!
Like this...
HUH?
...I HAVE BEEN DEVELOPING PLANS AND STRATEGIES.
チラッ
ゴツ..
HUH?

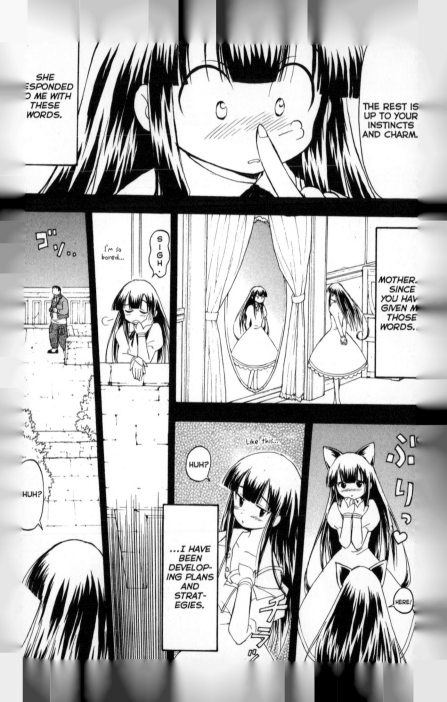

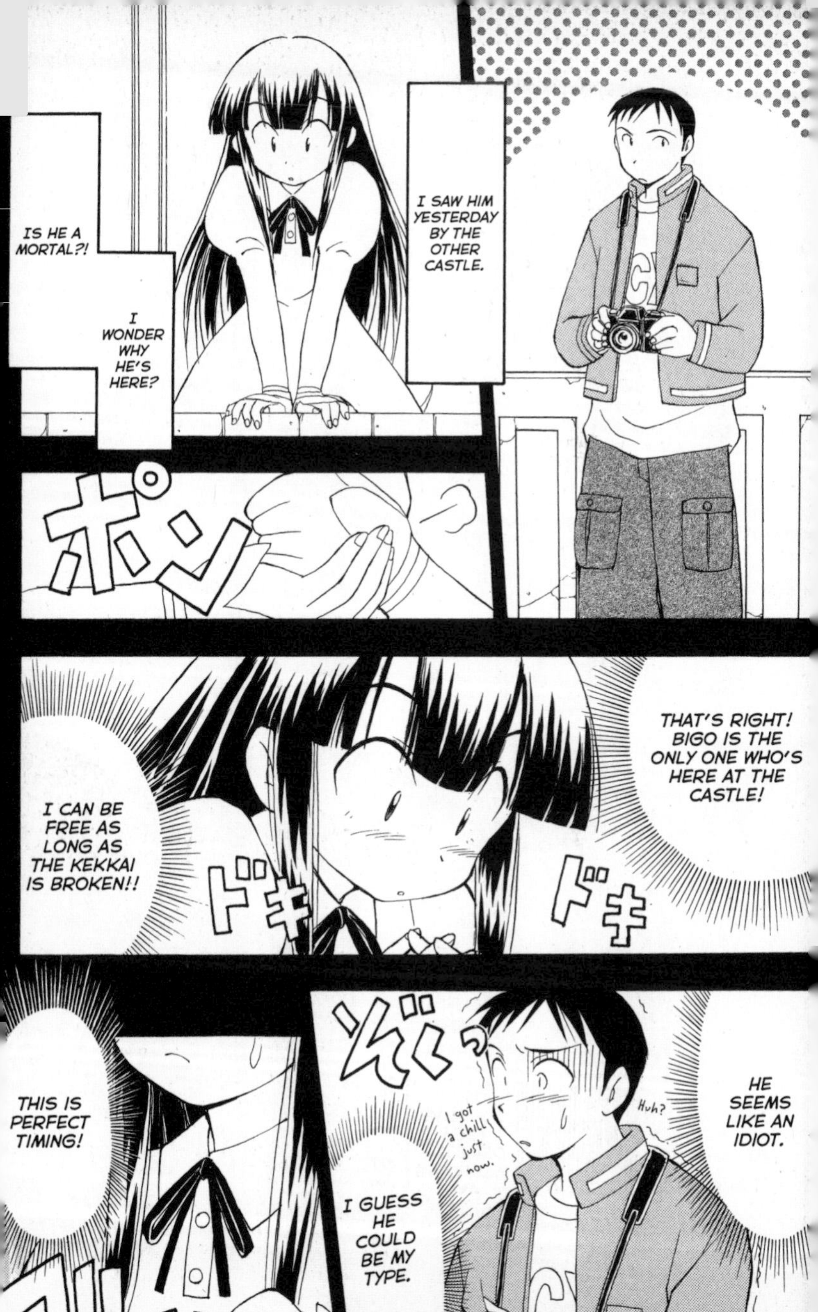
I SAW HIM YESTERDAY BY THE OTHER CASTLE.
IS HE A MORTAL?!
I WONDER WHY HE'S HERE?
ポン
THAT'S RIGHT! BIGO IS THE ONLY ONE WHO'S HERE AT THE CASTLE!
ドキ
ドキ
I CAN BE FREE AS LONG AS THE KEKKAI IS BROKEN!!
HE SEEMS LIKE AN IDIOT.
Huh?
I got a chill just now.
んぐっ
I GUESS HE COULD BE MY TYPE.
THIS IS PERFECT TIMING!

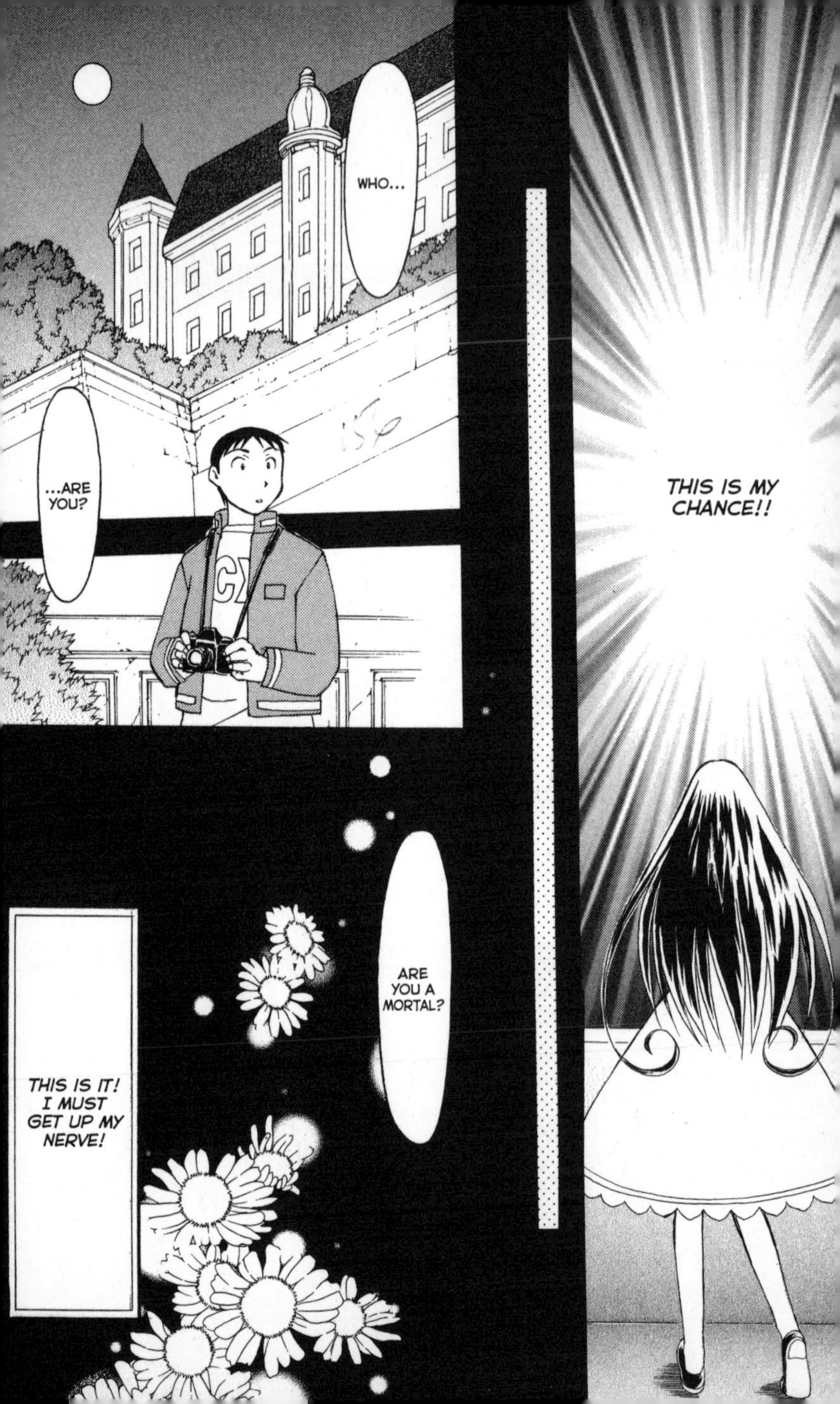
THIS IS MY CHANCE!!
WHO...
...ARE YOU?
ARE YOU A MORTAL?
THIS IS IT! I MUST GET UP MY NERVE!

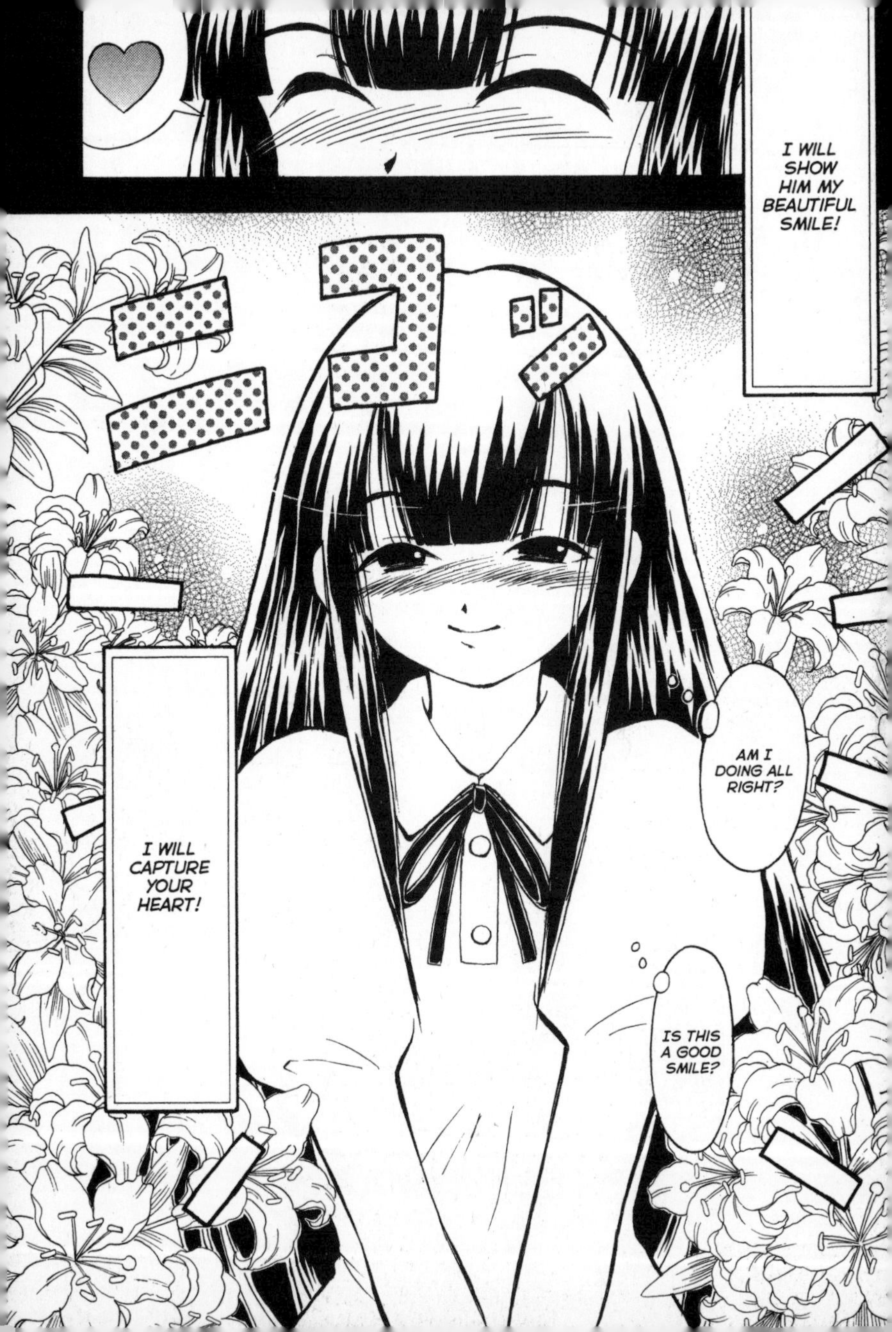
I WILL SHOW HIM MY BEAUTIFUL SMILE!
AM I DOING ALL RIGHT?
IS THIS A GOOD SMILE?
I WILL CAPTURE YOUR HEART!

POSTSCRIPT

MY EDITOR TOLD ME TO WRITE A POSTSCRIPT AND I AM HAVING A HARD TIME DECIDING WHAT TO WRITE. RIGHT NOW, MY LEFT HAND IS GETTING SEXUALLY HARASSED BY MY CAT, RAMUNE, WHO IS NOT NEUTERED YET. I'D RATHER BE SEXUALLY HARASSED BY A GIRL LIKE HAZUKI WHO HAS CAT EARS AND CRIES "MEOW." PLEASE DO THAT FOR ME!! I WILL GIVE BACK EVEN MORE! WELL, PLEASE LET ME HAVE THIS FANTASY. PLEASE! PLEASE MAKE ME FEEL SATISFIED! NO? I SEE.

KEITAROU ARIMA

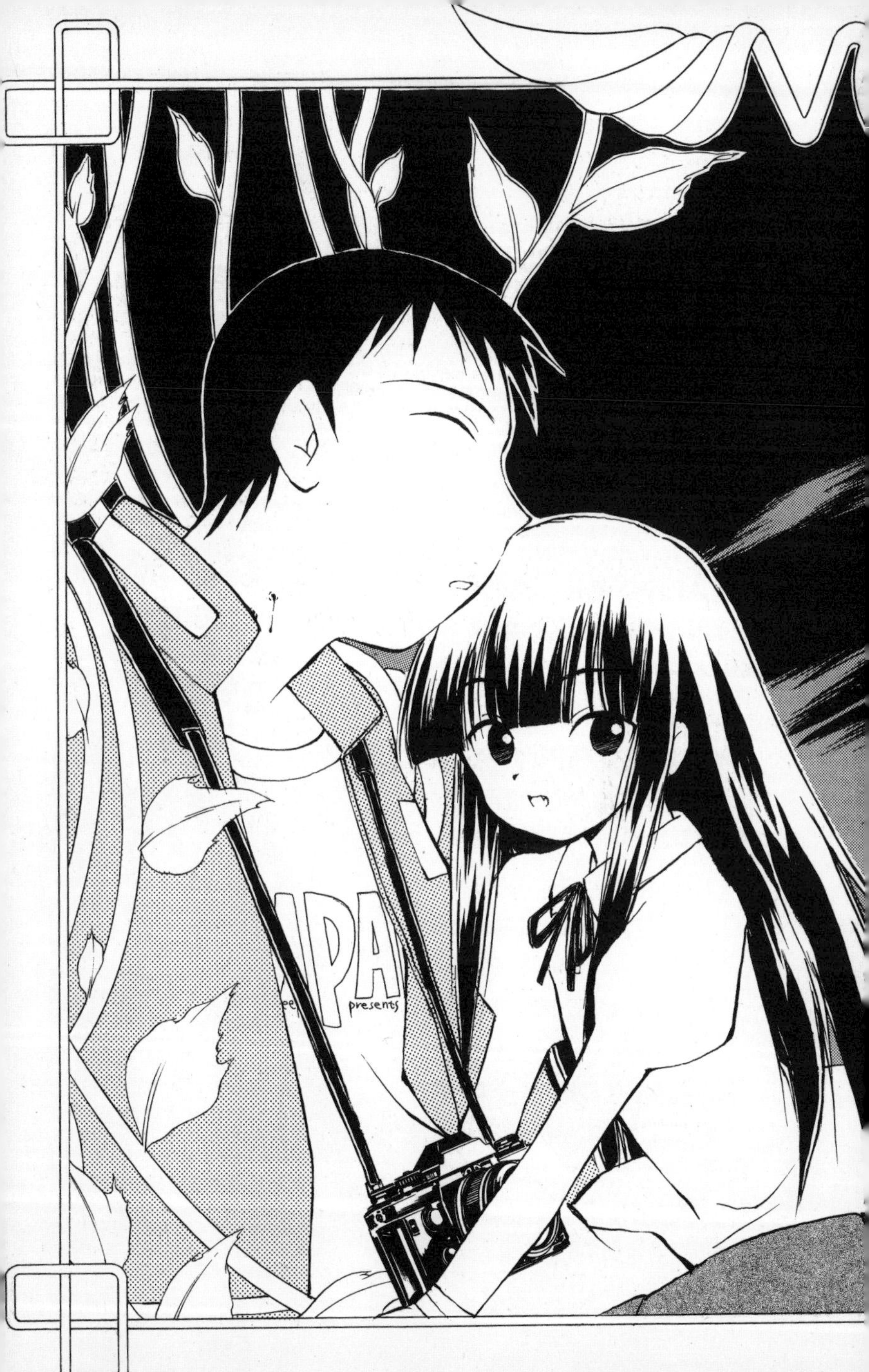
presents

IN THE NEXT

TSUKUYOMI
Moon Phase 月詠
VOLUME 2

AFTER TWO WEEKS
OF DOING CHORES IN
KOUHEI'S GRANDFATHER'S
ANTIQUE SHOP, HAZUKI
ASKS HIM FOR A TASTE
OF BLOOD. NOT TAKING
REJECTION LIGHTLY,
HAZUKI FURIOUSLY
PROWLS THE STREETS
FOR A VICTIM TO SUCK
ON. HER BLOOD THIRST
LEADS TO A CHAIN
REACTION OF ILL-FATED
EVENTS. CAN HAZUKI
LIVE WITHOUT USING HER
MAGIC ON OTHERS?

TOKYOPOP® SHOP

WWW.TOKYOPOP.COM/SHOP

HOT NEWS!

Check out the TOKYOPOP SHOP! The world's best collection of manga in English is now available online in one place!

MARK OF THE SUCCUBUS

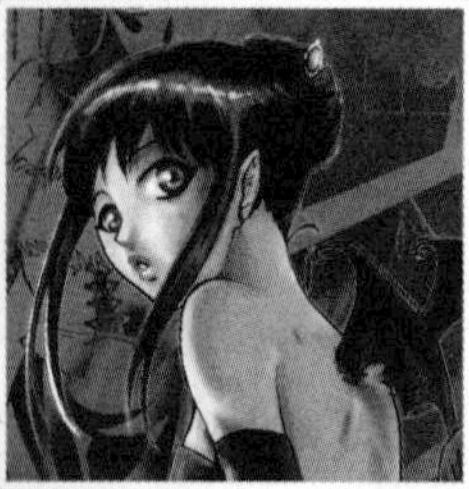

JUSTICE N MERCY

{A TOKYOPOP EXCLUSIVE ARTBOOK}

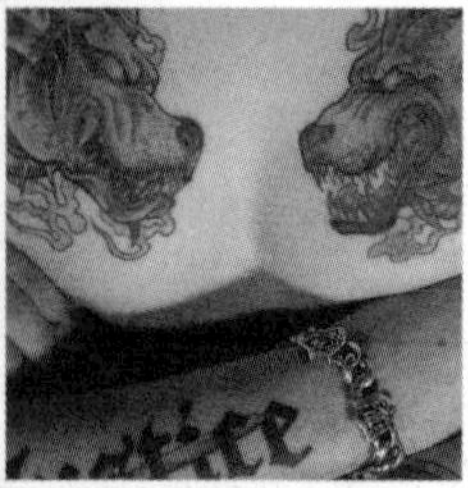

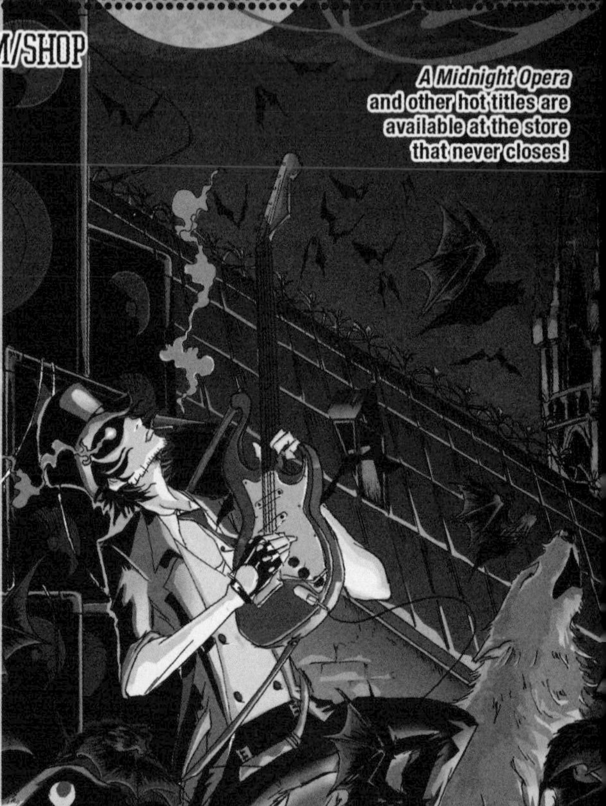

A Midnight Opera and other hot titles are available at the store that never closes!
A MIDNIGHT OPERA

- LOOK FOR SPECIAL OFFERS
- PRE-ORDER UPCOMING RELEASES
- COMPLETE YOUR COLLECTIONS

WWW.TOKYOPOP.COM/SHOP

0 00000 00000 0

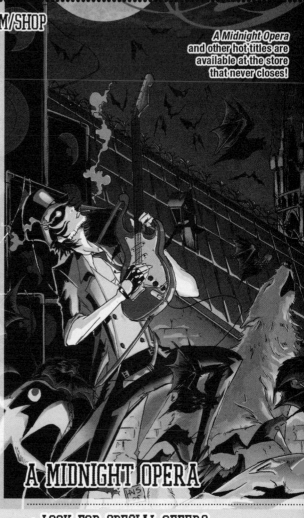

THE DREAMING

BY QUEENIE CHAN

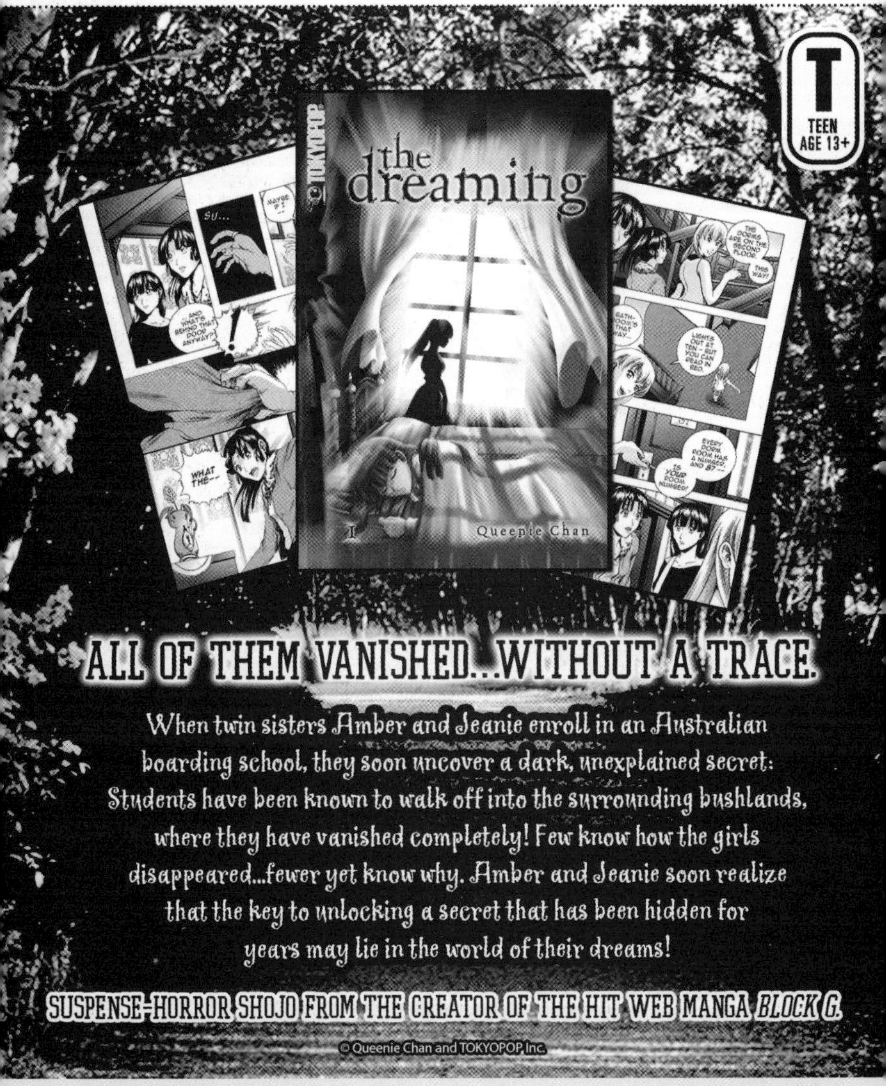
T
TEEN
AGE 13+
TOKYOPOP
the dreaming
1
Queenie Chan
THE DORMS ARE ON THE SECOND FLOOR.
THIS WAY!
BATHROOM'S THAT WAY...
LIGHTS OUT AT TEN -- BUT YOU CAN READ IN BED.
EVERY ROOM HAS A NUMBER, AND 87 --
IS YOUR ROOM NUMBER!
MAYBE IF I --
SU...
...AND WHAT'S BEHIND THAT DOOR ANYWAY?!
!
WHAT THE--

ALL OF THEM VANISHED...WITHOUT A TRACE.

When twin sisters Amber and Jeanie enroll in an Australian boarding school, they soon uncover a dark, unexplained secret: Students have been known to walk off into the surrounding bushlands, where they have vanished completely! Few know how the girls disappeared...fewer yet know why. Amber and Jeanie soon realize that the key to unlocking a secret that has been hidden for years may lie in the world of their dreams!

SUSPENSE-HORROR SHOJO FROM THE CREATOR OF THE HIT WEB MANGA *BLOCK G.*

FOR MORE INFORMATION VISIT: WWW.TOKYOPOP.COM/THEDREAMING

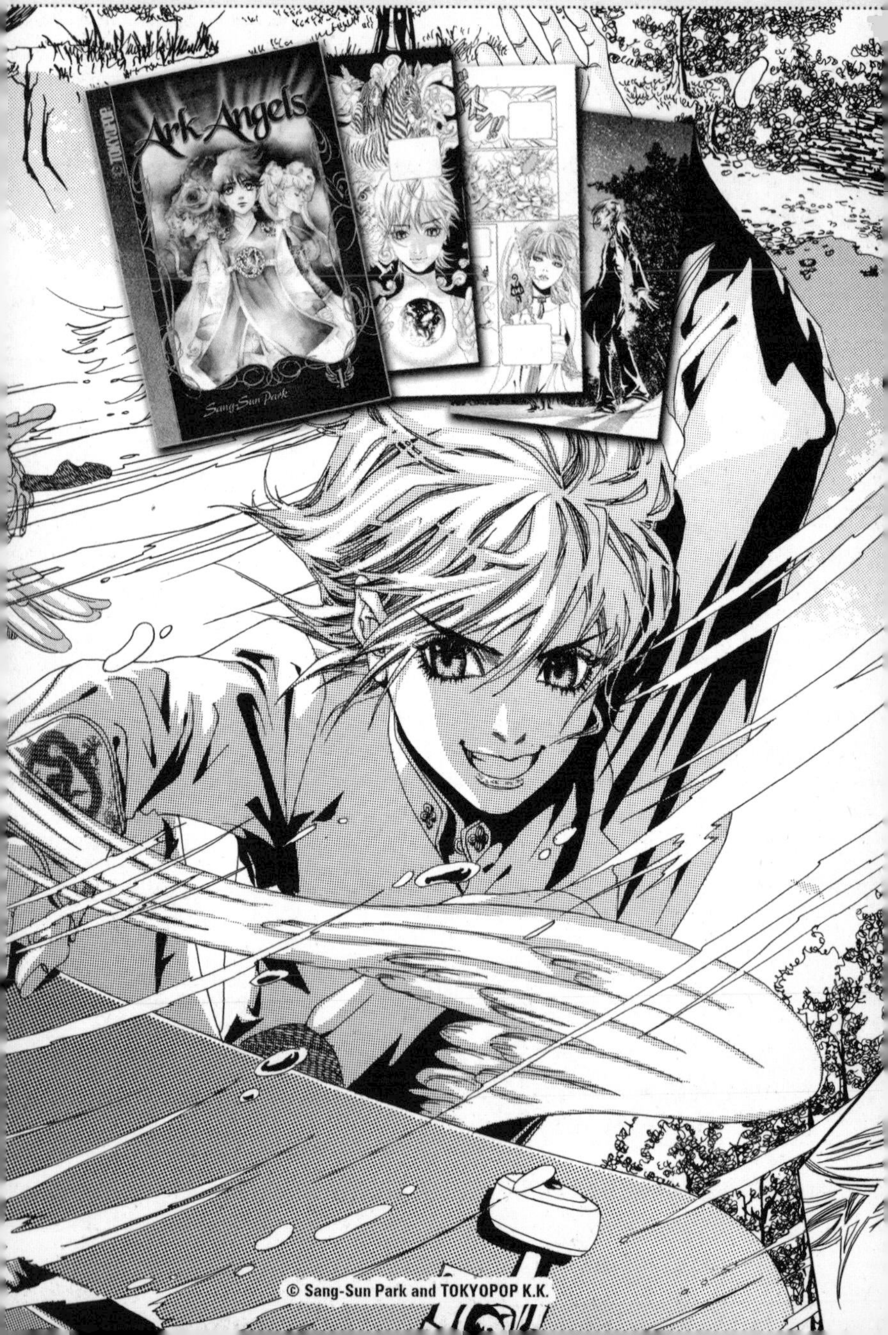
Ark Angels
TOKYOPOP
Sang-Sun Park

Ark Angels™

Girls just wanna have fun— while saving the world.

From a small lake nestled in a secluded forest far from the edge of town, something strange has emerged: Three young girls— Shem, Hamu and Japheth—who are sisters from another world. Equipped with magical powers, they are charged with saving all the creatures of Earth from extinction. However, there is someone or something sinister trying to stop them. And on top of trying to save our world, these sisters have to live like normal human girls: They go to school, work at a flower shop, hang out with friends and even fall in love!

FROM THE CREATOR OF THE TAROT CAFÉ!

T
TEEN
AGE 13+

STOP!

This is the back of the book.
You wouldn't want to spoil a great ending!

This book is printed "manga-style," in the authentic Japanese right-to-left format. Since none of the artwork has been flipped or altered, readers get to experience the story just as the creator intended. You've been asking for it, so TOKYOPOP® delivered: authentic, hot-off-the-press, and far more fun!

DIRECTIONS

If this is your first time reading manga-style, here's a quick guide to help you understand how it works.

It's easy... just start in the top right panel and follow the numbers. Have fun, and look for more 100% authentic manga from TOKYOPOP®!

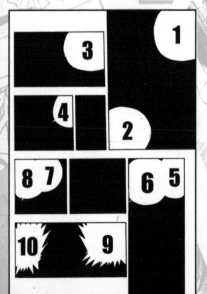